PATHWAYS IN SCRIPTURE

Pathways in Scripture

A Book-by-Book Guide to the Spiritual Riches of the Bible

DAMASUS WINZEN

The St. Paul Center Studies in Biblical Theology and Spirituality
SCOTT HAHN, GENERAL EDITOR

CHARIS

SERVANT PUBLICATIONS
ANN ARBOR, MICHIGAN

Charis Books is an imprint of Servant Publications especially designed to serve Roman Catholics.

Servant Publications—Mission Statement

We are dedicated to publishing books that spread the gospel of Jesus Christ, help Christians to live in accordance with that gospel, promote renewal in the church, and bear witness to Christian unity.

Scripture quotes represent the author's own translation.

Servant Publications
P.O. Box 8617
Ann Arbor, MI 48107
www.servantpub.com

Cover design: Alan Furst Inc. Minneapolis, Minn.

03 04 05 06 10 9 8 7 6 5 4 3 2 1

Printed in the United States of America
ISBN 1-56955-364-5

Library of Congress Cataloging-in-Publication Data

Winzen, Damasus, 1901-1971.
  Pathways in scripture : a book-by-book guide to the spiritual riches
of the Bible / Damasus Winzen.
      p. cm.
Includes bibliographical references and index.
  ISBN 1-56955-364-5 (alk. paper)
 1. Bible--Introductions. 2. Bible--Criticism, interpretation, etc.
3. Spiritual life--Biblical teaching. I. Title.
  BS475.3 .W56 2003
  220.6'1--dc21

                                                          2002154272

Introduction to the St. Paul Center Studies in Biblical Theology and Spirituality

Scott Hahn, General Editor

The St. Paul Center Studies in Biblical Theology and Spirituality are a series of books designed to help Christians in their study of the Word of God. Dr. Scott Hahn serves as general editor, and the St. Paul Center for Biblical Theology, founded by Dr. Hahn, cosponsors the series with Servant Publications.

Each volume helps to fulfill the mission of the St. Paul Center, which is to promote life-transforming study of Scripture in the Catholic tradition. The Center serves clergy and laity, students and scholars, with a variety of research and study tools, from books and publications to multimedia programs and a fully stocked Web library. All efforts promote an integrated study of the Word of God: the Old Testament with the New; the Bible within the liturgy; Scripture illumined by the Tradition and the Magisterium.

We believe that every generation of disciples should know Jesus in the breaking of the bread (see Lk 24:13-37) and exclaim, as his first-generation disciples did: "Did not our hearts burn within us while he talked to us on the road, while he opened to us the Scriptures?"

Marvelous is the profundity of Thy Scriptures. Their surface lies before us, flattering us as we flatter children. But marvelous is their profundity, o my God, marvelous is their profundity. To gaze into it is a shuddering, the shuddering of awe, the shudder of Love. I hate its enemies mightily: o, if Thou wouldst slay them with "a two-edged sword," that it might have no enemies. I would love them to die to themselves that they might live to Thee.

St. Augustine
Confessions, XXII, 4

Contents

Foreword

It was a flow tide of providence that brought Fr. Damasus Winzen to American shores.

Through the 1930s and '40s, Germany's Nazi regime had grown increasingly hostile to the Catholic Church, and the monks of the great Benedictine abbey of Maria Laach considered what they should do in the event of a sudden shutdown. How could they ensure that their work—the labor of nine hundred years of biblical and liturgical studies—would survive Hitler's murderous reign?

Just before the outbreak of World War II, the abbot sent three monks to the United States to prepare for the reestablishment of the monastery. If the final persecution should come, those three men would serve as bearers of the abbey's tradition. One of them was Damasus Winzen.

Thank God that last persecution never came for Maria Laach. But thank God, too, that Fr. Damasus traveled to America, for here he continued his work in the great tradition.

Fr. Damasus was a rare biblical scholar for his time, capable of profound literal-historical study, yet also able to expound the spiritual sense of the Scriptures. At midcentury, interpreters of the Bible tended to fall into two camps: Some emphasized literal-historical research to the exclusion of the Bible's spiritual senses; others practiced a fanciful spiritual or allegorical exegesis that sometimes ignored the literal meaning of the text.

11

Damasus Winzen, however, read the Bible in the Church's tradition, which acknowledges the moral, allegorical, and heavenly senses of Scripture, but which also says (with St. Thomas Aquinas) that "all other senses of Sacred Scripture are based on the literal." The Bible's literal-historical sense is foundational. Without adequate attention to the literal sense, spiritual exegesis is built on shifting sand.

Pathways in Scripture is a work faithful to Damasus Winzen's Benedictine, patristic, and medieval heritage. Yet it is also, in many ways, far ahead of its time. It anticipates, for example, the great "reunion" of historical and spiritual exegesis that would come in the 1960s with the Second Vatican Council (see *Dei Verbum*) and in still later magisterial documents, especially the *Catechism of the Catholic Church* (see nn. 115-119).

Fr. Damasus read the Bible as a true Benedictine, finding its life in the liturgy, in the liturgical year, and in the cycle of readings. In a sense, this was his fidelity to a tradition that had fallen out of fashion. Yet it also foreshadowed the day when scholars would teach the Bible's liturgical setting with renewed vigor. The Pontifical Biblical Commission stated in its 1993 document on *The Interpretation of the Bible in the Church:* "It is above all through the liturgy that Christians come into contact with Scripture.... In principle, the liturgy, and especially the sacramental liturgy, the high point of which is the eucharistic celebration, brings about the most perfect actualization of the biblical texts.... Written text thus becomes living word."

It's that living word that Damasus Winzen helps us to find in the words of the Bible. For him—for the Church—and for every Catholic, the Scriptures must be a liturgical reality, a historical reality, a spiritual reality, and a personal encounter.

Scott Hahn
General Editor

Introduction

The purpose of the introduction I have been asked to write is neither to sum up in advance the contents of this book nor to recall personal memories of my long friendship with Fr. Damasus Winzen. It is to try, using the primary meaning of the word, to "introduce" into his work, to lead the reader into it.

Such an undertaking is not superfluous: Each theologian worthy of the name has his own way of reacting to the mystery revealed for all and of expressing his thoughts in order to transmit the universal message. Fr. Damasus is not a difficult or obscure author, but he is unique and original, inasmuch as he had a strong personality. To seize his "style," to enter his mentality, it is good to have known him, to have heard his voice, to have seen him make his enthusiastic gestures and often laugh like a child of God.

Fr. Damasus wrote a generation ago, and this fact, in our times, can be enough to create between him and our contemporaries a real distance. Yet his doctrine remains contemporary, on condition that we make the effort that the expression he has given it requires of us. The greatest books—those that do not die—are not the easiest but those whose content, clothed in the culture of a particular age, is alive for all times.

Each of the chapters of this book, after the first, is a kind of introduction to one of the biblical books. Fr. Damasus' way, at once critical and theological, of reading the "stories" of the history of salvation

13

is especially timely in that it fills a void created by many generations of an exegesis which is purely critical, at least in intention. In a work in which erudition equals penetration, *The Eclipse of Biblical Narrative* (Yale, 1974), Hans W. Frei has shown how the excess of realism, of literalism, of empiricism, of historicism, in the seventeenth century and especially in the eighteenth, led, after the end of the period, at first in Germany and then everywhere, to a reaction in favor of a more interior, more experiential, more romantic (in the best sense of the word) interpretation: The religious man was no longer satisfied by this dry philology.

Today a like phenomenon is seen: The biblical sciences have brought a progress in religious knowledge which is one of the great achievements of the twentieth century. But the cycle of two centuries ago is being repeated. This scientific benefaction must be completed by a dimension of interiority: A new synthesis between knowledge and fervor is needed, among all the gifts henceforth accessible to our generation.

Fr. Damasus' way of writing about the Scriptures is nothing else than the traditional monastic way of "meditation": not stirring up ideas, no matter how perceptive, but careful study of the literal sense, the discovery therein of a content hidden because spiritual, the desire of accomplishing it. It is, therefore, to bring together thought and love, to participate in that meditation of the Church which is the celebration of the Eucharist, in which "thought and action merge in a perfect unity."

Throughout this book one will find this way of reading the Bible in the light of the fathers in the liturgy, without neglecting history and all that provides a solid basis for an objective spiritual interpretation. Throughout there are parallels between the Old and the New Testaments, between the patriarchs and prophets and Christ, between Israel and the Church: links of varying strength, but always suggestive.

Contrasts, poetic images, abound; and, sustaining the whole, there is a tone of joy, of enthusiasm, of confidence, of the spiritual optimism which characterizes the man of God, one whose faith is solid, his hope certain, his love unshakable. The chapters are pervaded by this security that comes from the fact that God has revealed himself, that Christ has risen, that the Spirit is at work in the world.

How timely is this message of confidence in a society, in a period, where there are so many reasons for losing heart, where the absurd and despair are the rule in a whole literature, in works of philosophy, of the theatre and of film. Fr. Damasus was, and is still, one of the prophetic voices by which God proclaims Good News that no power in this world can suppress.

When one reflects that the liturgically based theology that is expressed in these pages was thought out and lived before the official liturgical reform of Vatican II, one can judge the extent to which the Council was anticipated and prepared by a generation of humble prophets and men of God whose memory must not be allowed to disappear. Fr. Damasus was one of them, and it is good that his message be maintained among us, according to his words, both "present" and "active."

Jean LeClercq
Abbey of Clervaux, Luxembourg

Pathways in Scripture was first written in the late 1940s as a series of articles, when Fr. Damasus was chaplain to the Benedictine nuns of Regina Laudis Monastery in Connecticut. They were printed one by one, following the liturgical seasons, and distributed to subscribers. A second series provided the introduction by Jean LeClercq and dealt with books then scarcely read liturgically. The series was never finished.

In the Holy Year of 1950, while on pilgrimage to Rome, Fr. Damasus and his companions received the indult establishing the Monastery of Mount Saviour. From the spring of 1951, when monastic life was begun on a hilltop outside Elmira, New York, Fr. Damasus' work was the building up of this Benedictine community. He spent himself in giving conferences, teaching, and dealing with the day-to-day events concerning his monks, guests, the dairy farm, shops, and the interests of the surrounding community and of the whole Church. He always found speaking easier than writing, and there was never time to complete the *Pathways* and revise them for a new edition. After his retirement as prior in 1969 he turned his attention to the Psalms, and he was tape-recording commentaries on them up until his death on June 26, 1971.

In 1975, the twenty-fifth anniversary of the founding of Mount Saviour, his spiritual sons reissued the incomplete series. Some small changes were made. The spelling of biblical names conforms to recent translations of the Bible, and references to the Psalms follow the Hebrew (rather than the Vulgate) numbering. Where recent biblical scholarship has questioned or revised the traditional attribution or dating of a biblical book, a new footnote has been added; in a few cases the text has been amended to reflect modern critical opinion.

"Spiritual interpretation" of biblical texts as practiced by Fr. Damasus may seem to some readers independent of scholarly and historical considerations. This is not the case. Even when they appear most free, they are based on an adequate knowledge of the literal sense and an awareness of the interpretations put forth over the centuries by the great teachers of the Church. The first duty of a reader of the Bible is to apply himself to understanding the text, using all the resources of scholarship available to him. Such application to the author's intended meaning, as well as holiness of life, may open to him an extended interpretation, which has then to be tested by the Church's tradition.

Pathways is printed according to the usual order of the books of the Bible. In the Office of Readings in the new *Liturgy of the Hours,* the old practice of reading particular books in the major seasons of the year is retained: for example, Isaiah in Advent, the Acts in Eastertide. A new principle is used, however, for the remaining "weeks of the year." The books of the Old Testament are read in their historical order, mingling historical, prophetic, and wisdom literature in a single account of God's action. This is spread over two years, interrupted at intervals for the reading of St. Paul's letters, so that the Church's official prayer now takes in nearly the whole of the Bible (with the exception of the Gospels read at Mass and repetitive parts of the Old Testament).

At Mount Saviour selections have been used as public readings. It is the hope of those who have worked to bring out this edition of *Pathways* that many outside his own monastic family may profit by Fr. Damasus' insights into the mysteries of God as expressed in the Scriptures.

Words of Eternal Life:
How to Read the Scriptures

When we consider the number of books that are being published in our days and the number of people who read them, we might be moved to call our time the "Age of the Book." However, mass production has made the book such a common thing that we no longer value it and have lost the feeling for its "mystery." This is especially true of the Book of books, the Bible, which we put on a shelf together with all the other books; we let it stand there without even realizing what it means that this book is the "Word of God." The following remarks may help us to appreciate better the unique divine gift of the Scriptures and to read them in the Spirit in whom they were written.

The Word of God has expressed itself in three different ways: in creation, in the Scriptures, and in the sacred humanity of Christ. This visible creation is the first "book" that God's Word has written, and in it the wisdom, the goodness, and the power of the Creator are set forth. "For the invisible things of him since the creation of the world are clearly seen, being perceived through the things that are made, even his everlasting power and divinity" (Rom 1:20).

Why then did God add to the order of nature another medium to express himself, the Scriptures? If God speaks to men, he certainly does not do so in order to "chat" with them about something or other. God's Word always aims at the very existence of the one to whom it is addressed. "For he spoke, and it was done" (Ps 33:9).

The new word that God addresses to man must be a new creation, a "word of life," opening to man a new dimension. It was the fall of man that gave God the opportunity to speak a new word, the word of mercy and forgiveness. While this visible world may be well suited to praise the wisdom and glory of its Maker, no star, no mountain, no beast, no tree, no sunshine, no rain, will ever be able to announce to man that his heavenly Father has forgiven him his sin. The natural law will impose the death sentence upon those who rebel against the Creator; absolution can only come to man as a personal word issuing from the very heart of the Father and directed to the heart of the Prodigal Son.

People who think it is below the dignity of God to "speak" to man, besides and beyond the word that he has uttered in creating the world, do not realize that the fall of man has opened a new chaos, out of which the new word of God creates a new world, infinitely more beautiful and more sublime than the first.

Had God spoken his word of forgiveness only to an individual, like Adam or Eve, it would not have become Scripture. God's word of reconciliation took the form of a book because it was given to the chosen people. The spoken word passes with the sound. The letter gives the word that eternal, public, and authoritative character it needs to become the firm basis for the life of a community. The letter saves events of the past from oblivion and gives to laws their binding authority. The book, therefore, fulfills in the life of a community the two functions of memory and of conscience, assuring continuity of history and unity of action.

The two basic forms of books are, therefore, annals and codes. Holy Scripture has exactly this twofold function in relation to the people of God. It appears as the "book of the covenant" containing the laws God's people are to keep (Ex 24:7). But before this God had already ordered Moses to write a book "for a memorial" (Ex 17:14).

The Old Testament had to become a book of history because God's word of reconciliation was first given to men as a promise of a redeemer who, at the end of time, would crush the dragon's head (Gn 3:15). God is a faithful God; his promise is a sure promise. The fact that God ordered his promise to be put down in writing and to be repeated again and again in every generation gives it that rocklike quality that alone is able to reflect the eternal charity upon which the promise is based.

The Promise Fulfilled

God's word of reconciliation was not only a promise and a hope. It was also a presence. But as long as the promise remained a hope, God was present among his people only through the manifestation of his holy will in the form of the Law. When God fulfilled his promise and sent the Redeemer, a new commandment was given, not written on stone, not filling the pages of big books, but written into the hearts of God's children by his Spirit. The letter ceased to take the place of the presence. It was absorbed into it.

To Moses the writing was an essential part of his office as a mediator between God and his people. The Moses of the new covenant, Christ, did not write, and with the exception only of the Apocalypse, we do not hear that any of the books of the New Testament were written on explicit divine command. The Gospels, the Acts of the Apostles, and the letters of the apostles grew quite naturally out of the living tradition of the Church, which is not, like the chosen people of the Old Testament, a community gathered around a book.

Israel of old had the altar in the court of the temple, while the Law took the place of the presence in the Holy of Holies. The new Israel has the altar in the sanctuary of the church and places the book on the altar. This means that the writings of the New Testament grow out of, lead to, and are fulfilled by the sacramental presence of the sacrifice of Christ in the celebration of the holy Eucharist.

The letter in the New Testament is no longer the guarantee of a sure promise pointing to the future, nor the mere record of a historical past, but it is a continuation of the Incarnation, through which the Christian enters into the spiritual presence of Christ's work of redemption. "The mystery of the passion has been opened to us by the text of the Gospel in such a clear and luminous way, that to pious and God-fearing hearts it is the same: to have heard the words read and to have seen the event."[1] Therefore, the book of the Gospels is treated like Christ, and when the lesson from the Gospel is read, "all stand in awe and reverence."[2]

The close relationship between "word" and "action" that is so characteristic of the Old Testament becomes an identity in the New. When St. Paul uses the term "Word of God," he does not refer to a special message from God but to Christ himself, as he died and rose for us. The many "words of God" of the Old Testament have been replaced by the one Word whom John describes in the Apocalypse: "I saw heaven standing open, and behold a white horse and he who sat upon it is called faithful and true, and his eyes are a flame of fire and on his head are many diadems, and he is clothed with a garment sprinkled with blood, and his name is called 'the word of God'" (Rv 19:11-13).

This Word is indeed "living and active and keener than any two-edged sword" (Heb 4:12), able to save our souls (Jas 1:21). It is not a concept, not an idea. It is an action: Christ's "passover" through this world and through his death on the cross into the glory of his resurrection.

Likewise the "book" receives a new meaning in the New Testament. It is the scroll John saw upon the right hand of him who sits upon the throne, written within and without, sealed with seven seals. No one in heaven or on earth was worthy to open it, except the Lion of the tribe of Judah, the Root of David, the Lamb, standing as if slain in the midst of the throne (Rv 5:1-8).

Approaching the Scriptures

This vision reveals the true meaning and the "mystery" of the Scriptures. They are the earthly sign and sacrament of those eternal designs and decisions in which God has planned the "economy" of our salvation, according to which the whole body of sacred history develops in the course of time. To read the Scriptures means, therefore, to enter into this "mystery" of a new creation, which the Lamb of God works in us in the very moment in which we open our hearts to it. We see how vital it is for us to follow the solemn warning that the Church addresses to us morning after morning in the Invitatory of Vigils: "Today if you would hear his voice, harden not your hearts!" (Ps 95:8).

If the words of Scripture are "spirit and life" (Jn 6:63), the flesh will never be able to understand them. We are "flesh" as long as we read the Scriptures for worldly and selfish reasons.

"The Word of God is God, and the word of the world is world," says Macarius of Egypt.[3] We have to leave the world when we turn to the Word of God. We have to renounce any desire to be "entertained."

More still do we have to surrender our pride. It pleased God to destroy the wisdom of the wise and to save the world through the word of the cross: foolishness to those who perish but the power of God to those who are called (see 1 Cor 1:17-25). We cannot understand the Scriptures with a sophisticated mind and a self-complacent attitude. We must be ready to be recreated by God's Word. "I look on him that is poor and of a contrite spirit, and trembles at my word" (Is 66:2).

We must be willing to serve. "In the head of the book it is written of me: to do your will, O Lord!" (Ps 40:7-8). The "head of the book" is Scripture as a whole, summed up in this one sentence: "To do your will, O God!"[4]

The Word of God gives glory to the Father. To read the Scriptures is an act of worship. He who seeks his own glory will not understand them. Here lies the great danger of all those who approach the Bible merely from the point of view of the scholar and study it as an interesting historical or philological document. Those who are not willing to come to Christ that they may have life will search the Scriptures in vain. Such scholars have not the love of God in them (see Jn 5:39-42). "The sole end of the Scripture is love,"[5] so a mind set on controversy, imbued with hatred, will only bend the Scriptures its own way.

The Word of God is whole, truly comprehensive, creating heaven and earth; and the Spirit that emanates from it "fills the whole world" (Wis 1:7). No biased mind can grasp it. One must be at peace, free from hatred and pet ideas, to become a pure mirror of the Word, which is truth and light and peace.

In fact, no individual person, only the whole body of the Church, is large enough to receive the fullness of the Word of God. The Christian will, therefore, not consider the Bible his private and exclusive possession, as if he alone would own it, he alone understand it. He will be guided in his interpretation by the authority of the Church. He desires to be molded by the word of Christ into a member of his body, instead of using that Word as a foil to fence with the rest of the world.

Humility, obedience, prayer, and peace of mind dispose the soul to understand the Scriptures. How then do we go about the practical task of reading them?

Getting Started

The Fathers of the Church insist that every Christian should devote some time every day to the reading of the Bible. St. Caesarius advises its use as table-reading in families during the meal, if there is not enough leisure otherwise.[6] Some families read a short paragraph from the Scriptures before the meal to remind them that man does not live from bread alone but from every word which proceeds from the mouth of God.

The greatest difficulty for beginners is that they are tempted to start reading the Bible from the beginning. The Fathers always warned against this, insisting on a more gradual approach. In one of his letters[7] St. Jerome outlines a plan that has not lost anything of its practical value. One should start, he says, with the Psalms, because there one finds everything Scripture teaches in the easy and appealing form of song. The Psalms fit right into our lives, and at least the majority of them are self-explanatory.

After the Psalms the wisdom books should be read, because they also are relatively easy to understand. They teach the right way of living, and much in them is just sound common sense. With Ecclesiastes the reader begins to ascend to a higher level. Here he learns detachment from the things of the world.

This detachment will grow with the study of Job. The most perfect of all the books of the Bible from the poetic viewpoint, Job paints the true picture of the everlasting man, while at the same time it opens the way to faith and hope. The features of the Redeemer become dimly discernible in the person of this great sufferer.

The mind of the reader is now prepared for the reading of the Gospels, Acts, and the letters. The light of Christ kindled in our heart will open to us the understanding of the prophets who announced him, first of all Isaiah, who is rightly called the evangelist of the Old Testament.

St. Jerome recommends that only now should the beginner turn to the five books of Moses and to the other historical books of the Old Testament, while the Song of Songs is reserved for the mature and spiritually minded.

One can easily see why St. Jerome prefers to have all the historical books read in their historical order. It is indeed absolutely necessary for every student of the Bible to get a clear picture of the whole history of salvation. He should see as soon as possible the whole panorama, and he should beware of getting stuck in some difficult passages in a vain effort to understand everything at once.

Reading patiently Genesis and Exodus from chapter to chapter—leaving out, maybe, Leviticus and Numbers, and even Deuteronomy—he should proceed to Joshua, Judges, Samuel, Kings, Ezra, Nehemiah, and Maccabees. The reader should try to keep in mind the essential stages through which God leads his people to the "fullness of time," when the Messiah appears.

There are the first eleven chapters of Genesis, clearly set off as the magnificent overture that foreshadows the basic motifs of the whole history that follows: Highlights of these chapters are the Creation and the fall of Adam, and the judgment of the Flood, with Noah emerging as the first figure of the Redeemer.

With Abraham we enter into the light of history, beginning with the era of the patriarchs, which is the age of the promise, instilling faith and hope into the hearts of Abraham and his posterity.

With Exodus Moses appears, the great deliverer and lawgiver. He opens the age of the covenant, based on the law of the love of God and of neighbor (Deuteronomy). Joshua, abounding in courage and fortitude, is the fulfillment of the promise in the age of conquest.

Judges leads to the era of David. The people enter into the rest. The "house of David is built," with the temple and the city. Then another "flood" destroys all that had seemed eternal (in the Books of Samuel and Kings).

The Babylonian exile is the school in which the remnant is set to learn that God's promise is not fulfilled in any earthly king nor in any earthly country, but only in the spiritual kingdom of God, with the "suffering servant" (Isaiah) and the "son of Man" (Daniel) as king. This lesson of the Exile was confirmed by the history of the restoration and the building of the second temple (Ezra, Nehemiah), which in its humble and precarious existence remained a disappointment (see Maccabees). Then the true King came to the temple, offered by Mary the virgin and received into the arms of Simeon.

The Gospels are the glad tidings of the coming of the King, who brings the kingdom, teaches its mystery, is crucified, and rises as King. Upon his entering into his kingdom at the Ascension, the Church is born and conquers the world (Acts). She is the body of Christ (epistles), looking forward to the coming of the Bridegroom at the end of times (Apocalypse).

Meditating on the Word

After this first acquaintance with the Scriptures, the real "opening of the Book" in meditative reading may begin. In the Old Testament, whence the term has been taken, to meditate means to think in such a way that love makes thought so heavy with reality that it bursts out in some kind of inarticulate utterance, similar to the cooing of the dove.[8] The Church's meditation is the celebration of the holy Eucharist. There thought and action merge into a perfect unity. There the Lamb of God, present "as if slain" on the altar, opens the book.

Christ's *pascha*, his passing through death into life, is the focal point where the history of the chosen people, the laws and the ceremonies of the Old Covenant, the prophecies, the teaching and the earthly life of Christ, the life of the Church, and the life of every individual Christian converge. The Church has, therefore, grouped the meditative readings of the Scriptures during Vigils in such a way as to fit into the liturgical seasons.

Through this arrangement the Church directs the attention of the reader immediately to the spiritual sense of the Scriptures. There is much confusion in the minds of many as to what this spiritual sense really is. Arbitrary allegorical interpretations of even the most minute details of the sacred text have caused a reaction that sometimes even goes so far as to deny the existence of a spiritual sense altogether.

However, Christ himself mentions Jonah (Mt 12:39), Solomon (Mt 12:42), the brazen serpent (Jn 3:14), and the temple (Jn 2:19) as "signs" pointing to him. St. Paul explains Hagar and Sarah, with their sons Ishmael and Isaac, as "allegories" of the two Testaments (Gal 4:21-31). The Letter to the Hebrews calls the tabernacle and its ritual "types and shadows of heavenly realities" (8:5) and refers to the whole law as a "shadow of the good things to come" (10:1). These instances do not only prove the existence of the spiritual sense, they also reveal its nature. St. Thomas Aquinas defined this spiritual sense as "the mode by which the things signified by the words further signify other things," while the literal or historical sense is "the mode by which words show the meaning of things."

[The spiritual sense] has a threefold division. As the Apostle says (Heb 10:1), the ancient law is the figure of the new law; and the new law itself, as Dionysius says, is a figure of the future glory; also in the new law the things which were done in the person of our Head are signs of what we ought to do. Hence, insofar as things of the ancient law signify those of the new, we have the allegorical (or typical) sense; insofar as the things done in Christ, or the things which signify Christ, signify the things which we ought to do, we have the moral sense; while according as they signify the things which belong to eternal glory, we have the anagogical sense.[9]

The various kinds of the spiritual sense are all founded upon the literal sense and can therefore be discovered only through a careful study of the text itself.

There can be no doubt, however, that the "things" the Scriptures speak of have been arranged by the Holy Spirit in such a way as to point to Christ in whom "all things are summed up, the things in the heavens, and the things upon the earth" (Eph 1:10).

"The sense of the Scriptures is their direction," says Paul Claudel.[10] To find the spiritual sense of the Scriptures is to enter into their direction toward Christ.

"Read the prophets without Christ in them, what is more tasteless and more flat? Find Christ in them, then they will not only taste well, they will make you drunk."[11] Drunk indeed with the new wine of the Holy Spirit, which renews our souls every day through the meditation of the Word of God.

ONE

Genesis 1–11: Primeval History

Before the liturgical reforms following the Second Vatican Council the Church's cycle of Scripture reading began on Septuagesima Sunday—the Sunday a nominal seventy days before Easter that was observed as an anticipation of Lent. This custom went back to a time when the Church did not yet have an ecclesiastical year different from the civil year.

In ancient Rome the beginning of the year was celebrated early in spring, when, after the lull of winter, life and light were again on the ascendancy. The Old Testament shows that the Jews once followed the same custom by calling the month in which the spring feast of Passover is celebrated "the first month of the year" (Ex 12:2).

Many passages in the writings of the early Fathers and in the liturgy indicate that the Christians of old considered Easter the "first day" or "head" of the year. Because Lent and the pre-Lenten season belong to Easter as a time of preparation, Septuagesima Sunday was really the day when for the first time we would scent the holy spring of Easter in the air. That is the reason why the Church would read the book of Genesis then. She wanted us to contemplate the beginnings of the world in the light of Christ, who "has appeared at the end of the ages" (Heb 9:26) to redeem it. It is the same Son of God through whom all things received their first being and through whom they were reestablished on Easter. The work of creation foreshadowed the work of redemption, because Christ is the Alpha and the Omega, the beginning and the end of history.

The Torah

The Book of Genesis is the first of the five books of Moses,[1] which are also known as the Pentateuch or Book of Five. The Jews call the Pentateuch *Torah*—that is, the Law, or better, divine teaching. It is held in highest esteem because it contains God's message to Israel: the revelations, promises, and laws on which the faith, the claims, and the life of the chosen people are based. The Pentateuch holds in the Old Testament the position that the four Gospels have in the New.

The names that are now used for each of these five books have been taken from the Septuagint, the first translation into Greek of the books of the Old Testament. They indicate the central theme of each book. The first is called Genesis, "origin," because it deals with the creation of the world, the beginnings of mankind, and specifically with the origin of the Hebrew race. The second book, Exodus, "going out," describes the birth of the Jewish nation through the deliverance from bondage in Egypt and through the giving of the Law on Mount Sinai. The next one, Leviticus, receives its name from Levi, the priestly tribe of Israel, because it regulates the official worship of the people. Numbers gives an account of the holy army of Israel, its numerical strength, and its marching orders on the way through the desert. The last of the books of Moses is Deuteronomy, which means "recapitulation of the Law," written in the form of three addresses which the aging Moses delivered to his people shortly before he died.

A Different Kind of History

The first eleven chapters of Genesis form a whole quite apart from the rest of the book, and in modern commentaries they are usually referred to as "primeval history" because they trace the history of mankind from the beginning of creation to Abraham.

We should be aware, however, that these chapters do not give the kind of history that modern scholars present in their writings. No attempt is made in these chapters to give a complete account of "historical developments" in prehistoric times. The author of Genesis does not register historical events in their chronological order. He does not think in terms of centuries but of "generations." The Book of Genesis is divided into ten "generations" (see 2:4; 5:1; 6:9; 10:1; 11:10; 11:27; 25:12; 25:19; 36:1; 37:2). The first five of these make up the primeval history in the following order:

1. the generations of the heavens and the earth: the history of Paradise and the Fall (2:4–4:26)
2. the generations of Adam: the history of the Sethites (5:1–6:8)
3. the generations of Noah: the history of the Deluge (6:9–9:29)
4. the generations of the sons of Noah: the building of the tower of Babel and the dispersion of the peoples (10:1–11:9)
5. the generations of Shem: the genealogy from Shem to Abraham (11:10-26).

We see that the word "generation" is really the key word of Genesis. It means the handing down, from father to son, of a totality of life, the "seed." The family receives from the father a common stock in which each member participates and which unfolds in the life of the sons. The father is the "root" out of which the family grows like the branches of a tree.

Adam, therefore, is not only the first of a series of individuals but the root out of which the whole tree of mankind grows. His life affects all his posterity. His fall becomes in them "original sin."

History in the Old Testament is therefore the progressive unfolding of an original "soul" which repeats in each generation basically the same pattern of life. As the rabbis say: "The lives of the patriarchs foreshadow the story of their descendants." The life of Abraham, for example, anticipates the whole history of the Jewish people, and later on the life of Christ becomes the pattern imitated in the lives of his "generation."

The common life that in this way fills each generation is never produced by the father but has always been received or handed down from an ancestor. The first of these ancestors could come into being only through an act of creation, through which God himself sets the absolute beginning of the chain of generations. Creation exists only to make generation possible. Therefore, the generations of Genesis are preceded by a "creation" in which they are all rooted.

For this reason the Book of Genesis must be explained not in the light of geology or paleology but in the light of the history of the chosen people as it is presented in the other parts of the Old Testament and fulfilled in Christ. There we find unfolded what is contained, in a "primitive" form, in the first chapters of Genesis. The "beginning" in which all things were created (Gn 1:1) is the Word of God, the Son. "All things have been created through him and unto him. He existed before all things and he sustains and embraces them all" (Col 1:16-17). The Creation, therefore, is an expression of the infinite love that later manifested itself in the work of redemption: "For it has pleased God the Father that ... through his Son he should reconcile all things to himself, whether on the earth or in the heavens, making peace through the blood of his cross" (Col 1:20-21).

Love Creates

This divine love, which at the end of the ages appeared in the "Lamb that has been slain from the foundation of the earth" (Rv 13:8), shows its eternal pattern clearly on the first pages of Holy Scripture. The majestic sentence, "In the beginning God created heaven and earth," excludes all attempts to turn the world upside down and leave it to its own poor self. It saves the universe from the blind urge of self-perfection and anchors it instead in the love that descends from God.

One should notice that it is not only "heaven" (in Hebrew, "what is above"—the spiritual world) that love has created but also earth (in Hebrew, "what is below"—matter). The world is created to offer room for God's love. The earth is that room for love, because it is "void and empty," covered with darkness and with waters (1:2).

The "Spirit of God" does not dwell in heaven but hovers like a mother bird in the darkness over the waters. Purposely so. This hovering of the Spirit over the abyss reveals the patience in which God's love will be waiting—giving room for repentance to the chaos of sin—until, through his creative Word, God calls light out of darkness (1:3).

Darkness, however, does not disappear altogether. Only God is all light. The world is created to be the scene of history where light and darkness alternate, so that every new day, rising out of darkness, is a repetition of the first manifestation of God's creative love, when he said: "Let there be light." Darkness itself receives a place and function in the workings of God's love. It is called "night" (1:5): That means it is the "mother" out of whom the light of the day is constantly reborn.

God's love now turns to the other element of chaos, the waters. Again it does not annihilate them, but it divides them through the solid dome of the sky into the waters above and the waters below (1:6-7). Mightily and gently they are forced into the service of love: the waters above to give rain, the waters below to well up in springs and rivers.

Descending once more, love gathers the waters below to let the dry land appear (1:9). On the earth, thus rising out of the waters, there is good land, fields and pastures, for the cattle to live on. There is wilderness with thickets and deserts for the wild beasts. Finally, there is dust, the lowest element, for the "crawling things" (1:24). It is significant that love takes the dust to form man in its own image and likeness (2:7).

Love continues to divide: "Male and female he created them" (1:27). The woman is second. But man will leave father and mother to cleave to her (2:24), thus foreshadowing the love that moved the

Son to leave the glory he had with the Father in order to die for his bride, the Church. The woman is the first to fall victim to the subtlety of the serpent (3:4-7), but she is also the first to receive the promise of salvation, that her seed will crush the serpent's head (3:15).

The First Generations

The separation into a higher and a lower part, which constantly opens new room for God's love, is continued in the sons of Adam, Cain and Abel (chapter 4). *Abel* in Hebrew means "the weak one." Abel is good only to tend the sheep; Cain is the stronger one. He helps his father till the soil in the sweat of his brow.

God's love, however, finds its true image in the weaker one and accepts his sacrifice. After Cain has become guilty of his brother's blood, he is poorer than his brother ever was, a fugitive on the earth. It is then that love turns to him, and puts a seal on his forehead as a sign of salvation (4:15).

The sons of Cain are "smart people." They bring to the world the blessings of civilization (4:17, 20-22). Selfless love, however, grows cold among them, and lust and violence move in to fill the vacuum. Cain's descendant Lamech was the first to take two wives, and in front of them he brags with the sword of vengeance in his hand (4:23-24). With Lamech the "mighty ones," the "sons of God," the "men of renown" (6:1-4), make their first appearance on the scene of history.

Because God's grace does not find any room in them, a new beginning is set with Seth, who like a new shoot rises out of the stump of Adam (4:25). His descendants do not contribute much to the progress of human civilization. The first is called Enosh, which means "weakling" (5:6). This name characterizes man in all his nothingness. "What is 'Enosh' that you should think of him, and the son of man that you should care for him?" (Ps 8:4). Because he has nothing to brag about, he is the first to call upon the name of Yahweh, the name that stands for God's mercy. "From the mouth of babes and infants you have established a stronghold of praise" (Ps 8:2).

Outstanding among the descendants of Seth is Enoch, the seventh generation after Adam. He lives as many years as the sun year has days, 365 years. His name means "beginning" or "initiation." It points mysteriously to the dawn of a new day. After his first son was born, he began to "walk with God" (5:22), setting an "example of repentance for all generations" (Sir 44:16). With him God interrupts the ever-repeated burden of this chapter, "and he died." This is to show that "if by one man's offense death reigned through one (that is, Adam), all the more will those who receive God's overflowing mercy and his gift of justice, live and reign through one, Jesus Christ" (Rom 5:17).

Saved From Deluge

The last in this line of generations of Seth is Noah, who "in time of wrath was taken in exchange for the world" (Sir 44:17). After the Deluge he planted, as the head of a new generation, the vine, symbol of blessing and of joy (9:20). Among all the "giants" of his age, he was the only one "in whom Yahweh was well pleased" (6:4, 8). These words are taken up by the voice from heaven that said of Jesus at his baptism: "This is my beloved son in whom I am well pleased" (Mt 3:17), thus indicating that Noah was "fulfilled" in Christ. This is all the more true because Christ's baptism evidently refers to the Deluge.

If we link the story of the Deluge with that of the Creation, we realize that the Deluge is a relapse, by reason of man's sin, into the original chaos. The waters above and the waters below cover again the dry land between them. If we link it with later events in the history of the chosen people, we realize that the opening of the Red Sea for the Israelites and its subsequent closing to drown the Egyptians is a "repetition" of creation and flood. The invasion of the Holy Land by the Assyrians in the eighth century B.C. was another "flood" (see Is 8:7).

But in all these deluges chaos never triumphs completely. Noah survives with his family in the ark. Moses divides the waters with his rod. The Assyrian flood and the Babylonian captivity leave a "remnant" that returns to the Promised Land.

There is only one moment in the history of salvation when chaos seems to conquer: the "hour of the Messiah," when the sun loses its light, the mountains quake, and the waters of the Passion cover both body and soul of the Saviour, who cries "My God, my God, why have you forsaken me?" The risen Christ is like the light that God called out of darkness on the first day of Creation. That is the reason why the Resurrection took place on a Sunday, the first day of the week. Christ in his Easter glory is like another rainbow appearing in the clouds after the flood has passed.

All this has become a concrete reality for us, because our baptism and confirmation are the "repetition" in us of what happened to the world in the beginning. "For God, who commanded the light to shine out of darkness, has shone in our hearts to give us the light of the knowledge of God's glory, that is on the face of Christ Jesus" (2 Cor 4:6). From the first "day" of Creation—through the Flood, the deliverance of the chosen people at the Red Sea, and the survival of the "remnant"; to the baptism of Christ in the Jordan, his death and resurrection; and to our baptism and confirmation—leads one of those "pathways" that link our own lives to the first pages of the Book of Genesis. It is the ever-repeated triumph of God's love over the powers of selfishness.

TWO

Genesis 12–50: The Patriarchal Period

With chapter 12 of the Book of Genesis we enter into a new phase in the history of our salvation, the period of the great patriarchs of the Jewish people: Abraham, Isaac, and Jacob. God's dealings with Abraham and his two sons, Ishmael and Isaac, are reported in chapters 12–25:18. Chapters 25:19–36:43 relate the story of Isaac and his sons, Esau and Jacob. Chapters 37–50 contain the story of Jacob's descendants, particularly of his son Joseph. The patriarchal period comprises, therefore, the time from the migration of Abraham, about 2000 B.C., to the settling of the Israelites in Egypt two or three hundred years later.

Although we are not able to give the dates of these events, recent excavations, such as those in Abraham's home country of Ur and those that brought to light the El-Amarna tablets and the archives of Mari, have shed more light on life in Mesopotamia and the adjacent regions during the early second millennium before Christ. W.F. Albright sums up the results of this work: "So many corroborations of details [concerning the Patriarchal Age] have been discovered in recent years that most competent scholars have given up the old critical theory according to which the stories of the patriarchs are mostly retrojections from the time of the Dual-Monarchy (ninth to eighth centuries B.C.)."[1]

However, it is not the purpose of *Pathways* to expound the historical aspects of the Old Testament but rather to read it in the light of Christ. We are interested in the personalities and the lives of the patriarchs because each of them foreshadows in his own way the coming Saviour.

Father Abraham

Abraham is in all things the "great father" (Sir 44:19) and therefore typifies Christ as the father of a new generation. Abraham becomes "a father of many nations" (17:4), not through the will of the flesh nor the will of man (Jn 1:13), but through the blessing he receives from God. The word *blessing* is the key word in the narrative of Abraham's call: "I will bless you,... and you shall be a blessing. And I will bless those who bless you,... and in you shall all the kindreds of the earth be blessed" (12:2-3).

This blessing is given to Abraham and to his seed (13:15), which, as St. Paul explains, is Christ (Gal 3:16). He is the greatest of the "sons of Abraham" (see Mt 1:1), and through him Abraham's blessing has reached us. "If you be Christ's then you are the seed of Abraham, and his heirs under the promise" (Gal 3:29).

If Abraham foreshadows Christ as the father of a new generation, his son Isaac points to Christ as the Son. All through his life Isaac remains the typical son. With childlike confidence he follows his father to Mount Moriah to be offered (see chapter 22; the word *son* is the key word of this chapter). He grows up to be a kindly and gracious but never a strong man. He serves his God not as a "friend" as his father Abraham did, but in the fear of an obedient child.[2] At the end of his life, "when his eyes were so dim that he could not see" (27:1), acting as a mere instrument in the hands of God, he hands down the blessing to the younger son, Jacob.

The history of the patriarchs culminates in the formation of the house of Jacob. As the patriarchs foreshadow Christ, so does the house of Jacob reflect the spiritual order of grace that in our era became embodied in the Church. God's call to Abraham to leave his country and his kindred and his father's house for the land that he would show him is really the beginning of the Church. The Greek word for church, *ecclesia,* means "community of those who are called out"—called out of a world in which man is the center into a new order established by God's grace and serving God's glory.

By birth Abraham, the first "convert," belongs to the man-centered civilization of Babel, which finds its typical expression in the tower put up by organized masses of men eager to reach heaven for the sole purpose of self-glorification (11:4). Abraham is called by God to sever his ties with this city and to seek another one "which has true foundations, whose builder and maker is God" (Heb 11:10). Guided by faith, he reached the Promised Land. Acting in all things as God's yeoman he symbolically takes possession of the country not by hoisting a national flag but by erecting altars. He knows that the Holy Land is given to his posterity for the higher purpose of the glorification of God. In the same spirit we see him, when he has achieved victory, bending his knees before Melchizedek, the priest-king of Salem (later Jerusalem), who foreshadows the royal priesthood of the risen Christ (see Gn 14:18-20; Heb 7).

The power that makes Abraham a father of many nations and a friend of God is his faith. "Abraham believed God, and it was reputed to him unto justice" (15:6). The Hebrew word for *believe* has the meaning of "trusting in another's power." The power that distinguishes God from all creatures is the power to create life. To believe in God means to accept him as the one "who slays and makes alive, who brings down to the land of the dead and raises up again" (1 Sm 2:6).

God's Promise and Covenant

The two great "signs" of God's life-giving power are the Virgin Birth and the resurrection of Christ. These two mysteries are foreshadowed in the two events in the life of Abraham through which God tested his faith: the birth of Isaac (chapter 17) and the sacrifice on Mount Moriah (chapter 22).

Abraham and Sarah believed in the grace of God as the source of all life when they accepted God's promise of a son, although they had passed the age of procreation (see Rom 4:19). Their "laughter" is the expression of the joy that fills the hearts of those who believe the glad tidings of Christmas and see the Day of the Lord (see Jn 8:56).

It is faith in the Resurrection that gives Abraham the strength to offer Isaac as a sacrifice. He has believed in God's promise that through Isaac he is to have descendants bearing his name (21:12). If he now is ready to sacrifice his son, it is only because he believes that God is able to raise men even from the dead, "and from the dead he did indeed, in a similitude, receive him back" (Heb 11:19). St. Augustine asks:

> In whose similitude but of him of whom the Apostle says: "He that spared not his own Son, but delivered him up for us all" (Rom 8:32)? On his account Isaac also himself carried to the place of sacrifice the wood on which he was to be offered up, just as the Lord himself carried his own cross. Finally, since Isaac was not to be slain, who was that ram which was offered in his stead? When Abraham saw it, it was caught by the horns in a thicket of briars (22:13). What then did it represent but Jesus, who, before he was offered up, was crowned with thorns?[3]

The new order of grace and of faith to be established in Abraham's city is foreshadowed, too, in the covenant between God and Abraham. This covenant is formally established through a sacrifice. The sacrificial animals are cut in half and the pieces are put opposite each other so as to form a "blood street" through which the partners can pass in confirmation of the covenant (15:10).

As the sun is going down, "a great and awful gloom" falls on Abraham (15:12). God lays upon the father of the chosen people the burden of the four hundred years of slavery in Egypt that his children will endure before they are allowed to settle in the Promised Land. In the midst of this darkness, which reminds us of the distress and dread that fell on Jesus on Mount Olivet (Mk 14:33), Abraham receives God's promise of future deliverance (15:14-16). To confirm it, a deeply significant manifestation of God's charity takes place: "When the sun had set and it was quite dark, a cloud of smoke and a blazing torch passed between the pieces" (15:17).

God and not Abraham passes through the "blood street" to show that he himself is the origin of this covenant of grace. The cloud of smoke and the blazing torch prefigure the "column of cloud by day" and the "pillar of fire by night" (Ex 13:21) through which God fulfills his promise to Abraham when he leads his people out of Egypt. Both signs are fulfilled in the sacrifice of the new covenant, when the Son of God, rather than passing through the blood street, shed his own blood in confirmation of the covenant, his charity shining like a blazing torch in the hour of darkness (see Lk 22:53).

The covenant between God and Abraham received its seal in circumcision (chapter 17), which is the outward sign of the internal circumcision of the heart, which Abraham possesses in his faith in God (Rom 4:11). The circumcision signifies, as St. Augustine says, "a nature renewed on the putting off of the old flesh."[4] That circumcision is to be done on the eighth day after birth (17:12) points to Christ, who rose on the first day after the week was completed. The very change of names of the parents (17:5) indicates newness of life. Circumcision is fulfilled in baptism, where the old man of the flesh dies with Christ that the new man may be born in the power of his resurrection (see Col 2:11-12).

Jacob's Lie

The same order of grace that appears in the story of Abraham and his sons is revealed again in the "generations of Isaac" (25:19–36:43). Like

Sarah, Isaac's wife Rebekah is barren until Isaac entreats God for her (25:21). In answer to his prayers twin sons are born to Rebekah. When the children struggle in her womb, Rebekah consults the Lord and receives the answer: "Two nations are in your womb,... and the older shall serve the younger" (25:23).

This sentence, one of the most decisive of the Old Testament, has authentically been interpreted by St. Paul in his Letter to the Romans (9:11-13): "Before the children were born or had done anything either good or bad, in order that God's purpose may stand out clearly as his own choice, which depends not on what men do but on his calling them, she was told: 'The elder shall be the younger's servant!' As Scripture says: 'Jacob I loved but Esau I hated.'"

To show that his love is the only source of salvation, God repeatedly reverses the order of birth. Cain is rejected, and Abel is chosen. Jacob is given preference before Esau. Of the two sons of Joseph, it is the younger one, Ephraim, who receives the blessing of Jacob (48:11-20). The story of Esau and Jacob was repeated with the twin sons of Judah (38:29). Samuel was ordered by God to anoint David, the youngest of the sons of Jesse, as king of Israel (1 Sm 16:1-13). Of the sons of David, Solomon, the last in order of succession, ascended to the throne of his father (1 Kgs 1).

We are moving here on one of those "pathways" that lead through the Old Testament straight to Christ. He resumes the theme of the older and the younger brother in the parable of the Prodigal Son, showing that it is the father's heart that makes him *prefer* the younger one: "This your brother was dead and is alive again; and was lost and is found" (Lk 15:32). Because God is charity, there is more joy in heaven over one sinner who repents than over ninety-nine just persons who do not need repentance (Lk 15:7).

For the same reason God's only begotten Son left his Father's glory to become the last by taking upon himself our sins and dying a criminal's death. Because the "children of the kingdom" refused to accept him as their king, they were cast out, and the *hoi polloi* were called from the east and west to sit down with Abraham, Isaac, and Jacob in the kingdom of heaven (see Mt 8:11-12).

Christ, taking upon himself our sins, bearing off, in a manner of speaking, the primacy of the synagogue, and transferring it to the Church of the Gentiles, is the key also to the famous story of Isaac's blessing (chapter 27). Jacob's lie, in passing himself off as his older brother in order to receive his father's blessing, has offered welcome material for criticism to the enemies of the Old Testament and has caused much embarrassment to many of its admirers. We should not be afraid, however, to admit the lie in the immediate, historical sense of the report as long as we are able to discern its spiritual meaning. According to the latter Jacob's "lie" points to another "disguise" which is not a lie but a mystery of divine charity: the incarnation of the Son of God and the crucifixion of the innocent Lamb bearing our sins. St. Augustine says:

> Assuredly, he covered some parts of his body with the skins of kids. If we judge this deed by its immediate cause, we shall account him to have lied; for he did this that he might be taken for the man he was not. But if this deed is judged by its final cause—its signification—then the skins of the kids stand for sins; and he who covered himself with them signified him who bore not his own sins but the sins of others. Therefore the true signification cannot in any sense be rightly a lie.
>
> The same is true of his words. For when his father said to him: "Who are you, my son?" he answered: "I am Esau." Now if this be taken in reference to those twin brothers it will seem a lie; but if it is taken in its deeper meaning, it has to be understood of Christ in his body, the Church, of which he said—in reference to this episode—"Behold, they are the last that were first, and they are first that were last!"[5]

Prophetic Lives

The mystery of the Incarnation and the death of Christ is foreshadowed also in other events of Jacob's life, as in the report of his flight (chapter 28). On leaving the Promised Land, tired as he was, he laid his head upon a stone. When he had fallen asleep, he saw in a vision "a ladder standing upon the earth and the top thereof touching heaven: the angels also of the Lord ascending and descending by it, and the Lord leaning upon the ladder" (28:12-13).

Jacob sleeping with his head on a stone is a vivid picture of the faithful who put all their trust in God's eternal love. The ladder that appeared to him when he was in this position is evidently a symbol of the incarnation of the Son of God (see Jn 1:51), whose resurrection and eternal priesthood are prefigured in the stone, which Jacob anointed and set up as a memorial.

On Jacob's return to the Promised Land another mysterious event took place, which also receives light from Christ's death and resurrection. "Jacob was left alone; and there wrestled a man with him until the breaking of the day" (32:24). The "man" refused to give Jacob his name, because the name of the Saviour is only revealed in the New Testament. He gave, however, a hint as to his identity when he said to Jacob: "Your name shall no longer be Jacob but Israel (wrestler with God), because you have wrestled with God and with man and have overcome" (32:28). God suffering to be overcome by man is Christ in his passion. He blesses mankind at the daybreak of his resurrection.

Among the descendants of Jacob (chapters 37–50), Joseph and Judah are outstanding—the former as a type of Christ, the latter as his ancestor. The story of Joseph is, from an aesthetic point of view, the unsurpassed jewel of Old Testament literary art. For one who reads it "in the Spirit" it is a story of the salvation of the world through Christ.

Joseph, the son of Jacob, who through the jealousy of his brothers is put into the pit, sold into slavery, imprisoned, then exalted to the throne of Pharaoh, saves not only Israel but Egypt as well. His life is the prophetic prelude to the history of the suffering servant of God, the one refused by all the sons of Jacob, the brother sold for thirty pieces of silver, who descended into hell and was exalted to the right hand of the Father.

At the blessing of Joseph's two sons by Jacob (48:8-20), divine love once again prefers the younger to the older. To put his right hand on the younger and his left hand on the elder one, Jacob needs to extend his hands in the form of the cross.

The words of the dying Jacob with which he blessed his son Judah clearly point to the Messiah-King who will spring from the tribe of Judah: "The sceptre shall not depart from Judah, nor the rod from between his feet, until the ruler comes to whom the nations shall be obedient.... He washes his robe in wine and his clothes in the blood of grapes" (49:10-11). The rule of the Messiah-King shall be universal. "His robe" signifies the Church, which he washes in the "blood of grapes" (49:11) by cleansing her with his blood on the cross and in the sacrament of the holy Eucharist.

Only from the fact that the Messiah will be a son of Judah can the attitude of Tamar, Judah's daughter-in-law, be understood (chapter 38). Her deed typifies the longing of the Church to be the mother (the bearer) of the Messiah. That her younger son, Perez, becomes the ancestor of David, and therefore of Christ, represents another one of those strange "twists of fate" through which the love of God asserts its superiority over the claims of birth.

THREE

The Book of Exodus

Genesis was the book of the fathers, of their generations and their blessings. Exodus is the book of the people, reporting its liberation and its constitution as an independent nation under God. With Exodus we leave the narrow circle of the family and enter into the arena of world history. The fathers, Abraham, Isaac, and Jacob, are succeeded by Moses, the great political leader and lawgiver of his people.

The entire first part of the book (1:1–15:21) is taken up with the struggle between the two great opponents, Moses, the liberator, and Pharaoh, the oppressor. The second part (15:22–31:18) is devoted to the covenant, through which the liberated people becomes officially the "people of God" by accepting freely the Law God gives them through Moses. The last part of Exodus (chapters 32–40) describes the restoration of the broken covenant.

The history of the Israelite people is a faithful picture of the history of mankind. As the Israelites were living in Egypt as oppressed and wretched slaves under a cruel tyrant, so are we by birth slaves, enslaved to the devil. As the Israelites were led by Moses out of Egypt, where they were strangers, to the country that had been promised to them as their own possession, so the Church is led by Christ from this world, where we live as exiles and strangers, to our real home, the heavenly Jerusalem.

It is inspiring to see how faithfully the events described in the Book of Exodus prefigure the history of our own liberation. It has long been the Church's practice to read this book during Lent, when the whole Church is fighting with greater intensity in the old battle against the

49

devil for man's spiritual freedom. In that season every detail of the Book of Exodus takes on a new meaning and bears an immediate relation to our own lives.

We cannot read about Moses in those days without realizing that he set the pattern of the fast of forty days and forty nights, which later was fulfilled by Christ and his Church. We cannot hear about the paschal lamb, the Red Sea, the march through the desert, the feeding with manna, and last but not least, the manifestation of God on Mount Sinai, without seeing all these marvels transpire again in our churches and in our souls during the days of Lent when we recall Christ, our Paschal Lamb, being immolated.

The tremendous amount of material contained in the Book of Exodus might suitably be divided into the following eight sections.

1. Birth and early years of Moses (1:1–2:25). The blessing God bestowed upon Abraham and his seed shows its power in an extraordinary vitality that makes the Jews increase rapidly, like shoals of fish (see Gn 1:20; 48:16). On the other hand, the purely human civilization of the Egyptians gradually reduces their vitality (Ex 1:19). Pharaoh becomes alarmed, and the old and the ever-new play of power politics begins: first oppression through slave labor and concentration camps (1:11-14), then some primitive kind of "birth control" (1:15-21), finally open mass murder (1:22).

Humanly speaking, the situation of the Jews is hopeless, because they have no arms to defend themselves. God, however, chooses the weak to scatter the proud in the conceit of their hearts. A mother, a sister, and Pharaoh's daughter become the instruments of salvation.

The liberator is born, a lovely child; but there is no room on this earth for him (see Lk 2:7). His mother puts him into a little "ark" (the expressions used in Exodus 2:3 are the same as those used in Genesis 6:14 to describe Noah's ark). The child then becomes really a "Moses," which means "one drawn out" (2:10), out of the water, by Pharaoh's daughter.

Who would not think here of Noah and the Flood, of the people and the Red Sea, of Christ's baptism in the Jordan, of our own baptism? Every Christian is a "Moses" because he has been drawn out of the water.

Adopted by the princess, Moses is reared in Pharaoh's palace until the time comes when the spirit of the Saviour begins to descend upon him. Seeing the affliction of his people, he leaves the glory of the palace to take the part of the oppressed, "esteeming the reproach of Christ greater riches than the treasures of the Egyptians" (Heb 11:24-26). He points to the coming Saviour, who will leave his Father's heavenly glory "to take on the nature of a slave" (Phil 2:7).

2. The call (ordination) of Moses (3:1–7:13). Moses was called by God when he was living as "an exile in a foreign land" (2:22), thus anticipating the characteristic fate of his people. "The angel of the Lord appeared to him in a flame of fire, rising out of a thornbush" (3:2). In this "great sign" the whole history of our salvation is contained.

The fire is a symbol of God, who is "a consuming fire, a jealous God" (Dt 4:24). The thornbush, in its lowliness and worthlessness, represents the Israelite people and the whole of mankind in this state of fallen nature. The "angel of the Lord" is in the Old Testament, very often the Son of God. The fire that does not consume the thornbush foreshadows the Incarnation, which leaves intact the human nature of Christ.

The apparition in the burning bush initiates a new period in the history of our salvation. The time has come when God will fulfill the promises made to the patriarchs. It is this new activity that is indicated in the revelation of a new name of God. As long as the fathers of Israel wandered about in the Promised Land as strangers and guests, God made himself known to them under the name of *El Shaddai*, which usually is translated "God Almighty," to show that he was able to fulfill his promise (Gn 17:1; 28:3; Ex 6:3). The fulfillment itself, when

God leads his people into Canaan to take possession of it, stands under the sign of the name Yahweh, which means "I am that I am" (3:14). This name reveals the absolute truthfulness of God, whose promise of salvation will never be revoked. He is the "Yes" and "Amen" to all his promises, the Alpha and Omega, the first and last letter in the alphabet of human history.

Moses dreads his mission (4:10), as centuries later Jeremiah dreaded his (Jer 1:6). No true apostle is self-appointed. If he is called by God, however, he participates in his power (see Mk 16:17-18). As symbol of his apostolic power Moses receives "the rod of God" (4:20; 17:9), which he may use to heal or to strike. The rod clearly points to the cross of Christ, the powerful scepter in the hands of the Son of God made man with which he strikes Satan and heals mankind.

Two other events in this connection are of typical importance. The first is that Moses receives Aaron, his brother, to help him (4:14). The divine apostolate is exercised through the cooperation of two men. Our Lord practices the same system, sending out his apostles "two by two" (Mk 6:7). The greatest of all apostles, St. Paul, is never alone. Important parts of the Acts of the Apostles are written in the first person plural (see Acts 20). The reason for this is evident: The success of any apostolic activity does not depend on the personality of the preacher. He acts in everything as a member of the community of God's saints.

The other incident reported here and closely connected with Moses' mission is the strange encounter between him and God when he is with his family on his journey to Egypt (4:24-26). The incident shows that Moses cannot enter upon his mission without "having fulfilled all justice" (see Mt 3:15). An apostle is never an anarchist who wants to create something completely new by first destroying what has been built before. God's ways with men are not marked by overthrows and revolutions but by continuity through tradition, because God remains always faithful to himself. For this reason Moses, the mediator of the new covenant of Mount Sinai, has to fulfill the covenant of the circumcision. Likewise the Founder of the New Testament is circumcised (Lk 2:21), and baptized (Mt 3:15), and he does not want to take so much as a comma from the Law of Moses (Mt 5:18).

3. The plagues of Egypt (7:14–11:10). Very often we ask ourselves, "Why does God give so much power to his enemies?" God's dealing with Pharaoh, as described in these chapters, gives the answer. It is set forth in God's message to Pharaoh: "This is why I have spared you: to show you my power, and to have my glory recounted throughout all the earth" (9:16). For this purpose God "hardens the heart of Pharaoh" (11:10) and increases the plagues, until finally all have to confess, "This is the finger of God!" (8:19). Christ makes it clear which conclusion the wise men of Egypt and their Pharaoh should have drawn from this confession when he quotes this word: "If it is with the finger of God that I am driving the demons out, then the kingdom of God has overtaken you" (Lk 11:20).

Notwithstanding all the power of Pharaoh, no real struggle ensues between him and God. Frogs, mosquitoes, and locusts are sent out against him. "He that sits in the heavens laughs at them, the Lord makes sport of his enemies" (Ps 2:4).

This divine glory, however, is like a thin veil over God's wrath. God is not mocked (Gal 6:7). When the "angel of destruction" passes through the land to slay all the firstborn of Egypt, Pharaoh and his people will see that it is indeed "a fearful thing to fall into the hands of the living God" (Heb 10:31).

4. The liberation (12:1–15:21). The hour of death for the firstborn of Egypt is the hour of freedom for the "firstborn of God," the Israelite nation (4:22-23). The month of liberation is called "the first month of the year" (12:2) because it is the beginning of a new era. The night of salvation is to be celebrated as "a vigil for the Lord by all the Israelites throughout their generations" (12:42).

Needless to say, here we stand at the cradle of the Christian Easter vigil and of the whole ecclesiastical year. Christ celebrates this vigil at the Last Supper. Offering himself, the "firstborn" of the Father, as the true Paschal Lamb for the sins of the world (1 Cor 5:7), he fulfills the prophetic night observance of the Old Testament and replaces it with another "memorial," the Mass.

St. John reports that on the tenth of the month Jesus enters Jerusalem (Jn 12:1, 12), the very day when the paschal lamb has to be provided (12:3-6). It has to be kept until the fourteenth day of the same month, "and then the whole assembly of the community of Israel must slaughter it in the first evening" (14:6), that is, between three and five o'clock. On the same day, at three in the afternoon (Lk 23:45), Jesus dies. The soldiers do not break his legs, to fulfill what the Scripture provides for the paschal lamb: "Not one of his bones shall be broken" (12:46; see Jn 19:33-36). One of the soldiers opens his side with a lance, and immediately blood and water flow out. This shows that the sacraments of baptism (water) and of the Eucharist (blood) have replaced the Passover of the Old Testament (Jn 19:34).

Led by the column of cloud by day and of fire by night, the Israelites leave Egypt, only to see themselves caught between Pharaoh's army and the Red Sea (14:10). In this desperate situation Moses rises to his full stature. "Fear not!" he says. (How often do we hear this word repeated by God's messengers in the New Testament? See Lk 1:30; Mt 28:5.) "Stand still and see the salvation of the Lord. The Lord will fight for you, while you only have to keep still!" (14:13-14).

To keep still is the attitude of those who believe. Like another Moses, Isaiah repeated these words when he exhorted his people in a similar danger: "For thus says the Lord God, the Holy One of Israel: If you will sit still and be at rest, you shall be saved. In quietness and confidence shall be your strength" (Is 30:15). For the Israelites at the Red Sea "it was good to wait in silence for the salvation of the Lord" (Lam 3:26).

In their silence Moses raises his rod, the sign of the cross, and God moves the sea away by means of a strong wind—reminiscent of the Spirit of God moving over the waters (Gn 1:2) and of the wind that abates the waters of the flood (Gn 8:1). The Israelites pass through the Red Sea unharmed. The pursuing Egyptians are drowned. "And the people stood in awe of the Lord and believed in the Lord" (14:31). Thus they are "baptized in the cloud and in the sea" (1 Cor 10:2).

The first fruits of the new God-given freedom are the divine praises. Moses, the liberator, intones the song of triumph: "Let us sing to the Lord for he is highly exalted. The horse and its rider he has thrown into the sea!" (15:1). The whole people join him in song. Miriam, Moses' sister, takes a timbrel in hand, and all the women go out after her with timbrels and with dances (15:20).

This is the hour when the Divine Office is born. The joy of salvation must find its expression in the liturgy, meaning the common, public worship of God's people. Isaiah has announced God's rule in an admirable passage in which he draws a line from the first victory of God over the waters of chaos (Gn 1:2), to the deliverance at the Red Sea and further to the "Assyrian flood" of his own time:

> Awake, awake, put on strength, O arm of the Lord! Awake, as in days of old, as in generations long gone! Was it not you that did hew chaos in pieces, that did pierce the dragon [creation]? Was it not you that did dry up the sea, the waters of the mighty deep, that did make the depths of the sea a way for the redeemed to pass over [the Red Sea]? So the ransomed of the Lord will return by it [that is, from the Babylonian exile], and will come to Zion with singing, and with everlasting joy upon their heads.
>
> ISAIAH 51:9-11

That this same pattern of events is not confined to the Old Testament but determines the history of the Church down to the last days is solemnly attested to by John in his Apocalypse. He sees the dragon persecuting the woman and her child by pouring water from his mouth like a river (Rv 12:15). In the next vision he sees the seven angels ready to pour the seven plagues, prefigured in the plagues of Egypt, over the world "to complete the expression of God's wrath" (Rv 15:1). At the same moment he sees "those who have overcome" standing upon the sea of glass. They have harps that God had given them, and they are singing the song of Moses and the song of the Lamb: "Great and marvelous are your works, Lord God Almighty!" (Rv 15:3). We see that the ultimate purpose of salvation is the glorification of God through his people.

5. The march through the desert (15:22–18:27). The years in the desert are the years of childhood for Israel (Hos 11), when the divine Father teaches his firstborn its first steps. They are the years of "the first love," when the divine Bridegroom leads his bride "into the wilderness to speak to her heart" (Hos 2:14).

The barren desert is the place where Israel learns to depend exclusively on God. When the water is bitter, God points out a tree that will sweeten it (15:23-25). For the hungry he rains manna from heaven and gives quail for meat. He makes water pour forth from the rock for the thirsty (16:4-21; 17:6). He protects them from the fury of Amalek by ordering Moses to lift up his hands in the form of the cross (17:11).

"All these things were written to instruct us," St. Paul says (1 Cor 10:11). They foreshadow the way God deals with his Church during her days of pilgrimage on this earth. The manna, the rock, the rod of Moses—they are all "prophetic." The manna points to the "bread from heaven" which Christ gives to the world (Jn 6:32-40). The rock is Christ, and the water is the Spirit which he will give to those who believe in him (Jn 7:37-39). We see the cross typified in the tree that sweetens the bitter waters and in the rod with which Moses strikes the rock.

6. The covenant (19:1–24:18). Fifty days after the passage through the Red Sea, the Law is given to the people and the covenant made through which Israel becomes God's "own treasure," a "kingdom of priests and a holy nation" (19:6). Fifty days after Christ had passed through his passion and death, the Holy Spirit descended on the apostles and the new Israel was founded, bound together not by the common observance of a law hewn on tablets of stone but by the Holy Spirit writing the new law in their hearts.

The solemn act of concluding the covenant is clearly distinguished in four different phases. It is preceded by three days of preparation (19:3-15). Because Israel is now free, it is first asked if it is willing to accept God's Law. Israel's answer, "Whatever God says, we will do" (19:8), reminds us of the answer that Mary gave to the angel when the new covenant was going to be made: "Be it done unto me according to your word" (Lk 1:38).

Although God will descend now upon Mount Sinai, he will remain the Lord, the Holy One. Therefore the people must be sanctified. Their clothes have to be washed, and the mountain of God's presence marked off (19:10-15).

This act of preparation is followed by the awe-inspiring manifestation of God's majesty. The whole mountain is wrapped in smoke because God descends upon it in fire (19:18). Abraham's vision (Gn 15:17) is now fulfilled. The Israelites stand far off in fear and trembling; only Moses and Aaron are allowed to come up and receive the Law (19:24). Entering the cloud of the divine presence, they hear the voice of God: "I am Yahweh your God." The essence of all true divine revelation is expressed in these words: "Without ceasing to be what I am, I become yours."

The voice that promulgates the decalogue is really the voice of love. That there may be true love between God and man, the glory of God has to be kept separate from all earthly things and human happenings. "You shall make no molten gods," that is, "When you think of God, you should really think of *him,* and not of a molten god which you have made in your own image."[1] As long as the glory of God is firmly established "in the highest" (commandments 1-3) and his fatherhood (see Eph 3:14) is reverently acknowledged in our earthly parents (commandment 4), peace will reign among men (commandments 5-10).

The Law was given to prepare men for the grace of Christ (see Jn 1:17). Therefore the promulgation of the law is followed by the offering of a sacrifice (chapter 24). The altar, which for this purpose is built at the foot of the mountain, prefigures Christ, who descended upon this earth. The twelve pillars surrounding the altar point first to the twelve tribes of Israel and further to the twelve apostles who were gathered around the table at the Last Supper.

Acting as mediator, Moses sprinkles one half of the blood of sacrifice upon the altar and the other half upon the people, thus indicating the intimate communion of life between God and his people. To make it clear that he has fulfilled this ceremony through his own sacrifice, Christ at the Last Supper takes up the same expression: "This is my blood of the new covenant." His blood, however, is not sprinkled only on the Israelite people but is "shed for the many," for the mass of the gentiles as well (Mk 14:24).

After the sacrifice Moses, Aaron, and the elders of Israel are invited into the presence of God to participate, on the top of the mountain, in the holy meal. This meal seals the intimate union between God and his people (24:9-11).

The four phases in the solemn conclusion of the covenant on Mount Sinai—preparation, promulgation of the Law, sacrifice, and meal—correspond exactly to the various parts of the Mass: the preparation, the readings, the sacrifice, and Communion. The public assembly of the people of the new covenant is the fulfillment of the great assembly of Israel.

However, we are not come to a mountain that may not be touched, or to a blazing fire, to blackness, darkness, and storm. We do not hear the trumpet blast or the voice whose words made those who heard them beg to be told no more, for they could not bear them (see Heb 12:18-19). We hear the glad tidings of redemption from the mouth of the Word of God made man. And instead of trembling with fear, we greet them with the singing of the alleluia.

For we have come to Mount Zion, the city of the living God, the heavenly Jerusalem, to the company of countless angels, to the solemn gathering of all of God's firstborn. We have come to Jesus and to the shedding of his blood (see Heb 12:22-24). No fence separates us from the presence of God.

On the contrary, we may follow the loving invitation: "Come and eat: this is my Body!" Through this comparison between the old and the new we realize our great privilege as Christians, and we say: "Let us, therefore, be thankful that the kingdom given us cannot be shaken, and so please God by worshipping him with reverence and awe; for our God is a consuming fire" (Heb 12:28-29).

7. The tabernacle and its servants (25–31; 35–40). God does not impose a law upon the people without assuring them of his presence in the "tent of meeting." God himself shows Moses its pattern. It is a copy of the whole universe. Its three divisions—the court, the sanctuary, and the Holy of Holies—represent the unredeemed world, the Church, and heaven.

The altar of the burnt offerings (27; 38:1-7) is placed in the court (40:6), that it may point to the sacrifice of Christ, who "suffered without the gate" of Jerusalem (Heb 13:12) to redeem the world. The bronze laver between the altar and the tabernacle (30:18) foreshadows the sacrament of baptism, which, through the purifying power of the sacrifice of Christ, enables men to enter the sanctuary of the Church. The golden altar of incense, the candlestick, and the "bread of the presence" (see 1 Sam 21:1-6) in the sanctuary represent the three great spiritual treasures of the Church: the light of doctrine, the sacramental bread, and the spiritual sacrifice of prayer.

The Holy of Holies symbolizes "the inner heart of heaven." The light of this world is not allowed to enter it. It contains the ark of the covenant with the tablets of the Law, surmounted by the "throne of grace" (37:1-9), to indicate that God's mercy will fulfill his justice.

This happens at the death of Christ, when the veil that bars the entrance into the Holy of Holies is rent "from the top even to the bottom" (Mt 27:51). No human hand—which would start at the bottom—but only God's descending love in the death of Christ gives us access with confidence to God's throne of grace to receive his forgiveness (see Heb 4:16).

Not only the tabernacle but also the vestments and the consecration of the servants of the sanctuary point to Christ and his priestly office. The priestly tunic of white linen, all woven work (39:27), reminds us of Christ's tunic, which is described as "white and glittering" at his transfiguration (Lk 9:29) and as "woven from the top throughout" at his crucifixion (Jn 19:23). That the priests at their consecration are washed in the laver and anointed with oil (29:4, 7) points to Christ's baptism in the Jordan and to the anointing with the Spirit right afterwards, through which his priestly dignity is made known to the world.

If we see our Christian baptism and confirmation against the background of this Old Testament ordination, we realize that these sacraments are meant to be an ordination to the common priesthood of all Christians. The white tunic that the neophytes receive at their baptism not only symbolizes their purity of heart and freedom from sin but also shows their priestly dignity.

8. *The broken covenant (32–34)*. While on top of the mountain God is showing Moses the glorious gifts that his love is going to bestow upon his people, the latter grow impatient over Moses' absence and make a visible and therefore more "reliable" god, the molten calf (32:1-6). The

covenant is broken before it has been put into effect. God uses the sin of the people, however, to manifest his love still more gloriously.

Moses shows himself in all his greatness as the true mediator between God and the people. He does not try to excuse the Israelites, but he appeals to the God of Abraham, Isaac, and Jacob, to the God who has pledged everlasting love to his chosen people (32:11-13). In this he succeeds. The lack of stability and faithfulness in the hearts of the Israelites causes God to disclose the "rock" of his everlasting love (33:21).

The rock upon which Moses has to stand to see the "back" of the Lord is a symbol of this "covenant love" of God. The "back" also means not the unveiled glory but the mercy which was made flesh in Christ Jesus. Standing on the rock of his faith in God's charity, Moses hears the name of God proclaimed: "Yahweh, Yahweh Elohim, merciful and gracious, patient and of much compassion and true" (34:6-7). It is like a reflection of this divine love in Moses, the mediator, that he offers to be blotted out of the Book of Life rather than see his people condemned (32:32).

In this same love Christ dies on the cross for the sins of the world. St. Paul wishes himself to be accursed and cut off from Christ for the sake of his brothers, his natural kindred (Rom 9:3). And St. Peter, the "rock" on which the Church is built, lays down his life for his sheep.

Moved by Moses' entreaties, God lets mercy triumph over justice. Instead of sending an angel, he himself goes with his people (33:2; 34:10). The Book of Exodus ends with the description of the glory of God descending upon the tabernacle and filling it with the cloud of the presence (40:34). Likewise the passover of Christ ended with the dedication of the Church on Pentecost when the strong wind and the fiery tongues of the Spirit descended upon the apostles.

Since then, the Christian has been a "temple of the Lord" (1 Cor 3:16). The Greek term used here by St. Paul does not mean "temple" only but "Holy of Holies." Thus the "sign" of the tabernacle is "fulfilled": Every Christian is a Holy of Holies!

FOUR

The Book of Leviticus

Of all the books of the Old Testament, Leviticus is probably the least known among Christians. Those who try to read this vast mass of statutes and rules about sacrifices and purifications will probably say, with the contemporaries of Origen, "Why should those things be read in Church? Of what use are Jewish observances to us? Those things concern the Jews; let the Jews worry about them."[1]

Indeed, we cannot read the first seven chapters of Leviticus, which deal exclusively with laws relating to sacrifice, without remembering what our Lord said to the Pharisees: "Go and learn what this means: 'I will have mercy and not sacrifice'" (Mt 9:13).

Likewise, chapters 11–15, which contain the laws relating to cleanliness, would seem to have no importance for disciples of Christ, to whom the Lord has said: "Have even you no understanding yet? Can you not see that whatever goes into the mouth passes into the stomach and then is disposed of? But the things that come out of the mouth come from the heart, and they pollute a man" (Mt 15:16-18). Was not St. Peter warned by a voice from heaven not to call what God had cleansed unclean (Acts 10:15), and did not the apostles decree at their first solemn council in Jerusalem: "The Holy Spirit and we have decided not to lay upon you any burden" (Acts 15:28)?

Even the third part of the Book of Leviticus, the so-called "law of holiness," which is chiefly concerned with the sanctification of the heart (chapters 17–26), is first of all a law for the Israelites living in the Holy Land and therefore seems to be of no concern to gentiles.

The Spiritual Sense

In his commentary on Leviticus, Origen tried to solve this difficulty by explaining the whole book according to his principle that the law is spiritual, and its interpretation should therefore rise above the literal sense.

> As the visible and the invisible things are related to one another: the earth and the heavens, the soul and the flesh, the body and the spirit, so that this world consists of the combinations of these elements, so also does holy Scripture consist of visible and invisible elements. Like one body it is composed of the visible letter, the soul—the meaning of the letter—and the spirit insofar as it contains also some heavenly things, as the apostle says: "They serve unto the example and shadow of heavenly things."
>
> HEBREWS 8:5

According to his threefold division of body, soul, and spirit in the nature of man, Origen distinguished the literal, moral, and mystical senses of the Scriptures.[2]

Some of his contemporaries criticized Origen's method as disregarding the "historical truth." Henri de Lubac, S.J., in his brilliant introduction to a French translation of the Homilies of Origen on Genesis,[3] has shown that Origen himself certainly did not have any intention to neglect the literal sense of the Scriptures. There can be no doubt, however, that during the Middle Ages the allegorical interpretation was greatly abused and became in many cases a refuge of ignorance. People who lacked the thorough familiarity with the letter of Holy Scripture that Origen possessed let their imaginations run wild whenever they were faced with difficult texts.

We may take as an example the commentary that the good Abbot Rupert of Deutz wrote on Leviticus. He explains the kinds of animals to be used for sacrifice as representing the various states of life. The bullocks, powerful but without much brains, are according to him an image of the ruling classes, the princes and the higher clergy. The doves and turtledoves represent the contemplatives, because they are moaning all the time. The doves do this in company, the turtledoves alone by themselves, which points to the two main kinds of religious, cenobites and hermits. The amusement that such explanations may give us cannot compensate for the feeling of frustration over arbitrary interpretations that have lost all contact with the letter.

Occasional abuse, however, is no reason to abandon altogether every attempt at sound spiritual interpretation of the Scriptures. In the case of Leviticus it is an absolute necessity to rise above the letter. A Christian who would recognize only the literal sense of Holy Scripture either has to deny the divine authority of Leviticus or has to adopt Judaism. He cannot do the first, because our Lord said, "I tell you, as long as heaven and earth endure, not one dotting of an i or crossing of a t will be dropped from the law until it is all observed" (Mt 5:18). Neither can he become a Jew, "for in Christ Jesus neither circumcision nor the want of it counts for anything, but only faith acting through love" (Gal 5:6).

The spiritual interpretation of Leviticus is, therefore, the only way to avoid denying the Scriptures without actively practicing Judaism. Actually, a Christian who grasps the spiritual understanding of the Law becomes in some sense a Jew, "for the real Jew is not the man who is one outwardly, and the real circumcision is not something external in the flesh. The real Jew is the man who is one inwardly, and real circumcision is that of the heart, a spiritual, not a literal thing" (Rom 2:28-29).

Moral and Mystical

If therefore a spiritual interpretation of Leviticus is indispensable, the question arises, How should it proceed? Origen distinguishes two spiritual senses of Scripture, the moral and the mystical. The latter reveals the "heavenly things" contained in the letter; the former understands the events recorded in the Old Testament as referring to rules of conduct, to sins and virtues making up the moral life of the Christian.

To take an example: Jerusalem in the literal sense is the earthly city chosen by David to be the capital of the Jewish kingdom. In the *moral* sense it signifies the faithful soul. In the *mystical* sense it is the heavenly Jerusalem, the Church militant and triumphant.

A spiritual interpretation of the Book of Leviticus will have to use the moral as well as the mystical sense. The first half of the book containing the levitical rites of sacrifice and of clean and unclean (chapters 1–16) offers "examples of shadows and heavenly things" (Heb 8:5) and is, therefore, full of mystical meaning. The laws of sacrifice and of purgation are evidently also signs and symbols of our spiritual approach to God and therefore offer a wide field to moral interpretation.

The second half of Leviticus, the so-called "law of holiness" (chapters 17–27), is a repetition of the decalogue, with many additional precepts and statutes, sanctifying the whole realm of human life. If we compare this material with the laws and customs of contemporary heathen civilization, as well as with the new law of Christ, the superiority and spiritual grandeur of revelation will become more evident to us and will confirm in our hearts the love for the heavenly Father, who so wisely and lovingly leads his children into the fullness of the divine life.

The sacrificial legislation of Leviticus is determined by two decisive ideas: representation and mediation. The animal in sacrifice represents the offerer. He cannot complete the sacrifice without the mediation of a priest. Both representation and mediation were fulfilled in Christ, who as priest and victim entered into the Holy of Holies of heaven with his own blood, having obtained for us eternal redemption (Heb 9:11-12). But before we approach this last mystical sense of the levitical rites, we have to understand the immediate spiritual meaning suggested by the letter of the Old Testament itself.

The prophets were not the first to discover that sacrifices in themselves are nothing in God's eyes if they do not express a total surrender of the heart to God. That truth is proclaimed on page after page all through the Old Testament. We forget too easily that the offering of sacrifices is, according to the levitical legislation, confined to those who are "pure." Sinners who have purposely broken the covenant or, as the law says, have "sinned with a high hand"—we would say those who have committed a mortal sin—are excluded from the altar (Num 15:31).

The Old Testament sacrifices have no grace-giving power. They express feelings and states already existing; they do not create them. They make atonement only for offenses committed unwittingly or out of negligence (chapters 4–6). Their purifying power, therefore, is limited to the external sphere, which is not identified with but is symbolical of the heart.

We have to keep this in mind if we want to understand rightly the constantly repeated admonition: "Sacrifice and offering you did not desire" (Ps 40:6). Sacrifices, according to the Old Testament, are really not a divine institution at all. Their history starts with Cain! "And in process of time it came to pass that Cain brought to the Lord an offering of the fruit of the ground" (Gn 4:3). The sacrificial legislation of Leviticus opens with the words: "When any man of you brings an offering" (1:2).

It is, therefore, literally true that God did not "desire" sacrifices, and Jeremiah's statement in his famous temple address—"I spoke not to your fathers, nor commanded them ... concerning burnt-offerings or sacrifices; but this thing I commanded them saying: Hearken to my voice and walk in all the ways that I command you" (Jer 7:22-23)—has nothing revolutionary in it. He only restates the old truth that God, in allowing sacrifices to be offered, has no delight in the blood of bullocks or the fat of fed beasts (Is 1:11) but only in the one essential thing expressed by them: the hearkening to the voice of the Lord.

"What does the Lord require of you, O man, but to do justly and to love mercy, and to walk humbly with your God?" (Mi 6:8). Without this total surrender to God sacrifices are of no purpose (see 1 Sm 15:22; Ps 50:8-9).

The Sacrifices

The true meaning of the sacrificial legislation of Leviticus is not, therefore, to institute sacrifices but to give to this universal custom a form that will remove from it all pagan superstition and at the same time make it a symbol of the very essence of the Law, which is to serve God with the whole heart and the whole soul (Dt 10:12). The very term that the Mosaic Law uses for sacrifices in general, *korban,* does not suggest the idea of a gift to God but rather that of approaching or drawing close to God. Further, the things that are to be offered are those that belong to the life of man, being raised by him and serving him for food: domestic animals or cereals. They represent the person of the offerer.

Leviticus names three kinds of animals as eligible for sacrifices and gives each of them a definite function. The first kind, the animals "of the herd" (1:3) or the cattle, are working animals. They use their strength under the yoke of their master and therefore represent the offerer as actively working in God's service.

The second kind of sacrificial animals are those "of the flock" (1:10), goats and sheep. These live on pasturage, under the care of the shepherd. They represent the offerer as dependent on God as the

Good Shepherd (Ez 34:31). The lamb, the most helpless among them, characterized by silent obedience, is used in sacrifices for the whole people and for individuals without distinction, for the paschal sacrifice, and for the daily morning and evening sacrifice that is offered in behalf of all Israel (Num 23:3-8). The ram—hard, fast and strong, stubborn against strangers, accustomed to lead—is used, like the bullock, as sacrifice for people in leading positions, such as priests and rulers (9:2-3).

The third kind of animals used for sacrifice are the fowls (1:14), birds without talons and are unfit for attack, but able to escape easily the attacks of others by lifting themselves up into the air. They represent "God's poor," who live without provisions and means of defense but remain happy and secure from one day to the other because they have wings to bear them up from this earth into God's sky (see Ps 124:6-7). The turtledove, as bird of passage and harbinger of spring in Palestine, is a picture of the chosen people, whose return from exile into the Holy Land ushers in the spring of the Spirit (see Ps 74:19; Song 2:12). The pigeon is used for sacrifice when still young (1:14) and in need of the care of the parent birds, as Israel is like a fledgling under the care of God, as the mother bird hovering over the young, spreading out her wings, and taking her young on her pinions (see Ps 90:4).

The turtledove and the pigeon are the sacrifice of the poor as well as of those who have escaped sickness (5:7; 12:8). The fact that God accepts them as sacrifice shows that he finds pleasure not only in the sacrifice of the strong and in the loving confidence of the weak but also in the sufferings of those stricken with poverty and sickness. The way in which the turtledoves and pigeons are sacrificed emphasizes the idea of suffering: The priest shall wring off the bird's head, drain the blood out on the side of the altar, remove its crop and its feathers, split it open with his hands without completely dividing it, then burn it on the altar for a soothing odor to the Lord (1:15-17). Only at this sacrifice does the priest himself do the killing, which is to indicate that God draws the poor to himself through their sufferings.

Union With God

In the other sacrifices the killing is left to the offerer, who first has presented the animal at the tabernacle and, by laying, or better, planting his hands on its head, has made it his "support" to do atonement for him (1:4). The purpose of the sacrificial slaughter is not the death of the animal but the freeing of its blood. This symbolizes the fundamental act of renouncing one's own self and turning toward God, with which humanity's approach to God has to begin in this state of fallen nature. For this reason the offerer himself has to do the killing.

The function of the priest begins only with taking the blood and presenting it at the altar. "The blood is the life of the flesh" (17:11). Freed from the fetters of self-will through death, the blood is given *by God* upon the altar to make atonement for souls (17:11). "Atonement" has to be taken in its original meaning of restoring union with God.

The various ways in which the priest brings the blood into contact with the altar express various ways of nearness to God. At the usual burnt offering the blood is dashed against the altar to symbolize the wholehearted effort or resolution that accompanies the burnt offering. At the sin offering the blood is smeared on the horns of the altar—on the horns of the altar of burnt offerings for the laypeople, on the horns of the golden altar in the Holy Place for the priests. Because the horns of the altar stand for the strength of God and his power to raise up the fallen, the smearing of blood on the horns means a faithful, confident, abiding adherence to God.

The greatest nearness to God is achieved through the highest of sin offerings, on the Day of Atonement, when the high priest brings the blood for the priests as well as for the laymen into the Holy of Holies to sprinkle it (in Hebrew "to cause to leap up") on the mercy seat, the most sublime symbol of the grace-giving divine presence. This rite foreshadows the final, wholly spiritual union with God that is brought about by Christ, who as our high priest entered with his own blood into the Holy of Holies (Heb 9:11-12).

As the shedding of the blood in the levitical sacrifices symbolizes the freeing of the inner life of the offerer from selfishness and his union with God, so also does the use of the flesh at the sacrifices indicate transformation rather than destruction. The term Leviticus uses for the sacrificial burning of the carcass is not the ordinary secular word for destructive burning *(saraph);* rather, *hiqtir,* has the meaning of "causing to go up in sweet smoke." The fire on the altar of burnt offerings was a sacred fire. It came down from heaven in the first instance of Aaron's sacrifice (9:24), and it was never allowed to go out (6:12-13). It represents the holy will of God, who transforms our entire life, making it ascend to the level of the spirit, where it pleases God.

At the burnt offering (in Hebrew, *olah*—"that which ascends"), which expresses the desire of the offerer to dedicate himself wholly to God's service, the entire carcass is burnt. In the trespass and sin offerings, the fat, as the best part, is burnt. The rest is eaten by the priests, while the offerer, as a mark of penance, is required to abstain from the feast.

In peace offerings God, the priests, and the offerer with his kinsmen and guests have their portions to bind them together in the sacred bond of a shared meal. The peace offering expresses the enjoyment of the covenant privilege: solidarity in the nation or family under God's protection and blessing. It was offered in thanksgiving (7:12) or on festive occasions.

Christ Our Sacrifice

All the levitical sacrifices culminate in the solemn rites of the Day of Atonement (chapter 16). The office of the priests was to draw near every day to the Lord to offer sacrifices at the altar of burnt offerings and at the altar of incense. But once a year one of them, the high priest, was privileged to enter through the veil into the Holy of Holies to cleanse and hallow the priesthood, the people, and the sanctuary, that they may draw near on other occasions as a sanctified people.

It is the ritual of this day that the Letter to the Hebrews sees fulfilled in the sacrifice of Christ (Heb 9–10). The high priest, dressed in simple white linen tunic (16:4; see Jn 19:23), entering into the Holy of Holies once a year with the blood of bullocks, points to Christ, who as "High Priest of the good things to come" (Heb 9:11) entered once by his own blood into the sanctuary of heaven to cleanse our conscience from dead works to serve the living God (Heb 9:14).

The characteristic rite of the two goats, one of which is offered for the sins of the people, while the other is burdened with the sins of the people and then led into the desert (16:21-22), also was fulfilled in the passion of Christ. The two goats represent two ways: of life and of death, of repentance and of hardness of heart. Christ is prefigured in the goat offered as the sacrifice for the people. The "scapegoat," not offered but let free in the desert with the burden of sins, appears in the person of Barabbas, the murderer who was let free on Good Friday. The Fathers see also in the man who leads the scapegoat into the desert the figure of Christ,[4] who on the great day of propitiation entered into hell.

The last meaning of the sacrificial legislation of Leviticus is the symbolic expression of spiritual acts of repentance and self-surrender through which we may be reconciled to God. It wants to teach that this reconciliation can take place only through representation and mediation. A sinner dares not offer to God a polluted life, yet it is only by offering himself to God again that he can cleanse and reconsecrate his life.

The Book of Leviticus keeps awake in our hearts the sense of this fundamental dilemma. It shows also that the representation and mediation that it offers to solve this dilemma—the blood of animals and the service of human priests—are only a shadow of the "good things" of the messianic times, when the Son of God takes on the likeness of the flesh of sin and, becoming priest and victim at the same time, solves the dilemma by offering his own blood in the Holy Spirit for the sins of men. Through him the way is open for all who are incorporated into him to enter as priests into the Holy of Holies (Heb 9:12). On the day of Pentecost he sent his Holy Spirit in the form of fire to indicate that from now on the heart of the Christian has become the altar of burnt offerings.

> Now everyone who renounces all he possesses, takes upon himself his cross and follows Christ, offers a burnt offering on the altar of God. Now everyone who delivers his body to the glory of martyrdom offers a burnt offering on the altar of God. Now everyone who loves his brethren, who lays down his life for them, who fights for justice and truth, offers a burnt offering on the altar of God. Everyone who mortifies his members, so that the world is crucified to him and he to the world, offers a burnt offering on the altar of God.[5]

FIVE

The Book of Numbers

After the Book of Exodus has ended with the erection of the tabernacle for God to dwell in, and after Leviticus has shown the ideal
of holiness which the presence of the Holy One demanded from his
people, the Book of Numbers returns to historical reality by describing the vicissitudes of the Israelites on their march from Mount Sinai
to the border of the Promised Land. Again, however, Numbers is no
mere report of historical events during the journey in the wilderness.
Its aim is to show the order and the spirit which make the sons of Israel
an army ready to fight the battles of God.

The Book of Numbers is the book of the Church militant. On
every page it points beyond the historical reality of the Jewish nation
to the "new Israel," which, under the leadership of a "prophet" greater
than Moses, would reach what Moses was only allowed to behold from
afar: the Promised Land of eternal salvation.

The mystery of the Church appears already in the census with
which the book opens and from which its present title, Numbers, is
derived. It is not souls who are counted to find out the sum total of all
the "sons of Israel," but only men of "service age" (1:3). They are those
upon whom the Lord can count for responsible fulfillment of the Law.
They are the backbone of the people and constitute the "congregation"
in the strict sense of the word. More than six hundred thousand are
mustered for the service of the Lord "to fight the wars of Israel." The
course of events shows, however, that of all those who were registered,
only two, Caleb and Joshua, were found worthy to enter the Promised
Land (14:30).

Rebellion in the Camp

After three days of marching the people begin already to complain (chapter 11). Significantly enough, the rabble, who never have had anything good because they are not able to keep an orderly household, are the first to "fall alusting" (11:4) and to cry for meat and for the good things of Egypt. Infected by their discontent, the whole people start to lament throughout their families, "every man in the door of his tent" (11:10).

Moses is deeply discouraged: "Have I conceived all this people? Have I begotten them that you should say to me: 'Carry them in your bosom, as the nurse bears the suckling child'?... I am not able to bear this people alone, because it is too heavy for me" (11:12-14).

God sends quail to feed the people, but while the flesh is yet between their teeth, before it is chewed, the wrath of the Lord smites thousands of them, who are buried in the "graves of lust" (11:34). "They were protected by the cloud, and passed safely through the sea, and all ate the same spiritual food and drank the same spiritual drink.... Still with most of them God was not well pleased, and they were struck down in the desert. Now these things happened to warn us," says St. Paul (1 Cor 10:1-6). We Christians were saved through the waters of baptism. We have the spiritual food and drink of the holy Eucharist, but they will not be of any avail to us if we, forgetting the dignity of our Christian birth, give in to the rabble of our lower instincts.

Much more critical than the murmuring of the riffraff, who have not even been counted at the census, is the rebellion that breaks out among the "congregation" when the spies whom Moses has sent into the Promised Land return with their tale of horror. Lack of confidence in God has affected the imagination of the spies, so that in their eyes their enemies have grown into giants, and they themselves have shrunk to the size of grasshoppers (13:33).

At their report all those who have been registered to fight the battles of God lose heart and begin to complain: "Wherefore has the Lord brought us into this land to fall by the sword that our wives and our children should be a prey!" (14:3). They refuse to obey their divine leader and want a captain of their own choice to lead them back into the slavery of Egypt (14:4). It is an apostasy similar to the one at Mount Sinai, when they asked Aaron, "Up, make us a god who shall go before us" (Ex 32:1).

The covenant is broken. The wrath of God is kindled, but as at Mount Sinai, justice is turned into mercy through the intercession of Moses, who shows himself again the true shepherd of his flock. He does not want to be made the father of a new people of God. All he asks is that God would manifest his greatest power, his mercy (14:17-19).

Indeed the sentence God pronounces reveals the whole pattern of redemption: "As truly as I live, I swear that all men who have seen the miracles I worked in Egypt and in the desert and have not hearkened to my voice shall not see the land, and yet my glory shall fill the whole earth" (14:21-23). The rejection of the "old generation" and the calling in of the "little ones" (14:31) is really God's way of extending his salvation to the whole of mankind.

This pattern is fulfilled when, after the death of Christ, the refusal of the Jews brings the new generation of the gentiles into the promised land of salvation, extending the kingdom of God over the whole of mankind. We Christians are, therefore, the "little ones" to whom admission into God's rest is open.

To us is addressed the warning of the psalm: "Today, when you hear his voice, harden not your hearts as your forefathers did in the time of trial in the desert" (Ps 95:7-8). They saw the miracles of God; they had the good news of the Promised Land preached to them. But the message they heard did them no good because they did not accept in faith what they heard. Likewise we have seen God's glory and have heard the good news of the gospel preached to us, but we may still not be admitted to God's rest if we do not keep our confidence in Christ unshaken to the very end. Let us, therefore, as long as we can speak of "today"—that means, as long as the promise of admission to God's rest is still open—admonish one another: "Today when you hear his voice, do not harden your hearts!" (see Heb 3–4).

The Divine Hierarchy

When the census of the six hundred thousand takes place, the Levites are not numbered with them. They are chosen by God to be the custodians of the tabernacle and immediate helpers of the priests (3:6-7). Levi, their ancestor, is the third of the sons of Jacob (Gn 29:34), but God gives the Levites the place of the firstborn because they are the only ones who, when the people apostasize and adore the molten calf, remain faithful to God's Law (Ex 32:26-29).

The Levites, taken by God in exchange for the firstborn sons, are therefore another prophetic sign pointing to that great "revolution" that the mercy of God will work in the days of Christ. Then the "children of the kingdom," God's firstborn sons, will be cast out (Mt 8:12), and God will raise up children to Abraham out of the gentiles. By repeating this "pattern" time and again in the course of the history of salvation, God impresses upon us the fact that the order of salvation is not based on human blood but on God's grace.

The love that descends from God takes hold of men only through the medium of a divinely established hierarchical order. The people of God is not a "crowd"; it is a church, a legitimately constituted and organized assembly. The central part of the Book of Numbers, chapters 2–21, is mainly devoted to showing the external and the internal spiritual order of the people of God.

The center of this order is the tabernacle, where the Law is kept and the cloud of the divine presence appears. The tabernacle is strictly separated from the people, because the God of Israel is not the "incarnation of the national spirit" nor is his law the "will of the people" (see Ex 19:12-21). The Law is of divine, not human, origin, and God's presence among his people is the free gift of his sovereign will. For this same reason, those who are appointed by God to serve in the sanctuary are separated from the rest of the people to form an inner circle immediately surrounding the tabernacle. "And the common man that draws nigh shall be put to death" (3:10).

Within the priestly order itself there is a strict division of authority and function between the "sons of Aaron and the Levites." The former alone are priests in the full sense of the word (3:10), authorized to serve "within the veil" (18:7). The Levites "are wholly given unto Aaron and his sons from the children of Israel" (3:9), to help the priests before the tent (3:6-7) and to carry its furnishings on the march (chapter 4). They exercise their offices in strictest obedience. "According to the commandment of the Lord they were appointed by the hand of Moses, each to his service and to his burden" (4:49).

This divine order of authority, the very backbone of the life of the people of God, is threatened by Korah, Dathan, Abiram, and their followers (chapter 16). They rise up "in the face of Moses" and assemble themselves together against Moses and against Aaron, saying to them: "You take too much upon you, seeing all the congregation are holy, every one of them, and the Lord is among them; why then lift up yourselves above the assembly of the Lord?" (16:3).

Who will not recognize in these words the voice of the religious and political demagogues of all ages? And who would not feel the piercing power of Moses' sarcastic retort: "You take too much upon you, sons of Levi!" (16:7). In this rebellion the whole order of divine grace was at stake, not only for Israel but for all ages to come.

The destruction of the rebels had, therefore, to be such as clearly to reveal, once and forever, the divine purpose: that the priestly dignity of each member of God's people should never be used as a pretext to abolish divinely appointed authority. Exaltation of body and soul into heaven was the Father's answer to the voluntary self-abasement of the divine High Priest Jesus Christ. Here usurpers of priestly dignity were punished when "the earth broke asunder under their feet: and opening its mouth, devoured them with their tents and all their substance; and they went down alive into hell" (16:31-33).

Figures of Christ

That the vindication of priestly authority has taken place for the sake of divine charity and not of human tyranny is clearly demonstrated on this same occasion when the whole crowd, finding this punishment too hard, murmurs against Moses and Aaron: "You have killed the people of the Lord" (16:41). At this moment "wrath goes out from the Lord and the plague rages" (16:46), but Moses sends Aaron with the censer and fire from the altar to stand between the dead and the living, between the people and the wrath. "He prayed for the people, and the plague ceased" (16:48).

Aaron, sent by Moses, is the figure of Christ, whom the Father will send to stand between the people and the wrath, with the fire of his divinity and the incense of his humanity, to burn on the cross and to ascend in his resurrection as an intercession for his people. To make the messianic meaning of Aaron's priesthood still more evident, God confirms him by letting his rod, the symbol of the cross, "put forth buds and bloom blossoms and bear ripe almonds" (17:8).

The charity of Christ is the soul and fulfillment of all divinely appointed authority in the Old Testament. Moses, who has the highest authority because God has trusted him with all his house and speaks with him face-to-face (12:8), is "very meek, more so than all the men upon the face of the earth" (12:3). Completely selfless, he never considers his position a personal matter. When Joshua tells him that two men are infringing upon his privilege by prophesying in the camp, he gives the classic answer: "Are you jealous for my sake? Would that all the Lord's people were prophets, that the Lord would put his spirit upon them!" (11:29). All his life Moses is weighed down by the feeling of his insufficiency (see Ex 4:10). "I am not able to bear all this people, because it is too heavy for me" (11:14). He does not realize that his lack of natural assurance forms the "vacuum" that God's grace loves to fill.

He sees, however, that the final failure of his mission (20:12) is intended by God to point beyond Moses to the Messiah, as his successor and fulfillment. Therefore he asks that "the Lord, the God of the spirits of all flesh, set a man over the congregation who may go out before them and who may come in before them, and who may lead them out and who may bring them in; that the congregation of the Lord be not as sheep who have no shepherd" (27:16-17). Then, at God's command, he lays his hands upon Joshua, whose name he has changed prophetically from Hoshea—"the Lord has helped"—to Joshua—"the Lord will give plenty of room" (13:16)—which is the name of Jesus, the Messiah.

This Jesus, "when he saw the multitudes, was moved with compassion for them, because they fainted and were scattered abroad, as sheep having no shepherd" (Mt 9:36). He "goes out before them" in his death and "comes in before them" in his ascension. He "leads them out," and he teaches them to take their cross upon them and to follow him. He "brings them in" when he carries the lost sheep upon his shoulders into the pastures of eternal life.

That the office of Moses points to the Messiah Christ is also shown in the incident of the brazen serpent (21:4-9). When fiery serpents invade the murmuring crowd and many of Israel die, Moses prays for them at their request. But God commands him to set up a serpent of brass upon a pole. Everyone who has been bitten is ordered to look upon the serpent. If he does, he will live. Not Moses' prayer but a glance full of faith at the image saves the people.

Christ himself has revealed the meaning of this "sign." "As Moses lifted up the serpent in the wilderness, even so must the Son of Man be lifted up: that whoever believes in him should not perish, but have eternal life" (Jn 3:14-15). The fiery serpents are the symbol of the sins of men, and the brazen serpent foreshadows the One who took on the flesh of sins without sin, that through faith in his death for our sins we may be freed from death.

Besides the brazen serpent, the red heifer (chapter 19), is a figure of Christ, who bore our infirmities and died the death of a criminal to give us eternal life. The faultless red heifer has to be brought, like something unclean, outside the camp to be slain and burnt with cedar-wood and hyssop and scarlet. The ashes, mixed with spring water, then serve as purification from defilement with dead bodies.

"And so Jesus too," explains the Letter of the Hebrews, "in order to purify the people by his blood, suffered death outside the city gate. Let us, therefore, go out to him outside the camp, sharing the contempt that he endured" (Heb 13:12-13). The death of Jesus on Golgotha opens to his people the fountain of the Spirit, who, like living water, cleanses our conscience from dead works to serve the living God (Heb 9:14; 10:22).

The brazen serpent as well as the red heifer point to Christ as the humble Servant of God who heals our wounds by beating our infirmities. The last and the most solemn of the messianic prophecies of Numbers reveals him as the glorious king: the star of Jacob (24:17).

Balaam's Prophecies

When the children of Israel reach the country east of the Jordan, opposite Jericho, Balak, the king of Moab, tries to break their power by destroying the divine blessing that he realizes is the secret of Israel's strength (22:2-6). For this purpose he sends for Balaam, a famous sooth-sayer "from the mountains of the east" (23:7), to curse the people. Warned by God not to go but greedy for the "wages of unrighteousness" (2 Pt 2:15) that Balak offers him, Balaam saddles his ass and goes (22:21).

On the way Balaam is taught a lesson intended to break his pride and to make him, in the fear of the Lord, an obedient tool of the Spirit of God. The famous soothsayer must learn that his ass is a better prophet than he; it saves him from the sword of God's wrath just when it is being beaten itself by its blind and obstinate master (22:23-35).

Balaam becomes the faithful mouthpiece of God, who uses him to restate in a most solemn form the messianic blessing, which once was given to Abraham (Gn 12:3), which the blind Isaac then transmitted to Jacob (Gn 27:29), and which Jacob laid upon his sons (Gn 49:28). The essence of this blessing is the glorious messianic future of Israel, and what Balaam sees in his visions is the new Israel filled with the eternal life of the risen Christ (24:15-19). "Who has counted the dust of Jacob, or numbered the ashes of Israel? Let me die the death of the righteous, and let my end be like his!" (23:10).

We see right here the identification between the new Israel and his head, the Messiah, and the mysterious allusion to dust, ashes, and death as containing the secret of the risen life. All five prophecies of Balaam announce in fact the same glad tidings: that the irrevocable blessing of God—"When he has said, will he not do it?" (23:19)—is stronger than death. It covers Israel's sin—"None has beheld iniquity in Jacob, neither has one seen perverseness in Israel" (23:21)—and fills it with the power of the Resurrection, so that it "rises like a lion" (23:24) to battle and "couches like a lion" (24:9) in peace.

The real power of Israel, however, is its king. He is *God*—"The Lord his God is with him, and the trumpet call of the king is among them" (23:21)—and *man*—"A star shall rise out of Jacob, and a scep-tre shall spring up from Israel, and out of Jacob shall come a powerful ruler" (34:17).

A Divinely Ordered Life

Micah, the prophet, sums up in a few words the whole message of the Book of Numbers when he lets the Lord say to Israel: "I sent before you Moses, Aaron and Miriam. O my people, remember now what Balak, king of Moab, planned, and what Balaam, the son of Beor answered him ... that you may know the righteousness of the Lord.... He showed you, O man, what is good, and what the Lord requires of you: to do justly, and to love mercy, and to walk humbly with your God" (Mi 6:4-8).

Moses is the great hero of justice, Aaron of mercy, Miriam of a life hidden with God in chastity and humility. The three spiritual leaders of Israel represent the inner order of the life of God's people, of which the external order is the symbolic expression.

Justice, the foundation of the social unity of the people and of its material prosperity, has its field in the outer camp, where the "congregation" lives under its princes and standards (2:2). Humble walking with God in chastity and obedience, with contemplation as its fruit, characterizes the camp of the Levites. The sanctuary itself, where the sons of Aaron serve, is the place where the mercy of God meets the needs of men.

The three kinds of bodily uncleanness enumerated in the Book of Numbers (5:2) must be understood as symbolic of this same spiritual order. Leprosy, which excludes from the outer camp, is the mark of sins against unity. Sexual discharges exclude from the camp of the Levites because they are the bodily equivalent of sins of impurity. The touching of dead bodies bars priest from service in the sanctuary because it represents lack of faith in the mercy of God, who has the power to call the dead back to life.

The blessing the priests are commanded to pronounce day by day over the children of Israel (6:22-27) is like a divine seal that keeps and strengthens this inner order of life among the people.

The Lord bless you and guard you;

The Lord make his face to shine upon you, and be gracious
unto you;

The Lord lift up his countenance upon you, and give you
peace.

The three sentences of the blessing correspond to the threefold spiritual order: the first referring to prosperity and justice, the second to
spiritual knowledge and moral insight, and the third, the lifting up of
God's countenance, to the suppression of his anger in mercy.

The threefold order of justice, truth, and mercy, which the Book of
Numbers shows to be the foundation of the life of the Church, has
found its fulfillment in Christ. He is Moses, Miriam, and Aaron in
one, because he is the Way, the Truth, and the Life.

SIX

The Book of Deuteronomy

On Mount Sinai God lets his voice be heard by his people. Nothing as great as this has ever happened, nor has anything like it ever been heard of.

It seems incongruous that God, the eternal and infinite, should choose a certain day and a certain place to speak, and a certain group of people to address. If, in such an event, God remains God, who can hear him and live? If he enters the limitations of human hearing and human understanding, how can his Word remain God's Word? It must retain its infinite depth and at the same time be heard to the ends of the earth. It needs, therefore, a vehicle of a very special kind, able to keep its divine integrity and make it accessible to all men of all ages and of all races.

When the Word of God was made flesh, the Church and the sacraments were instituted to perpetuate its message and mission. The revelation of God on Mount Sinai possesses such a "sounding board" to carry it through the course of history into the depth of the human heart in the last of the five books of Moses: Deuteronomy. This Greek expression means "second law," or better, "copy (repetition) of the law."

Deuteronomy is indeed a recapitulation of the first law given on Mount Sinai. As Christ, before he left this world to enter into his Father's glory, instituted the eucharistic sacrifice as a living memorial of his entire work of redemption, likewise did Moses, before he died and before the people entered upon a new phase of its history, erect a memorial to all God's works and deeds in the sermons of Deuteronomy.

Exodus, Leviticus, and Numbers report the events and register the words of God. It is a long way for man's limited mind, however, from taking notice of a fact to realizing what it means. This is particularly true in things pertaining to God.

The Israelites see the fire, hear the voice on Mount Sinai, and readily give their assent to all that God has said. After a few days, however, they forget everything and dance merrily around the molten calf. Forty years of instruction and signs later, Moses has to confess: "You have seen all that the Lord did before your eyes in the land of Egypt under Pharaoh, to all his servants and to all his land: the great trials which your eyes saw, the signs and those great wonders; but the Lord has not given you a heart to know, and eyes to see, and ears to hear, unto this day" (29:2-4).

In a last attempt, therefore, to make them realize what has happened to them in the desert, Moses turns to his fellow countrymen and, from the brink of the grave, addresses them in sermons. In the majestic flow of their sentences, in the exalted maturity of thought, and in the smashing force of passionate appeal and denunciation, these sermons are unsurpassed in the entire Bible.

After a short preface, indicating the place and the time of these discourses of Moses (1:1-5), the book takes up an introductory address (1:6–4:40) containing an historical retrospect of the wanderings of the Israelites—from the mountain of Horeb or Sinai to the land of Moab, facing the Promised Land (1:6–3:29)—and ending in an ardent appeal to keep the commandments God himself has given to his people on Mount Sinai (4:1-40). A brief statement about the setting aside of three towns of refuge on the other side of the Jordan (4:41-43) separates the first sermon from the chief discourse (chapters 5–26).

This discourse opens with a preliminary exhortation to remain loyal to God, the Only One (chapters 5–11). Then follows the Deuteronomic code of laws containing the laws, statutes, and ordinances supplementing the Ten Commandments in regard to the new conditions that result from Israel's passage from the nomadic life in the desert to the agricultural setting in the Promised Land. A third discourse (chapters 27–30) details enforcement of the Law and the establishment afresh of the covenant between Israel and God.

The last chapters of the book relate the last days of Moses. He installs Joshua as his successor (31:14), delivers the Law to the priests (31:24), composes his last song (chapter 32), and gives his farewell blessing to the twelve tribes (chapter 33). Finally he ascends Mount Nebo, where the Lord shows him the goal of all his labors from afar and then "takes his life with a kiss" (chapter 34).

The Prophet

God's charity is the soul of prophecy. The Moses of Deuteronomy is a prophet because he has entered into the very heart of God's charity. For more than fifty years he has carried the burden of a numerous people. Now he is 120 years old, his eyes undimmed, his vigor unabated (34:7). Instead of clinging tenaciously to his office, as men in high station usually do when they grow old, he has risen to the height of complete detachment. Remaining true to the self-effacement that has distinguished his leadership from its very beginning, he has accepted God's irrevocable decision: "You shall not go over this Jordan" (see 1:37; 3:26; 31:2).

This refusal on the part of the Lord to let his faithful friend reach the goal of his most cherished hopes is more than mere punishment for his "slip" near Kadesh (see Nm 20:2-12). A secret lies hidden here, which a Jewish *midrash* (exposition of Scripture) indicates when it tells how Moses, crying to God for mercy, finally receives from him the answer: "Two solemn decisions I have made: one that you must die, the other that Israel never be destroyed. If I rescind one, I shall have to rescind the other. If you want to live, Israel must die."

Immediately Moses answers: "May a thousand Moseses die, if only Israel lives."

The Moses who speaks to his people in Deuteronomy bears an invisible crown of thorns on his head. His deep sorrow over not being allowed to enter the Promised Land, this supreme sacrifice, takes from him the last shadow of self-love and makes him a perfect likeness of God's only-begotten Son dying for the sins of mankind.

Through his complete union with God's charity, Moses finds himself standing "in the midst of times" (Hb 3:2). There he sees Mount Sinai "flaming with fire up to the very heart of the heavens" (4:11). Looking back into the past, he sees the history of his people rooted in the mystery of God's gratuitous election: "Even though the heavens to the highest heavens belong to the Lord your God, and the earth with all that is in it, yet the Lord set his heart on your fathers to love them, and chose their descendants after them, even you, in preference to all peoples" (10:14-15). "It was not because you were the greatest of all peoples that the Lord set his heart on you and chose you—for you were the smallest of all peoples—but it was because the Lord loved you" (7:7-8).

Moses sees in God's love for his people the key to the understanding of their wanderings in the desert as the training school where God has disciplined them, as a father disciplines his son. God led Israel into affliction, into hunger and thirst, and then fed them with manna and with water from the rock, that they might understand "it is not on bread alone that man lives but on every word that proceeds from the mouth of God" (8:3). He made them realize their lack of courage, of loyalty and trust in God, that they might not say of themselves, "My own power and the strength of my own hand have gained this wealth for me" (8:17), or, "It is because of my goodness that the Lord brought me into possession of this land" (9:4).

Moses wants to impress upon the hearts and minds of his fellow countrymen the same truth that the Moses of the New Testament,

Jesus Christ, taught his disciples: "It was not you who chose me, it is I that have chosen you" (Jn 15:16). God loved Israel first (see 1 Jn 4:19).

The same love that in the past has chosen Israel gratuitously fills the present with God's nearness. "For what great nation is there that has a god so near it as is the Lord our God whenever we call on him?" (4:7). Because the God of Israel is a personal God, he does not appear in visible forms, only in a voice (4:12). But "the word of God is not in heaven that you should say: 'Who shall go up for us to heaven and bring it to us and make us hear it, that we may do it?' Neither is it beyond the sea, that you should say: 'Who shall go over the sea for us, and bring it to us, and make us to hear it, that we may do it?'" (30:11). The word of God penetrates the heart of man. That is the place where it is kept.

> Hear, O Israel; the Lord our God, the Lord is One! And you shall love the Lord your God with all your heart [that is, the "inner man," the spiritual faculties], with all your soul [the "whole man," including his senses and his body], and with all your might [external possessions]. And these words which I command you this day shall be upon your heart, and you shall teach them diligently to your children, and you shall talk of them when you sit in your house, and when you walk by the way, and when you lie down, and when you rise up.
>
> DEUTERONOMY 6:4-7

The New Future

The one Lord of Israel is a jealous God who claims the exclusive loyalty of his children. His word, therefore, pierces like a sword to the very division of body and soul; it is like judgment. The day when it is announced is the absolute "today" mentioned in Deuteronomy not less than fifty-two times. It is absolute decision.

God's love cannot be met with delaying tactics. It does not tolerate procrastination. It opens the narrow pass between the mountain of blessing and the mountain of cursing. "See, I call heaven and earth to record this day against you that I have set before you life and death, blessing and cursing; therefore choose life that you may love the Lord your God and that you may obey his voice, and that you may cleave to him, for he is your life and the length of your days" (30:19-20).

Through the narrow pass between blessing and cursing (see 27:12-13) Israel will march into a new future. The God of Israel is a faithful God who keeps covenant and mercy with those who love him to a thousand generations (7:6-16). He will go with his people. He will not fail them, neither forsake them (31:6). The very nature of the Promised Land is seen by Moses in this light of God's grace and charity: "For the land that you are taking in possession is not like the land of Egypt from which you came, where you used to sow your seed and water it by hand. On the contrary, it is a land with hills and valleys, watered by rain from the sky, a land for which the Lord your God cares, the eyes of the Lord your God being continually on it, from the beginning to the end of the year" (11:10-12).

The eyes of Moses penetrate farther into the future, through the darkness of another exile (29:27-28) into the dawn of the messianic era. The charity of God has kept open for a disloyal people the door of repentance. In his compassion God will turn their captivity and gather them from all the nations whither he has scattered them. Then he will circumcise their hearts, that they may love him with their whole heart and their whole soul, so that God will again rejoice over them (30:2-9).

This is the time when the Lord will raise up a new prophet like unto Moses: "I will put my words into his mouth, and he shall speak to them all that I shall command him" (18:18). It is with clear reference to this prophecy that our Lord time and again confesses: "I have not spoken on my account; but the Father who sent me, he gave me a commandment what I should say, and what I should speak.... Even as the Father said to me, so I speak" (Jn 12:49-50; 8:28; 17:8; Acts 3:22).

In Christ the way of repentance is open to us. In him we have been gathered together from all the nations into the unity of the new Israel. In him we have received not a physical but a spiritual circumcision through the burning of our sins in baptism (Col 2:11; Dt 10:16; 30:6).

Moses' Final Song

Moses rises to his full stature as prophet only in the glowing effusion of his last song (chapter 32). In words rolling like thunder he reveals the secret of history: "I will proclaim the name of the Lord: the Rock. His work is perfect: a God of faithfulness and without falsehood."

Nine times in the course of this hymn is repeated this most expressive figure, which reminds us of the most critical moment in Moses' life when, after the breaking of the covenant by the people, God put him on the rock (Ex 33:21) and revealed to him the secret of his eternal love: "The Lord, the Lord God, merciful and gracious, long-suffering and abundant in goodness and truth, keeping mercy to the thousandth generation, forgiving iniquity and transgression and sin" (Ex 34:6-7).

It is God's charity that makes him the rock on which his people stand. When he assigns to all other nations their boundaries, he gives himself as the portion of his people (32:8-9). When the other nations build their comfortable homes in civilized countries, Jacob is found by God in the howling waste of the wilderness. "There he took Israel in his arms and taught him. As an eagle stirs up her nestlings, hovers over her young, spreads her wings, takes them thereon, and bears them aloft upon her pinions—the Lord alone did lead them, there was no strange god with him" (32:11-12).

When God's firstborn grows fat in the land flowing with milk and honey, however, he forgets the Rock that bore him and forsakes the God who gave him birth. When the Lord sees this, he casts away in anger those who were sons and daughters. The fire of his wrath blazes forth from him into the very depth of hell (32:22).

Nevertheless, when he sees that their power is gone, the Lord repents himself for his servants (32:36). He does not retain his anger forever, because he delights in mercy (see Mi 7:18). After a "little while" (see Is 54:7-8; Jn 16:16-24), he reveals himself as the God of the resurrection: "See now that I, even I, am he; there is no God beside me; I kill, and I make alive; I have wounded, and I heal; and there is none that can deliver you out of my hand" (32:39).

This verse is the burden of the whole history of salvation. Hannah, the mother of Samuel, repeats it in her song, which ushers in the new age of God's anointed one, David (1 Sm 2:6). We hear it from the lips of Job, the prophet of the Resurrection (Job 5:18). Hosea, the herald of God's charity, announces it (Hos 6:1). Tobit repeats it in his song of rejoicing over the glory of New Jerusalem (Tob 13:2), and the Book of Wisdom in its praise of God's providence in the history of his people (Wis 16:13).

We see that this word marks one of those pathways that lead straight to Christ. For the God who kills and makes alive can only be the Father of Jesus Christ, who sent his Son to die for our offenses and raised him up again for our justification (see Rom 4:25). With his coming the wall of partition will be torn down, and all the nations will praise the new Israel of God. At the Last Judgment the Lord will revenge the blood of his servants and will be merciful to the land of his people (32:43).

Thus Moses sees the whole history of Israel as one great manifestation of the love of God for his people. He gives it life and liberty. He saves it. He feeds it. He leads it. He protects it. He forgives it. Throughout all ages he remains its rock of salvation.

The Lawgiver

In history the Lord has chosen his people, that his people should choose him in keeping his Law (26:17-18). The observance of the Law is the people's answer to God's love. "Hear, O Israel, the Lord your God, the Lord is one: so you must love the Lord your God with your whole heart, with your whole soul, and with all your might" (6:5).

These words are the sum total of Moses' message, as prophet and as lawgiver. This message constitutes the unique beauty of Deuteronomy; that is, it recapitulates both the history and the Law of the chosen people in the light of the love of God. The Deuteronomic code (chapters 12–26) deals with the various fields of human life under the main headings of worship (12:1–16:17), of civil government (16:18–18:22), of criminal law (19:1–21:9), and of domestic law (21:10–25:19). It is the purpose of the following remarks to show how all these statutes and ordinances are formed by the spirit of love.

This claim may sound surprising to those who associate Deuteronomy with some vague recollections of stern measures against apostates and pagan worship and consider it, therefore, as the Magna Charta of intolerance, apt to become once more the grave of liberty should ever a militant Church succeed in securing a majority in a free country. It is true, the very word *inquisition* is derived from Deuteronomy (13:14); the witch hunts were justified by quoting Deuteronomy 17:2-7; the theocratic regimes that Calvin erected in Geneva and the Puritans created in early New England states such as Massachusetts were partly inspired by Deuteronomy.

On the other hand, it is easy to show that nothing is as opposed to the spirit of Deuteronomy as cruelty, that all its rules are inspired by the deepest respect for the dignity of the human personality. In fact, such great social reformers as Roger Williams, in his *Bloody Tenant of Persecution* (whose arguments for tolerance were "refuted" by his adversaries in Massachusetts in a pamphlet entitled *Mr. Williams'*

Bloody Tenant of Persecution Washed White in the Blood of the Lamb!), and Henry George, in his *Progress and Poverty,* were inspired by the legislation of Deuteronomy. If we try in the following to make the reader familiar with the salient points of the Deuteronomic code, we do so because we are convinced that it will make him realize how far our modern times have deviated from the Law, which the all-merciful God of Israel gave to his people through the hands of Moses.

The fundamental difference between Israel and all the other nations is that Israel's faith is a gift descending from God. It is not a human dream. It is not a glorification of the powers of nature.

Israel's faith was put to the test the moment it left the desert to settle in a country, entering into close relations with other nations. There was no greater temptation for Israel than to worship the gods of the country in the same way as the natives did. But Israel's whole existence, in fact the salvation of mankind, depended on its not being absorbed by its neighbors.

It was the divine mission of the people of God to witness to the universal truth that there is only one God, one Law, one faith, one people. It is the same principle for which St. Paul fought with all his might: "One Spirit—one body—one hope for your calling: one Lord—one faith—one baptism—one God and Father of us all, who is above all, and through all and in you all" (Eph 4:4-6). There is indeed no other possibility: If Israel's law is God's Law, then Israel cannot add to it nor take away from it (12:32). Any compromise here would immediately turn God's word into human opinion.

Deuteronomy shows great wisdom in pointing out the three eternal enemies of orthodoxy: intellectual seduction by false prophets (13:2-6), the pressure of family ties (13:6-11), and political power (13:12-19). If it imposes the death penalty on all those who try to undermine Israel's faith in God, it does not do so out of intolerance and national pride. On the contrary, as the history of the people shows, the false prophets and "dreamers," as Deuteronomy calls them, are always those who flatter the national pride at the expense of God's law (see Mi 3:5), while a true prophet such as Jeremiah must ask the people in the name of God to sacrifice their political independence. The death penalty for apostasy intends to impress upon the people that loyalty to God is Israel's life-nerve, that Israel's life is no more in its own hands but is God's property. It is not in Israel's power to change its God.

Every possible precaution is taken to prevent abuse of these laws: careful investigation has to precede the sentence (13:14); the witnesses have to take the responsibility for the execution of the sentence (13:9); no confiscation of property is allowed (13:17). (How wise is such a rule, if one considers that the confiscation of property has been one of the main incentives of religious persecution, from Henry VIII to Stalin!) There are, in fact, so many clauses attached to the laws against apostasy that they were seldom put into practice.

Taking the Land for God

Israel's attitude toward the Canaanites and their forms of worship is often considered the classic example of religious intolerance. One should read, however, the laws of warfare in Deuteronomy (chapter 20) and compare them with the "total war" of our times. Deuteronomy outlaws total war. Human kindness has to be shown even in war. Thus the betrothed is to be exempt from service. Peace has to be offered first to every enemy city. Destruction of the countryside is forbidden.

The Canaanites are requested to abandon idolatry and to adhere to the fundamental natural laws by the establishment of courts of justice and the prohibition of blasphemy, idolatry, incest, murder, robbery, and unnatural cruelty. We are apt to forget that the idolatry of the Canaanites was accompanied by all kinds of "abominations," such as temple prostitution and child sacrifices, which even in our days of religious toleration would bring about the intervention of the state (12:31).

The Israelites invade the Promised Land on the grounds that the idolatry of the Canaanites, together with their moral depravity, has deprived them of the right to possess the country. We have to ask ourselves if it really is such a heresy to think that a people could lose its right to a country by abusing it. The great majority of white nations today have conquered their present homelands by destroying the original inhabitants. Their only justification for this is their greater strength and their greater skill in exploiting natural resources. No ethical consideration whatsoever seems to interfere today with the right of the conqueror.

In contrast, when the Jews invade Canaan they are warned that they take upon themselves a definite moral and spiritual obligation: "You shall not do any of these abominations, that the land not vomit you out also, when you defile it, as it vomited out the nation that was before you" (Lv 18:26-28). A national god is more partial to his nation. He tells his worshippers that the law of national preservation overrides all other considerations, that the cruel extermination of millions of men, women, and children through mass starvation and atom bombs is perfectly licit as long as it saves the lives of conationals.

But the God of Israel never speaks that way. He only impressed upon his people that the preservation of their religious character is worth any sacrifice, even that of national self-interest. One need only compare the spiritual character of the worship of the one God of Israel with the gruesome cult of local gods to realize immediately that the extirpation of the latter is not a loss to mankind.

It is in perfect harmony with the truly supernatural character of Israel's religion that it is God himself who designates the place where he is to be invoked (12:5). He "puts his Name there," or, as it is said in Exodus 20:24, "where I cause my name to be mentioned." The God of Israel is not identical with nature. He is a free personality. His presence is not limited to a place, like the presence of a physical power. His presence is the spiritual presence of One who listens to the prayers offered to him in his name. It is the presence of the Father who loves to have his children gathered around him.

For this reason, God has appointed one place for all his family to offer corporate worship to him. There the Israelites will bring their offerings: "There you shall eat before the Lord your God, and you shall rejoice over all your undertakings, you and your households, in which the Lord your God has blessed you" (12:7).

God has given the Holy Land to his people that the right order of things should be restored in it, that it should serve the glory of God through the priestly service of man. The worship of the one true God is, therefore, the recapitulation of the entire life of the people under God as the head. It is the solemn proclamation of the presence of the kingdom of God. It does not, therefore, consist only of the silent prayers of individuals but includes eating and rejoicing, before the Lord, by the entire household: "And you shall rejoice before the Lord your God, you, and your son, and your daughter, and your manservant, and your maidservant, and the Levite that is within your gate, and the stranger, and the fatherless, and the widow, that are in your midst" (16:11).

Because God is the creator of nature, nature is to be held in reverence by God's children. The Israelites are not allowed to eat blood, because "the life is in the blood" (12:23), and life belongs to God. They shall not mutilate themselves (14:1), because they are God's own treasure. Never, especially not in the heat of war, should they give in to vandalism: "When you besiege a city a long time, you shall not destroy the trees thereof by wielding an ax against them. You may eat of them, but you shall not cut them down" (20:19).

Reverence for nature is shown not only in the control of brutal human instincts of man, but also in respecting God-given order. Man is not allowed to mix things in an arbitrary way: "You shall not sow

your vineyard with two kinds of seed; you shall not plow with an ox
and an ass together; you shall not wear material blended of wool and
linen; a woman must never wear man's clothes, nor must a man put
on a woman's garment, for whoever does these things is abominable to
the Lord your God" (22:5, 9-11).

The same sentiment of reverence toward God's creation forbids all
cruelty. The beautiful word of Proverbs, "A righteous man takes care of
his beast, but the heart of the wicked is cruel" (Prv 12:10), expresses the
attitude that the Law demands of God's children. "If you should happen
to come upon a bird's nest in any tree, or on the ground, with young
ones or eggs, and the mother sitting on the young or the eggs, you must
not take the mother with the young. You must rather let the mother go
and only take the young, that you may prosper and live long" (22:6-7).
The exercise of her function as mother makes the bird immune.

Love for the Poor

The right of property never makes man an absolute lord over God's
creation. The land especially remains always God's. "The land must
not be sold in perpetuity: for the land is mine, since you are only resident aliens and servants under me" (Lv 25:23).

The Israelites hold their land in trust. Every seventh year is a sabbath for the land, when it should rest from working for man and only
serve God—and the poor! The right of personal property finds its lim-
itation also in the needs of the poor:

When you reap your harvest in the field, and you have forgotten
a sheaf in the field, you shall not go back and fetch it: it shall be
for the stranger, for the fatherless and for the widow. When you
beat your olive-tree, you shall not go over the boughs again: it
shall be for the stranger, the fatherless and the widow. When you

gather the grapes of your vineyard, you shall not glean it after you: it shall be for the stranger, the fatherless and the widow. And you shall remember that you were once a slave yourself in the land of Egypt; that is why I am commanding you to do this.

DEUTERONOMY 24:19-22

A tenth of all the produce of the land belongs to God, and that means to the poor:

When you have made an end of tithing all the tithe of your increase in the third year, and have given it to the Levite, to the stranger, to the fatherless and to the widow, that they may eat within your gates and be satisfied, then you shall say before the Lord your God: "I have put away the hallowed things out of my house, and have given them to the Levite, the stranger, the fatherless and the widow, according to all the commandments which you have commanded me."

DEUTERONOMY 26:12-13

It is the eternal glory of the Mosaic Law that it unites the love of God once and forever with the love of neighbor. It does not separate piety from justice. On the contrary, justice is *the* form of piety, and the soul of justice is not the law of right proportion, as it was to the Greek, but mercy and compassion. Because every man has been created in the image and likeness of God, our love of God is shown in the love for his image here on earth.

More than that, however, the Law of Moses sees God's likeness rather in the underprivileged than in the "perfect specimens" of the human race. God chose Israel to be his people when the Israelites were slaves in Egypt. He will give glory to his Son dying the death of a criminal on the cross. Therefore, he commands his children to see his image and likeness in the lowly.

In the ancient world the slaves were the most unfortunate of all men, not even considered human beings by such enlightened minds as Aristotle. The Old Testament has no word for "slave." No man can really become the property of another man. "You must not turn a servant over to his master when he has escaped from his master to you: he shall live right in your midst with you, in any place that he chooses in one of your communities as being advantageous to him: you must not mistreat him" (23:15-16).

The same consideration is shown to the stranger: "If a stranger is residing with you in your land you must not mistreat him: you must treat the resident alien like the native born among you, and love him as one of your own, since I, the Lord, am your God; for you were once aliens yourselves in the land of Egypt" (Lv 19:33).

The likeness of God is also honored in the enemy: "You must not abhor an Edomite, because he is your kinsman. You must not abhor an Egyptian, because you were once a resident-alien in his land" (23:7).

Even the prisoner of war has not lost his rights and his dignity as a human person, as can be seen from the way in which a woman captive is to be treated (21:10-14). In the same way Deuteronomy protects the rights of the hired laborer: "You must pay his wages by the day, before the sun sets, so that he may not cry to the Lord against you, and you incur guilt (24:15). The stranger, the orphan, and the widow—they all enjoy the same protection of the Law of God (24:17), which thus prepares the way for the coming of Christ, the Son of Man:

[He] will take his seat on his glorious throne, and all the nations will be gathered before him, and he will separate them one from another just as a shepherd separates sheep from goats, and he will say to those at his right: "Come, you whom my Father has blessed, take possession of the kingdom which has been destined for you from the creation of the world. For when I was hungry you gave me food, when I was thirsty you gave me something to drink; when I was a stranger you invited me into your home; when I was naked you gave me clothes; when I was sick you looked after me; when I was in prison you came to see me."

MATTHEW 25:31-36

In Christ the Law of Moses is fulfilled, because the love of God and the love of neighbor have become one in the Son of God made man. It is certainly not by chance that our Lord took the three words with which he overcame the tempter from Deuteronomy (Mt 4:1-11). The forty days of Christ in the desert are the recapitulation of the forty years that the people, God's "firstborn," lived in the desert. As the sermons of Deuteronomy are the sum total of all that the people had received from God in those years of preparation, they are now taken by Christ as the rock upon which he will build his fulfillment of God's promises.

SEVEN

The Book of Joshua

I shall be with you, as I was with Moses, says the Lord. Take courage and be strong: for you are to bring my people into the land which flows with milk and honey. Be not afraid, for I am with you: wherever you go I shall not fail you nor forsake you. Take courage and be strong: for you are to bring my people into the land which flows with milk and honey."

This beautiful responsory from vigils of the fourth week of Lent—a combination of Deuteronomy 31:7 and Joshua 1:6—is the last vestige in our breviary to indicate that Deuteronomy and Joshua were once read toward the end of Lent. It strikes the key note of the Book of Joshua: "Take courage and be strong!"

The forty years of wandering in the desert produces a profound change in the hearts of the Israelites. A helpless, discouraged, inarticulate mass of people has passed through the Red Sea. Now a well-ordered community follows the leadership of Joshua in the spirit of courage and confidence on the road to conquest and victory. The Book of Joshua breathes on every page the spirit of Easter.

Joshua is closely connected with the Pentateuch as its crowning fulfillment. It relates the accomplishment of the two main tasks that Moses left to his successor: the conquest of the Promised Land and its distribution among the ten tribes that had not yet received their part from Moses (Nm 32:33). Accordingly, the first part of the book, chapters 1–12, gives an account of Joshua's campaign and victories over the Canaanite kings. The second part, chapters 13–22, shows Joshua, advanced in years, dividing the land by lot to the ten tribes—strictly speaking, there are nine and a half—which settle west of the Jordan. The book ends with an epilogue containing Joshua's last admonitions to his people, his death, and his burial (chapters 23–24).

The Book of Joshua is not only an end, the fulfillment of God's promise to give his people a home, but also a beginning: It is the first of the books of the Old Testament that describe the political development of the Israelite nation and show how the people lived up to their part of the covenant with God by keeping the Law. The book is a "beginning" in the sense this word always has in sacred history, whose author is the "I am who I am." It is comprehensive and universal, containing the entire future development and foreshadowing the end.

We do not find in Joshua a mechanical registering of events exactly as they took place during the first period of infiltration of the Israelite tribes into Canaan. It selects and sees the events that it relates in the light of the purpose, the "end" of the history of the chosen people. This history is essentially "prophetic." It has as its objective the establishment of God's kingdom among men.

This story differs from the history of the gentile nations which records one continuous effort to obtain prosperity and glory for themselves. Consequently they are not being guided by the light of divine wisdom. Their history is, in their own eyes, a matter of chance and luck and fate. They trust in soothsayers and diviners to guide them, blindly led by the blind.

Divine wisdom, on the contrary, chooses the prophets to make God's will known to his people. "The Lord your God will raise a prophet for you among yourselves, one of your fellow countrymen like me—it is he that you must heed" (Dt 18:15). Our Lord's contemporaries see this famous prophecy of Moses fulfilled in Christ, calling him "the Prophet" (see Jn 6:14; 7:40; Acts 3:22). Jewish scholars refer it to the prophets who in every period of Jewish history are the successors of Moses, beginning with Joshua (see Sir 46:1) and continuing with Samuel, David, Elijah, and so on.

For this reason the Jewish canon of holy writ classifies the books of Joshua, Samuel, and Kings as "prophetic," not "historical," books. A distinction is made between the "older prophets"—from Joshua to Kings—and the "younger prophets," beginning with Isaiah. Our Lord himself speaks of the "law and the prophets" (see Mt 5:17; Lk 16:16; 24:27).

Joshua is, therefore, the first of the prophet successors of Moses, and as such he immediately points to the last: Jesus. These two have, in fact, the same name, because *Jesus* is the English rendering of the Greek form of *Joshua*. It is the first name in the Old Testament formed with the name of Yahweh God, and it means "God will liberate" or "God will give room."

The name is, therefore, in itself a prophecy. It indicates that the conquest of the Promised Land under Joshua is more than a political event. Rather it foreshadows a spiritual liberation, the true nature of which is revealed when the same name is given to our Lord. The angel announces to Joseph: "She [Mary] shall bring forth a son, and you shall call his name Jesus, for he shall save his people from their sins" (Mt 1:21).

Jesus fulfills what Joshua prefigured. In the beginning of his public life as Saviour he goes to the banks of the Jordan, and at the spot where the ark of the covenant stood when Joshua and his people passed through the river, he receives from St. John the baptism of penance. Instead of standing on dry ground, as Joshua had done, he is immersed in the water to typify his death.

Jesus opens the passage from sin into the land of liberty by dying for the sins of the people. He is the Lamb who takes away the sins of the world. Joshua's courage is fulfilled in Christ's charity.

Preparing for Conquest

The Book of Joshua opens with the death of Moses (1:1), who did not enter the Promised Land. Thus the final revelation of God's ways is not in the Law given through Moses but in the grace and truth that came through Jesus Christ (Jn 1:17), who is foreshadowed by Joshua. Moses, a true servant of his people, spent himself in meekness, patience, and self-effacement, without reaching the goal of his hopes. Joshua leads with courage and strength, in the glory of victory.

The entire history of the conquest of the Promised Land is a prophecy of the spiritual conquest of the world through the Church under the leadership of the Messiah, Jesus. The immediate preparations for the passage through the Jordan (1:2–2:14) can only be understood in this light. Three times God admonishes Joshua: "Take courage and be strong!" (1:6–7, 9). The success of Joshua's mission rests on the foundation of the spirit of confidence and faith. Just so the apostles, when they set out to win the world for Christ, "were all filled with the Holy Spirit and fearlessly uttered the word of God" (Acts 4:31).

The two spies who are sent by Joshua to view the land point to the two heralds whom Jesus sent into the world to prepare for his second coming: the Law and the gospel. Jericho is a symbol of this world, of the old age, called "the moon town," it was subject, like the moon, to constant change from darkness to light, from light to darkness.

Rahab the harlot, who receives the spies and hides them in her house, and later is saved with her entire family when Jericho is destroyed, represents the Church of the gentiles. Renouncing the idolatry of her fellow countrymen and women and turning to the Lord God of Israel "as the God of heaven above and on the earth below" (2:11), she requests of the spies a sign that will assure her and all her family of salvation in the imminent fall of Jericho (2:12). At their advice she then ties a scarlet cord in the window of her house (2:21).

We first find the scarlet wool as a part of the ceremonies for the cleansing of a leper (Lv 14:1-7), the cleansing of a house (Lv 14:49-53), and the preparation of the water that purifies from the defilement caused by contact with dead bodies (Nm 19:6). The meaning of the sign is evident: The wool is taken from the sheep, the symbol of Israel and of the Messiah. The scarlet color is made of the blood of insects (kermes or cochineal). The scarlet wool is, therefore, Israel and the Messiah in their humiliation and their sufferings—the slaughtered Lamb of God.

The scarlet cord in Rahab's window is a sign of the universality of the saving power of the blood of Christ, shed not only for the children of Israel but "for the many" (Mt 26:28)—gentiles, harlots, sinners. These are invited to enter the kindgom of God by joining Rahab's house, the unity of the Church (6:22-25). What a great comfort it is to see this same sign also on Zerah, the twin of Tamar, who represents the chosen people (Gn 38:28)!

Dividing the Waters

The crossing of the Jordan (chapter 3) shows in every detail that this is not simply an "invasion" of a foreign country for the sake of political conquest. The ark of the covenant preceding the people into the waters of the river, carried by the priests and Levites, who embody the teaching office of God's Church, confirms the basic principle of spiritual conquest through the word of God. The ark is not a magic object. It contains the Law—God's holy will—which is "our sanctification" (1 Thes 4:3). That it is called here "the ark of the Lord of all the earth" (3:11, 13) is a reminder of the fact that it is the Lord of all the earth who gives this land to his people, and that taking possession of Palestine is only the figure of a more universal conquest: that of the entire world through the risen Saviour, who reigns at the right hand of the Father.

Wherever the word of God is announced to men, a division takes place, a "crisis" begins, symbolized here in the division of the waters of the Jordan (3:16). The waters at the right hand stop and form a mountain; those at the left ebb into the salty waters of the Dead Sea. In the same way, those who hear the Word of God are divided between those who keep it and form the mountain of the Church, and those who forget the Word, drop away, and get lost in the Dead Sea of this world.

This process will come to an end when "the Lord of all the earth" comes on the clouds of heaven and divides the sheep from the goats. He will say to the sheep on his right hand: "Come, you blessed of my Father, inherit the kingdom prepared for you from the foundation of the world," and to those on his left: "Depart from me, you cursed, into everlasting fire!" (Mt 25:31-46).

It is on the tenth day of the first month that the people come up from the Jordan and camp in Gilgal (4:19). This is the day when the paschal lamb is to be chosen and brought into the house, before it is killed on the fourteenth (Ex 12:3). Israel is the lamb, which now is being brought into the "home," not so much to conquer but to be an offering to the will of God in the spirit of unselfish love.

First the Israelites set up a memorial of twelve stones (4:1-18) to remember forever that they crossed the Jordan on dry ground through God's power and not their own. Their life in the new country should, therefore, be a continuous thanksgiving: "Not to us, Lord, not to us, but to your name give the glory, for your mercy and for truth's sake" (Ps 115:1).

Then they undergo, at the command of Joshua, the circumcision (5:3-9), which is the solemn pledge to overcome the selfishness of nature in order to serve God. Freedom from self enables them to celebrate their first Passover feast in the Promised Land (5:10), the feast of their independence and their salvation through the blood of the lamb. Through both these rites the Israelites profess that the possession of the Holy Land does not so much depend on shedding the blood of their enemies as on shedding their own blood in a sacrifice of redemption. The majority of them never understood this fundamental principle, though it was fulfilled by Jesus and applied to the new Israel of the Church through the sacraments of baptism and the Eucharist.

Capturing the Land

When they are thus sanctified, the "captain of the army of the Lord" appears to Joshua (5:13-15) to make it clear that behind Joshua is another One, greater than he, who is the real leader in this campaign. He shows the true nature of his power in the capture of Jericho (chapter 6), the first city to be taken.

This capture gives a picture of the Church's conquest of the world at the end of time. The six days the Israelites march around the city are a symbol, as the number six always is in the Old Testament, of this earthly time, which is given to mankind as an opportunity to hear the message of salvation, indicated in the blowing of the rams' horns by the seven priests. But the walls only fall on the seventh day, at the seventh procession around the city, when Joshua tells the people, who have kept silent until now, "Shout; for the Lord is giving you the city!" (6:16).

This is a picture of the spiritual power of the messianic age, in which the Spirit fills all and loosens the tongues of all. The walls of the world will not fall flat as long as the people of God leave the work of conquering the world to the priests. All have to participate. All have to raise the victory shout.

Jericho is offered as a firstling to the Lord. No loot is taken, but all valuables come into the treasury of the Lord (6:19). Achan, of the tribe of Judah, breaks the sacred ban by stealing some of the loot and burying it in the ground (7:1-26). He represents that part of the Jewish people which buries the treasure of God's grace in the ground of the

Holy Land and later on rejects the Messiah Jesus in order to keep "the people and the land" (Jn 11:48). The stoning of Achan and the salvation of the harlot Rahab already point, from here at the beginning of the sacred history of redemption, to the great "revolution" that the charity of Christ will bring about in the end, when the heirs of the kingdom will be thrown out into utter darkness while the prostitutes and tax collectors will be accepted (Mt 8:12; 21:31).

After the defilement brought on the Israelites by Achan has been removed, Joshua is able to conquer Ai, the second town in Canaan to fall to the Israelites. The inhabitants are put to the sword, and the king is "hanged on a tree [that is, crucified] and left until evening," but at sunset Joshua orders his body to be taken down from the tree (8:29). In the attack on Ai the Israelites use violence for the first time in their campaign to conquer Canaan. The battle against the five kings follows (chapter 10), and the defeat of the "kings of the north" (chapter 11). "And Joshua took and put to the sword and destroyed all the cities round about, and their kings" (11:12).

This war of extermination has nothing in common with the colonial wars which the white race fought during the last three centuries against practically all the rest of humanity. During the white conquest of colonial empires, whole nations were sacrificed to the white race's skill in exploiting nature. The war of Joshua, on the other hand, is directed against idolatry and sin.

Recent excavations have proved that Canaanite culture at the time of the Hebrew invasion had reached its lowest level and found itself in a state of complete moral corruption.[1] Temple prostitution, child sacrifices, and such were public institutions in these little city-states. Their extermination through Joshua is the demonstration of the absolute opposition between the holiness of God and the sin of man. The wages of sin is death, because the living God is holy, and he hates sin. It is the plant that the heavenly Father has not planted and which, therefore, shall be rooted up (Mt 15:13).

There is no essential difference between Joshua and the Messiah of whom David speaks: "The Lord said to my Lord: Sit at my right hand, until I make of your enemies your footstool [see Jos 10:24]. The Lord at your right hand has broken kings in the day of his wrath; he shall fill ruins, he shall crush heads in the land of the many" (Ps 110:1, 5-6).

But the Messiah Jesus has revealed a spiritual principle, here expressed in terms of war to be carried on by everyone in his or her own heart: "He that loves his life shall lose it; and he that hates his life in this world, keeps it unto life eternal" (Jn 12:25). True to his teaching, he has fulfilled Joshua by carrying the burden of our sins in his own body on the tree, that we might die to sin and live in justice (1 Pt 2:24).

The difference between the Book of Joshua and the New Testament is not that the former belongs to a more primitive stage of the ethical development of the human race, in which violence is still considered a legitimate means of spreading religion, while the latter is pacificistic. Rather, the difference is in the fact that Joshua hangs the evil kings on the tree, while Jesus takes on the likeness of sin and takes upon himself the death of the kings of Canaan. The difference between Joshua and Jesus is, therefore, that in Jesus charity has fulfilled justice, and death has been swallowed up in life.

Establishing the Kingdom

That the extermination of the Canaanites was not a matter of racial hatred or of political expediency is evident also from the treatment the Gibeonites receive when they come to make a covenant with Joshua (chapter 9). They disguise themselves as people coming from far away. Hastily, without asking the Lord—that is, for natural reasons only—the leaders of Israel receive them into the covenant. When their ruse is discovered, Joshua saves them and makes them hewers of wood and carriers of water for the sanctuary (9:21).

The Gibeonites have accepted the faith but have not changed the inner man, and therefore they do not obtain the true liberty of the children of God. The Gibeonites of all times are those who consider the Church and Christianity merely life insurance. Not living the positive fullness of the new life, they remain "servants," hewers of wood and carriers of water.

The weak Gibeonites are the first to be attacked by the enemy (chapter 10). Joshua comes to their rescue in the glorious battle of Gibeon, when he asks the sun to stop that the defeat of the enemy might be complete. This is a marvelous picture of the "Day of the Lord" which is constantly prolonged, far beyond the possibilities of nature, through the sacraments of the Church! The Joshua of the New Testament makes the sun stop when he institutes the sacramental memorial of his passion and his resurrection. And in his power every priest causes the sun of justice to stop when he says: "This is my body.... This is my blood."

The whole purpose of the conquest of Palestine by Joshua is the establishment of the kingdom of God. Therefore an altar is built as soon as a firm foothold has been gained in the land, an altar of unhewn stones to indicate that whatever serves God should be untouched by violence and corruption (8:31).

One God, one country, one people, one altar: This fundamental principle of the kingdom of God seems to be endangered when the tribes living east of the Jordan build an altar for themselves (22:10-34). All Israel is ready to fight against them (22:11)—until the eastern tribes explain that this altar is not being used to offer sacrifices, but only serves as a reminder to them that they also have the right to offer and that they also had "a part in the Lord" (22:27).

In these tribes living outside the Holy Land, Israel in exile is prefigured; their altar is an anticipation of the synagogue, which takes the place of the temple for the exiles. God's mercy is not limited by geographical border lines; his altar is wherever there are hearts to adore him. Thus the altar east of the Jordan represents all those who, although they have not been incorporated into the Church "physically" through the sacraments, have nevertheless the sincere intention, in good faith, to serve God, who is God in heaven and on the earth below.

After the conquest of the land Joshua distributes it by lot, which means through God's grace, to the nine and a half tribes that have not yet received their part from Moses (see Nm 32:33). This second distribution, in itself evidently a foreshadowing of the dispensation of grace through Jesus Christ that follows the old dispensation under the Law, is not too interesting a matter to read (13:1–21:43), but it is full of spiritual significance.

Take only the institution of the "towns of refuge" for those who have slain someone unintentionally, with the significant rule that the manslayer may return safely to his own city after the death of the high priest (chapter 20). According to the Law (see Nm 35:33), the blood of the innocent defiles the country and cannot be expiated but by the blood of the one who has shed it. If, however, blood has been shed unintentionally, the responsibility rests with the high priest, and his death expiates the land. We see the signpost pointing to the vicarious death of Christ, which makes possible our return to the Father's home.

In the last two chapters (23–24) Joshua renews the covenant, impressing upon the minds of the Israelites that the love of God, which has given them a land in which they have not labored and cities to dwell in which they have not built (24:13), does not take away their freedom of choice. They have to decide whom to serve: the God of their fathers or the gods of the Amorites. When the Israelites choose to serve the God of their fathers, Joshua tells them that they will not be able (24:19), but he and his house will indeed serve the Lord (24:15). A true prophet, Joshua sees the apostasy of Israel but also the loyalty of Jesus and his house, the Church.

EIGHT

Judges and Ruth

The conquest of the Holy Land under the leadership of Joshua marks the end of the first phase of Jewish history, which began with the liberation of the chosen people from bondage in Egypt. It is the age of Israel's childhood, when God calls his son out of Egypt, takes him by the hand, and leads him with cords of love (see Hos 11:1-4). With the conquest of Palestine Israel leaves the "kindergarten" of the desert and enters upon the trials and temptations of adolescence. These are described in the Book of Judges.

The youth who has escaped the bridle of the tutor and tastes for the first time the intoxicating sweetness of liberty and independence seems to forget at once what he has learned in school, until the experience of life teaches him to accept through his own conviction what external training has not been able to impress upon him. This is what happens to Israel. After Joshua's death a new generation grows up, which does not "know the Lord nor yet the work that he has wrought" (2:10).

Joshua's conquest has not been as complete and as final as it should have been. Many of the native tribes are left (1:27-36) "to prove Israel by them" (3:1). "They were as thorns in Israel's side, and their gods had become a snare to them. And the children of Israel did what was evil in the sight of the Lord, and served the Baalim" (2:3, 11).

In punishment for their faithlessness God repeatedly delivers them into the hands of their enemies. Then, moved by their repentance and their groaning, he raises up a series of judges from among them as their liberators. After the death of each judge the people relapse into their former servitude.

117

This cycle of apostasy, servitude, repentance, liberation, and relapse—repeated six times—forms the pattern of the first part of the Book of Judges (2:1–16:31). Three divine messages in which God reveals himself as the source of Israel's liberty divide the six cycles into three main groups.

The first message, brought by "the angel of the Lord" (2:1-3), opens that section of the Book of Judges in which Israel's struggle for freedom against the kings is described (chapters 3–5). Othniel liberates Israel from the yoke of Cushan-Rishathaim of Mesopotamia (3:8-11). Ehud, the left-handed Benjaminite, saves Israel from the oppression of the Moabites by killing their king Eglon, the fat one (3:12-30). Deborah, the prophetess, kindles the flame of resistance against Jabin, king of Canaan (4:1–5:31).

The second message, brought by a prophet (6:8-10), marks the beginning of Israel's liberation from the hordes of the Midianites (6:1–8:35) through the great champion Gideon. His rule is followed by the bastard Abimelech's abortive attempt to kill Israel's freedom from within by establishing a tyranny (chapter 9).

The third message is directed to Israel by God himself (10:11-13) as introduction to the third struggle: Israel's fight under Jephthah against the Ammonites in the east (10:17–12:15) and Samson's daring exploits against the Philistines in the west (13:1–16:31). Six outstanding leaders, usually called the major judges, are thus counted in the book. Six minor judges are inserted in between: Shamgar (3:31), Tola and Jair (10:1-5), lbzan, Elon, and Abdon (12:8-15). Our Lord had these twelve in mind when he said to his apostles, "Amen, I say unto you, that you, who have followed me, in the regeneration when the Son of Man shall sit on the seat of his majesty, you also shall sit on twelve seats judging the twelve tribes of Israel" (Mt 19:28).

Sent by the Spirit

It is a long way, however, from the twelve judges to the twelve apostles. The latter are sent out to establish the kingdom of the Son of God's love in the power of the Holy Spirit, who flows from the pierced heart of the "king of the Jews" and fills the whole house of the Church on Pentecost. The spirit of the judges never fills the whole house of Israel, nor does the Holy Spirit rest upon them. While the spirit of God in the beginning of creation moved over the waters of chaos, the spirit of God in Judges acts as an alien force, seizing the champion with violence and lifting him up above his natural strength, without, however, penetrating into the inner man and transforming the heart. He is the spirit of adolescence, not of maturity. We should not expect the judges to have the inner qualities we love in Jesus. They are not "saints" in our Christian sense. When we read their stories we should remember the words of St. Augustine: "The Spirit of the Lord worked the prefiguring and the preaching of the things to come through knowing people as well as through those who did not know. There is no reason, therefore, to call their sins non-sins, because God, who knows how to make good use of our evil deeds, has used even their sins to signify what he intended."[1]

The deeds of the judges are "signs" of the work of redemption to be wrought by Christ. As an example, let us take the story of Ehud, who kills King Eglon of Moab (3:12-30). Ehud's deed is not very edifying, and it would not be worth recording in the annals of God's kingdom if it did not have a spiritual meaning reaching beyond the naked fact.

Eglon, who is too fat to move, is the typical representative of that pompous spirit of self-confidence with which the great ones of the earth try to imitate the omnipotent Lord of heaven and earth. He stands for the "prince of this world." Ehud's saving deed points to the way in which the Saviour Christ frees mankind from the domination of the devil. Under the pretext that he has a "word of God" for Eglon, Ehud thrusts the sword, so that it goes in, blade and hilt, into the king's belly.

Now, the Word of God is very often called in Holy Scripture a "sword." The author of the Letter to the Hebrews writes (4:12), "The word of God is living and effectual, and more piercing than any two-edged sword; it reaches to the division of the soul and the spirit, of the joint also and the marrow, and is a discerner of the thoughts and intents of the heart." When we read these words, we may suspect that he has Ehud and his two-edged sword in mind.

Is the Law, with its two commandments of the love of God and the love of neighbor, not indeed a two-edged sword? Is it farfetched to see in the two natures of Christ, as Son of God and Son of Man, this twofold essence of the Law fulfilled?

Once we see Christ himself represented in Ehud's sword, we understand why the sword went into Eglon's belly blade and hilt, and why "the fat closed in upon the blade" (3:22). It prefigures the way in which Christ killed the prince of this world—by taking on the sins of men and women, by dying for them, and by descending into hell. Holy Scripture does not tell Ehud's story to recommend murder but to point to the mystery of Christ, who made the sacrifice of his innocent life the source of spiritual freedom for the new Israel.

Deborah

Israel's fight for liberty against the kings reaches its climax in Deborah's rising against Jabin of Canaan (4:1–5:31). Tyranny always was, always is, and always will be the fruit of idolatry. The *baalim* of the Canaanites are local deities. They merge, therefore, with the local political power of the king.

Israel's God, the one true God, stands for absolute justice for everyone. He frees his servants from the arbitrary rule of local tyrants. "Happy are you, O Israel! who is like you? A people made free by the Lord" (Dt 33:29).

This spirit of freedom under God is in danger of being suppressed under the iron rule of Jabin. His general, Sisera, resides in the fortress that has the significant name of Harosheth-ha-goiim, "silence of the nations." Sisera has silenced the voice of free nations with his police force of nine hundred chariots of iron (4:3).

All weapons have been confiscated. "There was no shield nor spear seen among forty thousand in Israel" (5:8). The people have gone underground. "The highways ceased, and the travelers walked through byways" (5:6). There are among the people no leaders: "The rulers ceased, they ceased" (5:7).

At this point a woman arises: "You did arise, Deborah, arise as a mother in Israel" (5:7). In a similar way, in the beginning of the New Testament, when a man is put to silence, the voice of a woman opens the gates of freedom for mankind (Lk 1:20-38). The song of Deborah breaks the silence of the nations (5:1-31). In the power of genuine inspiration, it praises the beauty of that freedom which only the Spirit of God is able to release in the soul of mankind:

When men let grow their hair in Israel,
When the people offer themselves willingly,
Bless ye the Lord! (5:2)

The service of the one true God is not a matter of violence and force. Those who serve him do so willingly, because he alone moves the hearts of men. His army is an army of volunteers. Deborah's trumpet call arouses everything that is noble and generous and magnanimous in Israel. From all sides they respond, banding together on Mount Tabor against the kings.

In the plain at the foot of the mountain Sisera's chariots hold free sway, and the poorly armed peasants would not have much of a chance if the Lord did not move heaven and earth to help them. "The stars in their courses fought against Sisera" (5:20). A sudden cloudburst turns the brook Kishon into a raging sea and the entire plain into a swamp. Thus horse and rider and chariot suffer the fate of the Egyptians in the Red Sea.

Alone, without his horse, Sisera found his way into the tent of Heber's wife, Jael. There, at the hand of a woman, he meets an inglorious death.

In a masterful climax the song of Deborah ends with a scene in the harem of Sisera's ancestral palace. There his mother and his wives wait for him to come back loaded with spoil. In the whole of human literature we do not find a more poignant picture of degraded womanhood, its freedom and dignity lost, than here. It forms the sharpest contrast to the noble, heroic attitude of the woman whom the Spirit of God has made "a mother in Israel."

The Israelite peasants of Deborah's days are the spiritual ancestors of the free Greek citizens who defeated the armies of Xerxes at Thermopylae, of the Swiss shepherds and farmers who descended from their mountain abodes to destroy the armor of Austria at Murbach, and of the volunteers who in the American war of independence gained victory over the Hessian mercenaries. The true meaning of Deborah's song, however, is the praise of the freedom that the Word and the Spirit of God give to the Church.

Deborah, the prophetess whose name means "the talkative one" and also "the bee," sends to Barak a call to rise against Jabin (4:8). She represents the voice of God, which in the Law and through the prophets calls the Israelite people (Barak) to battle against the powers of this world. Victory, however, is completed not by her but by Jael, who is described as the wife of a non-Jew (4:11, 17; 5:24) and therefore foreshadows the Church of the gentiles.

Gideon

Israel's struggle for freedom reaches its peak in Gideon's fight against the Midianites (6:1–8:35). One cannot read these pages of the Book of Judges without being deeply moved by this splendid document of the spirit of Israel's youth: how the Spirit of God puts on this man like a garment (6:34); how Gideon destroys the cult of the *baalim;* how he blows the trumpet and thirty thousand follow him.

But God tells Gideon: "The people that are with you are too many for me to give the Midianites into their hand, lest Israel vaunt themselves saying: 'My own hand has saved me'" (7:2). Then we see how Gideon makes sure that God truly will save Israel through his own hand; how of the thirty thousand finally only three hundred are left who do not bend their knees to satisfy their thirst; how these by night with flaming torches and with the war cry, "The sword of the Lord and of Gideon!" chase the enemy from bed and sleep into panic and flight; how, free from all vainglory, the saviour of Israel disarms the envious Ephraimites with a clever witticism (8:2).

Finally, in the greatest moment of all, we see how Gideon rejects the temptation to accept hereditary rule over Israel: "I will not rule over you, neither shall my son rule over you; the Lord shall rule over you" (8:23). All this so magnificent, of such consummate strength and clarity of faith, that we understand very well why Isaiah sees the day of the messianic liberation from all pressure and darkness in the light of the "day of Midian" (Is 9:4).

Magnificent as the spirit of Gideon is in the days of his campaign against the Midianites, it is still the spirit of Israel's youth—that violent, alien force that takes possession of its instrument without really changing the heart. The spirit does not stay with Gideon. He has scarcely rejected the rule over Israel when he establishes a little principality in his home town, with a "house god" made of the earrings of the Midianites (8:24-27) and with a large harem (8:29-31).

Out of Gideon's apostasy grows the evil shoot Abimelech, Gideon's bastard son from a Canaanite concubine (8:31). He establishes a tyranny by shedding the blood of his brothers (9:1-56). One brother, Jotham, escapes Abimelech's sword to reveal in a magnificent parable the true nature of tyranny, which is like a thornbush shooting forth fire to devour the very cedars that have made it a king over them (9:7-15).

The sad end of Gideon's glorious beginnings shows that the spirit of Gideon alone is not sufficient to make the "day of Midian" a prophetic picture of the day of the Messiah Jesus. His story, however, abounds in signs pointing to the two great mysteries of the day of Christ: the Incarnation and the *Pascha*. The Incarnation is foreshadowed in the salutation of the angel, which uses the very words Gabriel was to speak to Mary, "The Lord is with you" (6:12), and in the sign of the fleece (6:36-40). The beautiful words "and the spirit of the Lord clothed himself with Gideon" point in the same direction (6:34).

According to Jewish tradition, the night in which Gideon offers his sacrifice of a lamb and unleavened loaves is the paschal night.[2] We see indeed the mystery of Christ's sacrifice and resurrection indicated in the angel's touching the gifts with his staff, so that fire goes up from the rock to consume the flesh, and in the altar, which Gideon afterwards dedicates to "my Lord is peace." The cake of barley bread and Gideon's sword (7:13-14, 20) are symbols of the paschal new moon.[3]

Gideon's trumpet, the broken pitchers, the shining torches—they all indicate Christ's *pascha*. The trumpet points to the preaching of the glad tidings. The pitchers signify our earthly bodies formed from clay by the divine potter (see Gn 2:7). They are broken as Christ's human body is broken in his passion and as the bodies of martyrs are broken. The torches that shine when the pitchers are broken—what else do they foreshadow but the glorious life of the Resurrection radiating from Christ and from all those who participate in his death? The "day of Midian" bears indeed the prophetic marks of the day of Christ.

Jephthah

"The children of Israel did again what was evil in the sight of the Lord, and served the *baalim*, and he gave them into the hands of the Ammonites" (10:6–7). Then Jephthah the Gileadite, who as a youth had to flee from his brothers, was made the head by the elders of Gilead to lead them in the fight against the Ammonites. In the Spirit of the Lord (11:29) he defeated the Ammonites. On his return he offered his daughter in sacrifice, because he had vowed that if the Lord would deliver the Ammonites into his hands, he would offer whatsoever came forth from the doors of his house to meet him.

Many features of Jephthah's story remind us of our Lord. Christ also had to flee from his brothers, the Jews, who despised him as the son of a harlot (see Jn 8:41). He associated with sinners and publicans as Jephthah did in the "land of Tob" (11:3), the land of salvation and grace; and on the cross he was reckoned among sinners (Is 53:12). Christ fulfilled, as Jephthah did, the "vow of salvation" by offering his "daughter," his own flesh; and at the end of time he shall deliver up his Church, the "virgin chaste" (2 Cor 11:2), to his heavenly Father (1 Cor 15:24). But his enemies he will judge as Jephthah judged the Ephraimites at the ford of the Jordan (12:6).

Samson

Through his victory over the Ammonites, Jephthah has secured peace in the east. In the west the defeat of the Canaanites in the days of Deborah has freed the Israelites from any threat. But then a new power establishes itself in the fertile plains along the Mediterranean coast: the Philistines, from whom the whole country receives the name Palestine.

They come from the west, and they bring with them much of early Greek civilization. Their political life is much better organized than that of the native Canaanites. They excel in their metal work, of which Goliath's armor is the outstanding example (1 Sm 17:5-6).

Against them God raises up Samson, who is in every way the opposite of civilization, good manners, art, and politics. No ropes are strong enough to hold him. The abundance of his vitality is the only law of his actions. He does not gather wealth or power. He has no education, no training, but he excels all others in natural wit and sheer physical strength.

It would be wrong, however, to see in the Samson stories only a protest against civilization in favor of a "return to nature." The secret of Samson's greatness is his character as a Nazirite (13:5), a man who is separated from ordinary men to be consecrated to God. True, Samson's weakness does not allow him to keep the order of life the vow imposes on him, and therefore he ends in failure. But his death is, at the same time, the most glorious manifestation of his true nature as a figure of Jesus, the other great Nazirite (Mt 2:23). Both fight alone and singlehandedly, in complete disregard of human cunning, in the supreme liberty that is present where the Spirit of God is (2 Cor 3:17).

Samson reaches in the grandeur of his death that freedom of the spirit which neither unbridled nature nor civilization can secure, but only the sacrifice of self. Samson's death, through which he kills more of his enemies than he ever killed during his life (16:30), makes him truly a figure of Christ, who overcame his enemies through his death, and by his victory over Satan "solved" Samson's riddle: "Out of the eater came forth food, and out of the strong one came forth sweetness" (14:14).

The last chapters of the Book of Judges (17–21) follow as a kind of appendix showing how Israel's freedom is threatened, not only by external attacks but still more by the lawlessness that corrupts the inner life of the nation. The two incidents reported in these chapters—the apostasy of the Danites, who set up a graven image (chapters 17–18), and the crime of the Benjaminites (chapters 19–21)—stand for the two great dangers to which the inner life of the people is exposed: idolatry and adultery. They show, at the same time, that the political organization of Israel under the judges is insufficient, that the time is approaching when there should be a king in Israel (18:1) instead of having everybody do what is right in his own eyes (21:25). The Book of Judges thus leads to the main truth that the experience of adolescence has taught Israel: The Spirit of God, who moved all those years over the stormy waters of Israel's youth, must descend to rest upon God's Anointed.

The Book of Ruth

This truth is certainly the reason why the Book of Ruth has found its place in the canon of Holy Scripture after Judges. It leads us to Bethlehem, David's hometown and that of our Lord. There we meet Boaz, the father of Obed, the father of Jesse, the father of David, the father of Christ. This book focuses on the story of Ruth, the Moabite. Together with Rahab and Bathsheba, she has found her place in the genealogy of Jesus (Mt 1:5). We can say, then, with Theodoret, "Why was the story of Ruth written? In the first place for the sake of Christ the Lord, for from Ruth he sprang according to the flesh."[4]

The story of Judges and Ruth ends, therefore, with the dawn of a new day, the day of perfect union between God and humanity. The day when the Spirit of peace and love turns the servants of God into friends and lets them speak with Ruth (friendship): "Where you go, I will go; and where you lodge I will lodge; your people shall be my people and your God my God; where you die I will die, and there I will be buried; the Lord do so to me and more also, if anything but death part you and me" (Ru 1:16-17).

NINE

The First Book of Samuel

The Israelite people have received the promises God has made to the patriarchs (Genesis). The precious gift of liberty has been bestowed upon them (Exodus). The Law has been given to them (Leviticus, Numbers, Deuteronomy). The Holy Land has been delivered into their hands (Joshua). The period following the conquest of Palestine, that of the judges (divinely appointed and inspired leaders), has found the people loosely united as a republic of free men under God as their exclusive king, in constant battle against the power of the neighboring princes.

Nevertheless, the rule of leaders raised up by God as the occasion requires lacks one most important thing: stability. After the long period of wandering through the desert and of dwelling in the easily movable tabernacle, divine Wisdom is seeking a "resting place" (see Sir 24:7). This will be secured through the establishment of the royal throne of the house of David in Jerusalem. Hereditary kings, replacing temporary leaders, are the means God uses to bring about the necessary consolidation of the community-life of the chosen people after the period of conquest is over.

Time for a King

The king is more than a mere organ of God's will, more than only God's mouthpiece. He has an authority of his own entrusted to him. He must decide and act by his own wisdom. Moses was only the instrument God used to make his Word and will known to the people. Joshua acted as God's sword, and so did the judges. The king, however, is not anointed to act merely *from* God, but *for* God and *in* God's place.

A more intimate and organic union between the king and God must therefore replace the passing divine interventions by which the judges were led. Only a continuous, habitual "union of the heart" between God and his anointed one can bring about the stability for which the people are longing. Thus, the first two books about Israel's kings describe how God establishes the "eternal throne" in Jerusalem through David, who is, as his name—"the beloved one"—indicates, the "man according to God's heart."

The history of the kings of the house of David shows, however, that in none of them is God so absolutely pleased as to establish his throne forever. David's throne is eternal only in Jesus Christ, the "Son of David," in whom alone God is so well pleased as to anoint him publicly with the Holy Spirit (Mt 3:16-17) and to give to him the throne of his father David, to reign over the house of Jacob forever (Lk 1:32-33).

The first two books about Israel's kings are usually called the Books of Samuel, not because they were written by Samuel but because Samuel is the spiritual father of the period recorded therein. They describe the establishment and the consolidation of the messianic throne in the house of David.

First Samuel 1:1–7:17 can be considered a kind of introduction describing the rise of Samuel, the man whom God uses as his instrument to lay the foundation of the eternal throne of David. First Samuel 8:1–31:13 constitutes the first main part of the book, covering the period of preparation preceding the final establishment of the throne of David: Saul's election and rejection, and David's trials until the death of Saul. The second main part (2 Sm 1:1–20:26) relates the enthronement of David and the confirmation of his rule. Second

Samuel 21:1–24:25 appears as a kind of epilogue to the history of the rule of David. The report of the buying of Araunah's threshing floor (24:18-25) and the erection of an altar there point to the building of the temple, the central theme of the following First Book of Kings.

The birth of Samuel (1 Sm 1:1–2:11) finds the Israelite people in a state of complete disintegration. Politically their liberty and independence are threatened by the Philistines, who control most of the Holy Land. The Israelites, unarmed and divided as they are, are not able to take the strongholds of the Philistines. Spiritually things are even worse. The priesthood, under the old and weak Eli and his evil sons, is corrupt and in disrepute with all the people.

The catastrophe is unavoidable. When the Philistines muster against Israel for war, and Israel goes out to meet them in battle, thirty thousand of the Israelites are killed, and the ark of God falls into the hands of the enemies (4:10-11). The glory of God has departed from Israel (4:22). When Eli hears the sad tidings, he falls backward from his seat, breaks his neck, and dies (4:18).

Scripture does not spare any words to describe the old age of the priest (4:15-18). He stands for the old order of things that has come to an end. A new age is about to begin. We are reminded of the beginning of the Gospel according to St. Luke where Zacharias the priest, "an old man and well stricken in years" (Lk 1:18) loses his speech (Lk 1:22), while Mary, the young maiden, says the word initiating a new age: "Behold the handmaid of the Lord; be it done to me according to your word" (Lk 1:38).

This similarity between the first chapter of the Gospel of St. Luke and the beginning of the First Book of Samuel becomes more striking when we turn to the details of Samuel's birth. Samuel is raised up by God in such a way as to mark him "from birth as altogether an instrument of the Lord's providing."[1]

Hannah and Samuel

In the history of our salvation, as it is written by God on the pages of Holy Scripture, the dawn of a new age is always marked by a new manifestation of God's mercy. A holy woman usually stands at its beginning as the *porta salutis,* the entrance gate through which God's chosen one enters upon the scene. Samuel is born, as Isaac was, in answer to the prayers of a barren woman, in the power of Almighty God. Hannah, his mother, ranks with the great mothers of the Bible—with Sarah, Rebekah, Rachel, Elizabeth, and Mary.

The new age of salvation is ushered in on the wings of a woman's prayers. Hannah is indeed the great example and teacher of prayer. Her prayer is the word of her heart (1:13). It is poured forth from the innermost center of her personality, which has been torn open by her bitterness of soul (1:10). Nevertheless, her prayer is not a mere drifting of the heart on the waves of emotions. Her lips move (1:13), which means that her prayer consists of definite, formulated thoughts.

Deeply significant is the way she addresses God: "O Lord of hosts" (1:11). This is the first time in the Scriptures that a prayer is directed to God under this name. It signifies God as the Lord and Master, the leader and commander of the universe. The universe, in turn, is conceived as an "army"—not a changeless, impersonal combination of forces under a physical law, but an infinite variety of different beings, each of which has its own place and task as a soldier serving in obedience under the one supreme intelligence and will of the commander-in-chief.

Hannah approaches the Lord of hosts as his "handmaid," the key word of her prayer. Repeated three times in one verse (1:11), this word points clearly to Mary, who as a true handmaid was eager that it be done unto her according to the word of the Lord of Hosts (Lk 1:38).

Hannah's petition ends in a vow through which she solemnly binds herself never to forget that the child is the fruit of her prayers.

Although her prayer has risen "out of the abundance of complaint and grief" (1:16), it brings her already the assurance of God's mercy. "So the woman went her way and ate and her countenance was no longer sad" (1:18).

When the son is born Hannah calls him Samuel—"I have asked him of the Lord"—and in a beautiful *eucharistia*—hymn of thanksgiving—she pours forth her gratitude (2:1-10). Hannah's song is reechoed in the New Testament by the *Magnificat* of Mary (Lk 1:46-55). The two mothers understand that it is God's eternal design to save mankind not through power but through his descending, sacrificial love.

The God of Israel, the Father of Jesus Christ, is not the God of the mighty but of those who stumble (2:4), not of those who are full but of the hungry (2:5). He is the God of the barren and the God of the poor. But the real secret of his heart he shows when he takes his own Son, kills him and makes him alive again—bringing him down to the grave and up again (2:6). In this verse Hannah remembers the God of Moses, who brought his firstborn into the grave of Egypt only to give him a more glorious freedom.

From its first appearance in the song of Moses, this theme becomes the ever-repeated burden accompanying the whole of the Old Testament (Hos 6:1; Job 5:18; Wis 16:13; Tob 13:2). It is fulfilled at last in God's only begotten Son, who "died for our sins according to the Scriptures, was buried and rose again the third day according to the Scriptures" (1 Cor 15:3-4). In the Resurrection God "gave strength unto his king, and exalted the horn of his anointed" (1 Sm 2:10).

In the very beginning of this new age of the kings Hannah points as a true prophetess to the messianic King, in whom the idea of the divine kingship finds its last fulfillment. In Jesus Christ, who entered the "city of the great king" humbly riding on an ass, who conquered death by dying on the cross, who established his throne by shedding his blood for the remittance of our sins—in him the heavenly Father "raised up the poor out of the dust, and lifted up the needy from the dung-hill, to make them sit with the princes and inherit the throne of glory" (2:8). Hannah's and Mary's songs form part of the eternal *eucharistia* of the Church, in which she gratefully praises what proves to be the fundamental principle of salvation: "Not by arms, nor by force, but by my spirit, says the Lord of Hosts" (Zec 4:6), or as Hannah puts it, "By strength shall no man prevail" (2:9).

God's mercy, which manifests itself through the instrument of a barren woman, continues its work of salvation during the life of Samuel. As a child he is called by God, at a time when the word of God is precious, and there is no "open vision" (3:1). The seven-branch candlestick that burns in the tabernacle at night as a symbol of the eternal life of God's anointed (see Ps 132:17; 1 Kgs 11:36; 15:4) has not yet gone out (3:3) when God calls Samuel, through whom he intends to light the lamp of God's anointed king.

Shortly after, the great defeat takes place, when Israel loses the ark and Eli dies in sorrow. But the ark does not remain long in the hands of Israel's enemies. Not by force of arms but through two milk cows, it is brought home to Joshua of Beth-shemesh (6:7-14).

When a new catastrophe threatens at Mizpah, where Samuel officiates in his function as a judge, his prayers and his sacrifice of a suckling lamb save the people (7:9). That God on this occasion "thunders with a mighty voice" against the Philistines when Samuel is offering the holocaust (7:10) indicates that the suckling lamb is a symbol of Jesus, the Lamb of God, for whose glory God thundered over Jerusalem shortly before he was led to the slaughter (Jn 12:28).

Samuel is the great example of a servant of God completely forgetful of self. He is like John the Baptist: the friend of the bridegroom, the humble forerunner of the Saviour, the one who wants to decrease that another may increase. Without being in the least concerned over his own position and influence as the universally acknowledged judge of Israel, he obeys the voice of the people and the command of God to anoint the first king of Israel (8:9).

Saul

Saul is a king according to the heart of the people, "a handsome young man; and there [is] not a man among the Israelites more handsome than he. He [is] taller than any of the people from his shoulder upward" (9:2). By nature brave, daring, and resolute, he soon rallies the people around him and wins their favor by showing generosity toward those who first despised him (11:13). He fights successfully against all the enemies on every side and delivers Israel out of the hands of its plunderers (14:48).

Nevertheless, Saul owes his royal dignity to the impatient request of the people to have a king "like the other nations" (8:5). Samuel has pointed out to them that by their request they reject God as king over them (8:7). He has warned that only true fear of the Lord—on the part of the people as well as of the king—can prevent the monarchy from turning into tyranny (12:14-15). Here Saul fails.

With all the charming and fascinating qualities for which Samuel and David and all the others love Saul so much, he lacks one thing: the fear of the Lord. Religion is for him more an infection than a conviction. In the company of the prophets he prophesies (10:10). But his friends who know him better ask with a skeptical smile, "Is Saul also among the prophets?" (10:11).

Saul is not really a religious man. His is a complicated character, moody and fickle. One moment he summons the priest, the next he brushes him away (14:18-19), and in the end he kills them all (22:18). Seven days he waits for Samuel to come and offer sacrifice. Then at the last moment he loses patience and offers the sacrifice himself, against the commandment of God (13:8-10).

One day Saul, seized with an unreasonable religious zeal, puts the whole people under oath not to eat anything for a whole day of heavy fighting. He is ready even to kill his son Jonathan, unaware of his father's oath, for having taken a little honey (14:24). Another time he disregards the express command of God in order to please the people and his own vanity by saving the spoils and sparing his brother-king, Agag of Amalek (chapter 15). In the beginning of his reign he cuts off all the wizards from the land and puts a ban on superstitious practices, but he later asks the witch of Endor to divine for him by her talisman (28:3-25).

For all his natural virtues and talents, Saul lacks real faith in God. He has no deep-seated religious principles and convictions. What he possesses has come to him without effort. Therefore he neglects to develop it, and as a result we see his character deteriorate rapidly. He puts his own glory above everything else, and consequently jealousy over the successes of his son Jonathan and of David eats into his heart, making him cruel, resentful, and hardhearted. He sinks deeper and deeper into the abyss of gloom and hatred, until finally, surrounded by defeat and mortally wounded, he throws himself upon his own sword.

"His history," says Newman in one of his sermons, "is a lesson to us, that the 'heart of unbelief' may exist in the very sight of God, may rule a man in spite of many natural advantages of character, in the midst of much that is virtuous, amiable and commendable."[2] The Spirit of God, which seizes upon Saul so suddenly and gives him "a new heart" (10:9), has taken root. Therefore the evil spirit returns with seven others, and Saul's last state becomes worse than his first (see Lk 11:24-26).

A Jewish legend relates that when Saul's daughter Michal, who has become David's wife, sees her husband dancing before the ark of the Lord at its solemn entry into Jerusalem, she says to him: "The men of my house were much more dignified than you, because they never exposed a hand or a foot that other people might see it." David answers her: "You are right, the generation of Saul only sought their own glory. I am not anxious about my own honor, if I can magnify the Lord" (see 2 Sm 6:20-23).

David

Indeed, the essential difference between Saul and David is just this, that David lives and moves in the fear of the Lord. He is the "man according to God's heart" (13:14). He is the good shepherd and the sweet singer of Israel, who praises God and loves his people.

Saul is a "son of wrath." Of him it is said, "I gave you a king in my anger, and took him away in my wrath" (Hos 13:11). *David,* however, means "the beloved one."

David does not have the imposing outward appearance that Saul has. The Lord, however, does not see as mankind sees, for they look at appearances, but God looks at the heart (16:7). The youngest among his brothers, David is called from shepherding his father's flock on Bethlehem's fields to be anointed by Samuel. "And the Spirit of the Lord seized upon David from that day forward" (16:11-13).

It is said of the judges and of Saul that the Spirit of the Lord seizes them, but "from that day forward" is not said of any of them. In David wisdom finds a resting place. In him the stable, continuous union between God and the heart of the king becomes an accomplished fact.

In this David is the figure of the messianic king, of whom Isaiah says: "A shoot shall spring from the stump of Jesse [David's father, 16:1], and a sprout from his root will bear fruit, and the Spirit of the Lord will rest upon him" (Is 11:1). This prophecy finds its fulfillment in the Son of David, whom the Spirit descends upon as a dove and whom the voice from heaven solemnly proclaims as the beloved Son ("David") in whom the Father is well pleased (Mt 3:17).

Many other traits in the life of young David show him to be the prototype of Christ, especially his fight with Goliath (chapter 17). Faith and spirit have left the Israelites and their king, Saul. They do not dare to answer the giant's blasphemies. Then David jumps into the breach, without armor, a true soldier of his God, knowing that "not with sword and spear does the Lord deliver: for the battle is the Lord's"

(17:47). With a sling, a stone, and a stick, David overcomes all the most up-to-date might of Goliath (17:5). Who would not be reminded of Christ, the one who jumps into the breach to give his life for the whole people and conquers the power of Satan with the cross on his shoulders?

Jonathan

Another beautiful sign of the love of Christ prefigured in the life of young David is the friendship between him and Jonathan (18–20). Jonathan, who as son of Saul is heir to the kingdom, prefers to be disowned by his father rather than give up David, "whom he loves as his own life" (18:3). He takes off his royal cloak, his sword, his bow, and his girdle and gives them to David. By this act he renounces his natural right to the throne in favor of David. He entrusts his own life and that of his family completely to the good graces of his friend: "O may you, if I am still alive, O may you show me the kindness of the Lord!" (20:14).

In doing this Jonathan represents the portion of Israel that at the time of Christ will prefer to be banned by their own people rather than leave the Son of David, who through his incarnation has received the royal garment of Israel. It is this Jonathan-group among the Jews, the apostles, to whom Christ reveals the secret of his friendship: "Greater love than this no man has, that a man lay down his life for his friends. You are my friends" (Jn 15:13-14). The friendship between David and Jonathan is fulfilled in Christ, who does more for his friends than David or Jonathan ever do. He lays down his life for them.

David's friendship with Jonathan marks the beginning of those long years of trial that make him still more a figure of Christ (chapters 21–29). The desert becomes David's refuge. Abandoned by all—without arms, without food—he receives from the priest the holy bread of the Lord, which is always kept in the sanctuary (21:3-6), and the sword of Goliath, which also has been preserved in the tabernacle. At every turn God shows that David is his anointed one, the man according to his heart. David gives witness to the love of God working in his heart when he answers Saul's incessant persecution by sparing his life (24:6; 26:9).

Nevertheless, the most beautiful monument of a heart big enough to love its enemies is the dirge David sings when the news of Saul's death reaches him (2 Sm 1:19-27):

> Thy beauty, O Israel,
> > upon thy heights is slain!
> > > How have the heroes fallen!
> > > > O mountains of Gilboa, let neither dew fall, nor rain be
> > > > upon you, O fields of death!
> > > Saul and Jonathan, beloved and lovely!
> > > > In life and death they were not divided; swifter than
> > > > eagles were they, they were stronger than lions!
> O Jonathan! By thy death I am mortally wounded,
> > I am stressed for thee, my brother Jonathan;
> > > thou hast been exceedingly dear to me,
> > > > wonderful was thy love to me,
> > > > > passing the love of women.
> How have the heroes fallen,
> > and the weapons of war perished!

TEN

The Second Book of Samuel

In the fateful battle on Mount Gilboa, Israel's forces are scattered and some even annihilated, and the Philistines certainly suffer heavy losses. Because the seasoned troops of David have not taken any part in the battle (1 Sm 29), they are the only military force left intact. Consequently, David becomes automatically the decisive political factor in Palestine.

He takes up residence in Hebron, the capital of the southern part of the Holy Land, where he is soon proclaimed king of Judah (2 Sm 1–4). After the violent deaths of Ishbosheth, Saul's incapable son and successor as king of Israel, and his general, Abner, the way is free for David. He becomes king of all Israel (5:1-5).

David's achievements during the thirty years of his rule over the united kingdom (ca. 1005–972 B.C.) are of lasting importance. He frees Israel from the supremacy of the Philistines by breaking the power of that nation once and forever (8:1). By subduing the neighboring tribes, especially the Ammonites and the Syrians to the north and northeast of Palestine (chapters 8 and 10), David establishes Israel within its ideal boundaries, from Dan in the north to Beer-sheba in the south. He consolidates the union between Judah and Israel by making Jerusalem, situated on neutral ground between the two, the political as well as the religious center of his kingdom (5:6-12). When he finally sees his son Solomon following him on the throne of Israel, he can give thanks to God out of a grateful heart that he has "set in order all things and secured" (23:5) and given rest to his people.

"A Man After God's Heart"

The secret of David's political success lies in the unique position above the two rival parties of Judah and Israel that he has built for himself. David's reign is not, like that of Saul, exclusively national. The most important pillar of his power, the bodyguard of devoted personal followers he had formed when he fought against Saul as an exile among the Philistines, is predominantly gentile, composed of "Cherethites and Pelethites," Cretans and Philistines (15:18). Jerusalem, his capital, is not a Jewish community but a Jebusite town, and most of the inhabitants of the "city of David" are not of Jewish origin.

Unlike Saul, David grants freedom and protection to Canaanite communities in Palestine. His treatment of the Gibeonites, who are not "of the children of Israel, but have a covenant with them," and whom Saul has sought to slay "out of zeal as it were for the children of Israel and Judah" (21:2), is of highest significance. David asks them: "Wherewith can I make expiation, so that you may bless the inheritance of the Lord?" The Gibeonites answer that the man who crushed them, Saul, should be destroyed in his seven sons, who should be given to be crucified to the Lord.

David consents, and the men are crucified on a hill "before the Lord in the first days of the harvest, when the barley began to be reaped [that is, at Eastertime]. And after that God was propitiated toward the land" (21:9, 14).

A thousand years later Pontius Pilate, the representative of the Roman emperor, will, at the demand of the Jews, hang the Son of David on the pole "before the Lord" at Eastertime. The crucified Christ will break down in his flesh "the middle wall of partition" between Jews and gentiles and "reconcile both to God in one body by the cross" (Eph 2:14, 16).

David's policy of strengthening his rule over "all Israel" by grafting, as it were, the gentiles into the original olive tree of the chosen people points clearly to the other "Good Shepherd of Israel," who has "other sheep that are not of this fold." This Shepherd promises that they too will hear his voice, and he keeps his promise when he sends another Saul—whose name, however, has changed to Paul—to become the great "teacher of the gentiles." This Saul-Paul reveals to his own people the great mystery of God: that all Israel will be saved when the fullness of the gentiles has been grafted into the good olive tree (see Rom 11:17-24).

In order to be truly "a man after God's heart," David must not only reflect the universal love with which the Father of all mankind draws "the many" to himself; he must also show, in his life and his actions, that he is a child of God's grace. He shows it when he chooses the naturally insignificant Jerusalem to become the "city of the Great King," imitating the God of all mercies, who selected the smallest among all the nations to be his chosen people.

The prophet Ezekiel gives us the right interpretation of David's "stroke of genius" when he announces the oracle of the Lord over Jerusalem:

> By origin and birth you belong to the land of the Canaanites. Your father was an Amorite and your mother a Hittite. As for your birth, on the day you were born your navel-string was not cut, nor were you washed with water to cleanse you, nor were you salted or wrapped in swaddling clothes; no eye had pity on you to do any of these things out of compassion for you. But you were cast upon the open field, with no regard for your life, on the day you were born.
>
> Then I passed by, and saw you weltering in your blood; and I said to you, as you lay weltering in your blood: "Live, and grow like a plant of the field!" So you grew big and strong till you reached the time of your maturity....
>
> Again I passed by you, and saw that you had reached the age of love; so I spread the skirts of my robe over you, and covered

your nakedness, and I plighted my troth to you, and entered into a covenant with you. So you became mine. Then I bathed you with water, and washed your blood from you, and I anointed you with oil. I clothed you with embroidered robes, shod you with shoes of porpoise skin, wrapped you in fine linen, and swathed you in silk. I adorned you with ornaments,... and your beauty was perfect, because of the splendor that I had bestowed upon you.

EZEKIEL 16:3-14

Room for Grace

That to be a man according to God's heart means to be a child of his grace is brought home to David in the most striking way when he decides to build a house for the Lord. Nathan must bring him God's answer: "Should you build me a house to dwell in? ... I took you from the pasture, from following the sheep, that you should be a leader over my people; and I have been with you wherever you have gone, and I have cut off all your enemies from before you, and I will make for you a great name.... The Lord declares to you that he will build *you* a house" (7:5-11).

David will not build the Lord a house, but God will build David a house. It will be a gift of God's grace. It will not be a house of stone, however; it will be another "man according to God's heart," the "Son of David."

"And when your days are finished, and you are laid with your fathers, I will raise up your seed after you, who shall be born of your body. And I will establish the throne of his kingdom forever. I will be his father, and he shall be my son.... Your house and your kingdom shall be confirmed before me forever. Your throne shall be established forever" (7:12-16).

These words are fulfilled when the angel brings the glad tidings to Mary, the daughter of the house of David:

Hail, full of grace. The Lord is with you.... Do not be afraid, Mary, for you have found grace with God. And behold, you shall conceive in your womb and you shall bring forth a man, and you shall call his name Jesus. He shall be great and shall be called the Son of the Most High [see 2 Sm 7:14]; and the Lord God will give him the throne of David his father, and he shall be king over the house of Jacob forever, and of his kingdom there shall be no end.

LUKE 1:28-33

Jesus Christ, the "Son of God who was born to him according to the flesh of the seed of David" (Rom 1:3), is the "temple" God has built. Therefore he says, speaking of the temple of his body: "Destroy this temple, and in three days I will raise it up" (Jn 2:19-21). The risen Lord is the kingdom and the "throne established forever." He is the fulfillment of the "sure mercies of David" (Is 55:3). It is of him that David sings: "My flesh will rest in hope, because you will not abandon my soul to hell, neither will you let your holy one see corruption" (Ps 16:9-10).

Peter explains these words to the multitude on the Feast of Pentecost:

I may speak freely to you of the patriarch David, that he both died and was buried, and his tomb is with us to this day. But as he was a prophet and knew that God had promised him with an oath that he would put one of his descendants upon his throne, he foresaw the resurrection of the Christ, and spoke of this, for he was not deserted in death, and his body was not destroyed.... For David did not ascend into heaven, but he said: "The Lord said to my Lord: Sit at my right hand, until I make your enemies your footstool."

ACTS 2:29-35, see Psalm 110:1

The Son of David, who offers himself as a holocaust for God's enemies and whom God raises from the dead, is the "house" where God is now dwelling forever. All those who are incorporated into him by taking part in his death and his resurrection through baptism also belong as living stones to the house God is building, because "in him you also are built together into a habitation of God in the Spirit" (Eph 2:22).

David nearly destroys the house God is building for him when he sins with Bathsheba, the wife of Uriah (chapter 11). However, in his fall, even more than in his heroic deeds as leader of Israel, he shows that he is really a child of grace. His humility and his genuine contrition turn his guilt into an abyss into which the grace of God descends.

Because of David's repentance, the Lord takes away his sin. "Nevertheless, because you have openly spurned the Lord by this deed, the child that is born to you shall surely die," says Nathan to David. With fasting and weeping David beseeches the Lord to save the child. But this "son of David" must die, that David might live.

When the child dies, David, in perfect resignation to God's will, bathes and anoints himself, changes his garments, and goes into the house of the Lord to worship. He comforts Bathsheba, now his wife. The son whom she then bears to him is called Solomon. The Hebrew *shalom* means "peace," and peace, according to Jewish thought, is perfect communion of life, first of all between God and his creatures, and consequently between men.

Solomon's birth is for David the visible pledge that his communion with God, which was destroyed by his sin, has been restored. The love of God descends right into the very wound David inflicted upon his house, so that out of it a new shoot sprouts, upon which the Spirit of God will rest. God loves Solomon, and he gives him a name accordingly: Jedidiah, which means "the Lord's darling" (12:25). In his free and sovereign grace God makes his choice among the sons of David. The finger of his love points out the one to be David's successor on the throne of Israel.

According to the law of succession Solomon certainly is the last to expect the throne. He has many elder brothers, and all must have inherited from their father the beauty and personal charm with which David commands the loyalty of his followers. There is Amnon, whom David loves because he is his firstborn (3:2). But when Amnon in a fit of passion ravishes his half-sister Tamar, he is killed by Absalom, her brother.

Absalom himself is the born crown prince, brilliant and beautiful. When after long years of exile in punishment for his sin Absalom is admitted again into the presence of his father, David kisses him as does the father in the parable of the Prodigal Son. Absalom, however, does not have a heart of repentance. He uses the splendid gifts with which nature has endowed him to steal the hearts of the people of Israel away from David (15:6) and have himself proclaimed king in Hebron.

The Messiah Foreshadowed

The news of Absalom's revolt comes on David like a thunderclap out of a clear sky. He is unsuspecting and utterly unprepared. Yet this worst predicament he has ever known brings out his best qualities. Never does David show himself more truly a child of God's grace than in this moment of his greatest humiliation.

To spare the city, David leaves Jerusalem. Crossing the Kidron, he surrenders himself and his kingdom completely into the hands of God: "If I shall find grace in the eyes of God, he shall bring me back. But if he say: 'I have no delight in you,' then I am ready, let him do to me as seems good in his sight" (15:25-26). Then David goes up to the Mount of Olives, weeping as he goes, with his head covered and walking barefoot; and all the people who are with him cover their heads as well, weeping as they ascend (15:30).

Who would not be reminded here of another "King of the Jews," the true "Son of David," who crosses the Kidron as his forefather did (Jn 18:1)? Surrounded by the little band of his disciples, he goes up to the Mount of Olives and there prays in the agony of deepest sorrow: "Father, if you are willing, take this cup away from me. But not my will, but yours be done" (Lk 22:42).

Being a child of God's grace, David knows the power that the poor in their affliction wield over the heart of God. Therefore he suffers Shimei's curses to be added to his misery: "Perhaps the Lord may look upon my affliction, and the Lord may requite good to me for the cursing of this day" (16:12). Indeed, God, who loves to descend, bows the heavens and comes down. He sends from on high and takes David and draws him out of many waters, delivers him from his strong enemies and sets him free, for his delight is in him (22:17-20).

Absalom's army is defeated. The rebel is caught by his hair in a tree. According to the Israelites, the hair is the glory of a free man. Absalom's glory is thus his ruin.

In spite of all his son's treachery, David wants to save him and is disconsolate when the news of his death reaches him. "My son Absalom! Absalom, my son! Would to God that I might die for you, Absalom, my son, my son!" (18:33). Do we not hear in these words the voice of the Good Shepherd mourning over the lost sheep?

Through all this human confusion of defeat and victory, of treachery and loyalty, of disappointment and triumph, we can hear—if we have ears to listen—the quiet steps of God's fatherly love pursuing the path of redemption. The blundering of men God uses as the means of fulfilling his promise and of putting the chosen one of his love upon his father's throne, thus pointing to the Son of David, who after his death will be enthroned at the right hand of the Father.

David himself is the "Christ," the "anointed one" of the Lord (Ps 132:17). His name, David, "the beloved one" (see Mt 3:17); his birthplace—Bethlehem (see Lk 2:11); his youth as a shepherd (1 Sm 17:34-37); his beauty (1 Sm 16:12)—really everything in his life foreshadows the Messiah. He wins the hearts of his countrymen and women through his kindness, and the bond thus established between him and his people points to the new covenant of love between Christ and his Church. Indeed, what the tribes of Israel say to David the day he is proclaimed their king—"We are bones of your bones and flesh of your flesh" (5:1)—gives us the first inkling of the great mystery of the mystical body of Christ, which St. Paul is later to reveal.

David's wars and victories have also a messianic character. "It is God that girds me with strength, that teaches my hands to war" (Ps 18:32, 34). It is God who lights David's candle in darkness, by whom he leaps over the wall (Ps 18:28). His victories are anticipations of the great victory that the "Son of David" will win at his resurrection. The "sure mercies of David," of which Isaiah speaks (Is 55:3), are fulfilled in Jesus, the Son of David, who does not see corruption because God raises him from the dead (Acts 13:34-37).

It is this Son to whom David's eyes are turned at the end of his life in his beautiful "last words":

The saying of David the son of Jesse, and the saying of the man raised on high to be the anointed of the God of Jacob, and the sweet singer of Israel: The spirit of the Lord spoke by me, and his word was upon my tongue. The God of Israel said, the Rock of Israel spoke to me:

Ruler over men shall be the Righteous, even he that rules in the fear of God, and as the light of the morning when the sun rises, a morning without clouds; when through clear shining after rain the tender grass springs out of the earth.

For is not my house established with God? For an everlasting covenant he has made with me, ordered in all things and sure. For all my salvation and all my desire, will he not make it to grow?

But the ungodly, they are as thorns thrust away, all of them, for the man that touches them must be armed with iron and the staff of a spear; and they shall be utterly burned with fire in their place.

2 SAMUEL 23:1-7

The Psalms of David

This song contains the essential message of all the psalms that the Holy Spirit puts on David's tongue. It is the final victory of the Messiah-King, who will rise as the Sun of justice to bring the new day of salvation in which the house of David, the Church, will grow like the first grass in spring. Meanwhile the ungodly, *the civitas diaboli*, will perish through the very law of the sword under which they have always lived. The love of the Saviour gives life and growth to the family of the redeemed. The ungodly's hatred turns them into thorns, which will be raked together with an iron rake to be thrown into the fire.

David, the prophet and the sweet singer of Israel, is therefore really our father, not only because he is the ancestor of Christ but also because we live through his songs, the psalms. They become the prayer of his Son, during his life on earth, and through him they become the prayer of the Church on her pilgrimage to heaven. David's life, Christ's life, our lives, are welded together into one unity through those inspired songs of affliction and sorrow, of rocklike confidence, of victory and thanksgiving. These David has sung, Christ has sung, and we are now singing. How fitting it is that these songs should accompany the celebration of holy Mass, through which the death and resurrection of the Son of David sacramentally enters our lives, not ignoring our weakness but transforming it into victory and uniting us in the kingdom of God. Through the Mass and the Divine

Office, David's prophecy has been fulfilled: "God has kept me to be the head of the nations, a people whom I have not known serve me" (22:44).

His unshakable conviction that he is in all things a child of God's grace makes David's heart a harp for the Holy Spirit. Like a youth he is "whirling in a dance" when the ark of the Lord enters Jerusalem (6:14). Nothing can give us a deeper insight into the soul of the "sweet singer of Israel" than his answer to Michal, his wife, who scorns him for having "stripped himself in the sight of the maidservants, as a common rake exposes himself" (6:20).

David says to her: "It is before the Lord that I dance, who chose me rather than your father or any of his house to be ruler over the people of the Lord, over Israel. Before the Lord will I make merry. And I will be yet more vile than that, and I will be base in my own sight. But with the maidservants to whom you have referred I shall indeed be held in honor" (6:21-22).

David looks deep into the secret of the messianic rule, according to which children will enter the kingdom of God. The first will be the last and the last first; those who humble themselves will be exalted; and the one who rules must minister. His prophecy has indeed been fulfilled, and up to this day the Michals despise him and his Son, but the maidservants are holding both in honor.

Nothing could make David more Christlike than his playing like a child before the eternal Father, as a true image of the Son of God, who says: "When God appointed the foundations of the earth, then I was by him, as a nursling; as a ward of his; and daily was I filled with delight, as I played before him all the time, played in this world of his, and found my delight in the sons of men" (Prv 8:30-31). It is therefore only logical that his life, as that of Christ, should culminate in instituting the solemn, public *eucharistia* or thanksgiving with which the report of his life in the Book of Sirach closes:

Over all he did give thanks
   to the Holy One, the Most High, with words of praise.
He sang praise with his whole heart,
   and he loved his Maker.
He placed singers before the altar,
   to make sweet melody with their voices.
He gave dignity to the festivals,
   and he set the seasons in order throughout the year, while they
   praised God's holy name,
   and the sanctuary rang with it from early morning.

SIRACH 47:8-10

ELEVEN

The Books of Kings and Chronicles

The Books of Samuel and of Kings center around the solemn promise God made to David: "And when your days shall be fulfilled and you shall sleep with your fathers, I will raise up your seed after you and I will establish his kingdom. I will be to him a father and he shall be to me a son; and if he commit any iniquity I will correct him with the rod of men and with the stripes of the children of men; but my mercy shall not depart from him" (2 Sm 7:12-15).

The latter part of the Second Book of Samuel shows how God used the crooked ways of men, the jealousies and ambitions of the older sons of David, in order to put upon the throne of his father the youngest among his sons, the one whom God had chosen: Jedidia—"the Lord's darling," who is known to history under the name of Solomon, the peaceable.

The forty years of Solomon's reign are described in the first eleven chapters of the First Book of Kings. They constitute the most glorious period of Jewish history. The weakness of Egypt and Assyria, the two great powers on which the fate of Israel depends, gives Solomon an opportunity to reorganize the administration of his country (chapter 4), to fortify the towns (9:15-19), to set up industries and promote trade with foreign countries (9:26; 10:28), and to crown his work with the building and the dedication of the temple (chapters 5–9). "And Judah and Israel dwelt without any fear, everyone under his vine and under his fig tree, from Dan to Beer-sheba, all the days of Solomon" (4:25).

"The Sun King"

As "king of peace," reigning in glory, Solomon prefigures the other "Son of David," who on the cross became our peace (Eph 2:14) and in the power of the Resurrection established his kingdom. Israel's "Sun King," in the splendor of his court, foreshadows the gloriously reigning Christ, who sits at the right hand of the Father to judge the living and the dead.

The first sentence Solomon pronounces in his official capacity as judge of his people (3:16-28) is much more than a mere "illustration" of his wisdom. As the anointed one of the Lord, Solomon judges in the wisdom he has received from God as answer to his prayer (3:4-15). It is, therefore, typical of the way in which Christ, the Solomon of the New Testament, into whose hands the Father has delivered all judgment, will one day judge the peoples of the earth.

The procedure Solomon follows is not so much intended to establish the guilt as to answer the question, "Who is the true mother?" It is intended to reveal the "thoughts of the heart." For this purpose Solomon has the child delivered to the sword. Immediately maternal love is kindled in the heart of the true mother. She would rather give up her rights as a mother than see her child killed. Thereupon Solomon pronounces the sentence: "Give the living child to this woman; she is the mother" (3:27).

Solomon's sentence is "fulfilled" at the judgment on the top of Golgotha. There the child who had been mankind's hope through all the centuries is delivered to the sword. The false mother, the Pharisees and the priests, ask that the "prince of life" be killed and that the murderer be released: "Not this man, but Barabbas!" (Jn 18:40).

The true mother is also there, standing by the cross and witnessing the fulfillment of the prophecy she received when she offered her firstborn in the temple: "Behold, this child is set for the fall and for the resurrection of many in Israel, and for a sign which shall be contradicted.

And a sword shall pierce your own soul, that the thoughts of many hearts may be revealed" (Lk 2:34-35).

The death of her Son pierces her soul like a sword and reveals the heart of the true mother. She offers up her Son that Israel may live. The Son of David repeats, from the cross, Solomon's sentence: "Mother, behold your son!" (Jn 19:26-27). Mary is the true mother, representing the Church, and the living child is to be given to her.

This sentence of the Solomon of the New Testament will be repeated wherever people meet the crucified Christ and hear the glad tidings announced: "This Jesus whom you have crucified, God made both Lord and Christ!" (Acts 2:36). All those whose hearts are pierced by this message in true compunction and who turn to the child whom God has raised from the dead, who prefer his life to their own by saying with St. Paul, "Not I live, but Christ lives in me," they all are "true mothers" and "children of the resurrection."

The wisdom Solomon receives from God not only revealed the hearts of men; it is also the key to understanding the secrets of the world. David, the "sweet singer of Israel," offered his heart and all creation to God in prayer and psalm. Solomon, the typical representative of the second generation, turns his mind toward this world to reveal its secrets in proverbs. God gives him "largeness of heart, even as the sand that is on the seashore" (4:29). "And Solomon spoke three thousand proverbs. He spoke of trees, from the cedar that is in Lebanon to the hyssop that comes out of the wall; and he discoursed of beasts, and of fowls, and of creeping things, and of fishes" (4:32-33).

The wise king is like a one-man university. From all over the world people come to hear his wisdom (4:34). The most famous among the pilgrims is the queen of Sheba (10:1-10). She speaks to Solomon "all that she has in her heart" (10:2), and when she hears and sees his wisdom, "there is no more spirit left in her" (10:5).

When the Son of David, who is greater than Solomon, sees himself rejected by his own people, he warns them that the "queen of the

South" will rise in judgment against them. She came from the ends of the earth to hear the wisdom of Solomon, and this generation does not want to believe the One who is greater than Solomon (Mt 12:42).

The Word of God made flesh is indeed the sign and riddle that fulfills all the proverbs of Solomon. He is infinitely greater than all of them, because he answers the deepest secret of the human heart, that of human guilt. Instead of his own people, millions of gentiles come from the east and from the west, like the queen of Sheba, to tell the Solomon of the New Testament "all that is in their hearts."

When they hear his answer—"Your faith has saved you, go in peace" (Lk 7:50; 8:48)—and see his works—the blind receiving their sight, the lame walking, the deaf hearing, the dead being raised up, and the poor having the gospel preached to them (Mt 11:5)—there is "no spirit left in them," because they realize that "not by the works of justice which they have done, but according to his mercy, he saves them by the laver of regeneration, and renewal in the Holy Spirit" (Ti 3:5). Thus the wisdom of Solomon is "fulfilled" by the "foolishness of the cross" (1 Cor 1:21).

The Temple

The crown of Solomon's works is the temple, the beautiful symbol of a world restored to its original splendor as God's resting place. A Jewish proverb says: "The country of Israel is in the heart of the earth. Jerusalem is in the heart of Israel. The temple is in the heart of Jerusalem. The ark of the covenant is in the heart of the temple, and next to the ark is the cornerstone of the world." That cornerstone is Christ.

The temple is indeed a symbol and a promise that all creation will be restored under Christ as the head. The gold and silver of Arabia; the cedars of Lebanon; the wisdom of Hiram, king of Tyre—practically the whole world contributes to the building. The walls and doors of the temple are covered with reliefs of fruit trees and cherubim, reminiscent of the garden of Eden (Gn 3:24), which is itself a symbol of the world at peace with its Maker.

The heart of the temple, however, is a windowless room in cubic form, without any image. It is the "Holy of Holies," a symbol of the innermost sanctuary of heaven, where God dwells in darkness. As Solomon says at the dedication of the temple: "The Lord established the sun in the heavens, but he himself said that he would dwell in thick darkness" (8:12).

The windowless darkness of the Holy of Holies shows that God is the center of the universe but not a part of it. The Hebrew word for "Holy of Holies," *debir,* could be related to *dabar,* "word." St. Jerome therefore translated it as *oraculum,* "oracle," a place where the people listen to God and where God listens to his people. The only "object" in the Holy of Holies is the ark containing the Law. The ark is surmounted by the two cherubim facing each other and forming, with their outspread wings, the "mercy seat," ready to receive the divine presence (8:7).

Solomon's temple is not, like the temples of the heathen gods, a place for the God of Israel to dwell. At the dedication Solomon prays: "If heaven and the heavens of heaven cannot contain you, how much less this house which I have built. But have regard to the prayer of your servant and to his supplications, O Lord my God ... that your eyes may be open upon this house day and night, upon the house of which you said: 'My name shall be there'" (8:27-29).

Not an image but the "name" of God is present in Solomon's temple, as long as his word is kept by obedience to the Law and his name is invoked in prayer. It is "fulfilled," therefore, when the Word is made flesh and dwells among us.

Out of all the nations under the sky, God set apart one people to be his servant. From all countries of the world he selects one to be his Holy Land, and among all the mountain heights where people used to offer sacrifices he takes possession of Mount Zion, that from all over the world people might go to this one place to worship the one and only true God. Not because he is a local god, but because he is the one God of the universe, does the God of Israel choose Solomon's temple for his name and his eyes and his heart to be there (9:3).

One God, one nation, one country, one temple—to prepare the way for the One in whom the Father is well pleased, Jesus Christ, the Son of God and Son of David. He is God's chosen one, his Holy Land, and the temple of his presence. When he is come, people will worship the Father neither on Mount Gerizim nor at Jerusalem, but in spirit and in truth (Jn 4:21-23).

This, however, does not mean that Jesus will give everyone the license to worship the god of his fancy in the recesses of his heart. What Christ teaches the Samaritan woman at Jacob's well is not intended to abolish the one God, who promised to hallow the house Solomon built for him and to put his name there forever. It is meant to show that he who speaks to the woman is the Messiah foreshadowed in the temple. Speaking of the temple of his body, he says: "Destroy this temple, and in three days I shall raise it up" (Jn 2:19).

Since the Resurrection Jesus has become "the chief cornerstone, in whom all the building, being framed together, grows up into a holy temple in the Lord. In him we are all built together into a habitation of God in the Spirit" (Eph 2:20-22). The "one God, one nation, one country, one temple" of the Old Testament reveals now its true meaning as one Father, one Son, one Church, where men adore the Father in one Spirit and one truth.

Solomon's Fall

The house that Solomon builds on Mount Zion does not stand forever. "If you turn aside from following me, you or your children, and keep not my commands, but go and serve other gods, then I shall cast away from me the house which I have sanctified for my name" (9:6-7). Solomon turns aside. God has given him a heart as large as the sand on the seashore, but Solomon has allowed this largeness of heart to turn into illimitable love of the world.

He is "a lover of foreign women" (11:1). He has a thousand of them—a thousand being the number symbolic of the perfection of this material universe. They turn his heart after their gods, "and his heart is not whole with the Lord his God, as was the heart of David his father" (11:4). Largeness of heart destroys in him the simplicity of heart that is derived from faith in one God.

David, who had suffered so much during his life, found in his old age Abishag the Shunammite, a "maiden very beautiful" (1:4). She slept with the king and served him, but "the king did not know her"—the first mysterious dawn of virginal love in the Old Testament. Solomon, on the contrary, never has to suffer. He rules in glory without knowing the cross. Therefore earthly love destroys in him the love of God, and his throne cannot not be established forever.

When Solomon grows old and earthly love fails him, his days become dark and cold, filled with the groaning of this creation. The peaceable one changes more and more into a tyrant. The glory of his court becomes an unbearable burden to his people (12:4). Rebellions break out (11:23-40). The days come of which the preacher says: "The silver cord is severed, and the golden bowl broken, and the jar is shattered at the spring, and the wheel broken in the pit; the dust returns to the earth as it was, and the spirit returns to God who gave it. Vanity of vanities,... all is vanity" (Eccl 12:6-8).

Eros, the love of the world, kills Solomon because he has not known *agape,* the sacrificial love which alone is stronger than death. Only *agape* is able to make a heart large without destroying its simplicity. This the crucified Son of David teaches, and St. Paul applies it to our daily lives:

This, therefore, I say, brethren: the time is short. It remains that
they who have wives live as though they had none, and those
who mourn as though they did not mourn, and those who
rejoice as though they did not rejoice, and those who buy anything as though they did not own it, and those who use this
world as though they used it not: for the fashion of this world
passes away. I want you to be free from all anxiety.

1 CORINTHIANS 7:29-32

After Solomon's death only fatherly, condescending love can heal
the wounds that Solomon's "worldliness" has inflicted upon the
people. But Rehoboam, his son, follows in the footsteps of his father.
In fact he threatens, "My father beat you with whips, but I will beat
you with scorpions" (12:14).

The ten northern tribes refuse to obey and form the kingdom of
Israel under Jeroboam. Only the tribe of Benjamin remains with Judah
under the house of David; God says, "that there may remain a lamp
for my servant David always in Jerusalem, the city which I have chosen that my name might be there" (11:36). Benjamin's loyalty is like a
pledge that the time will come when all Israel will again be united in
one fold under one shepherd.

Judah and Benjamin constitute the southern kingdom of Judah
under the sons of David. Israel, which has rebelled against the "eternal
throne of David," is ruled by various dynasties, without any stability.
Rebellion is its constant companion.

The second main part of the First and Second Books of Kings,
1 Kings 12:1 to 2 Kings 17:41, gives us a synchronistic history of the
two kingdoms, which, however, is not intended to be complete. These
accounts show the development of history in the light of divine justice. God rewards faithfulness and punishes disloyalty; he fulfills his
promise to David: "I will be to him a father and he will be to me a son;
and if he commit any iniquity, I will correct him with the rod of men;

but my mercy shall not depart from him" (2 Sm 7:14-15). Indeed, despite the disloyalty of the people, God never rejects his "firstborn" completely. In every decisive crisis a "remnant" is saved.

The most critical moment for the worship of the one true God in the northern kingdom of Israel come during the reign of Ahab and his wife Jezebel, daughter of the king of Sidon. She induces her husband to make the worship of Baal, the town-god of Tyre, the official religion of the country (16:29-33). At this moment God raises up Elijah, the prophet (1 Kgs 17:1 to 2 Kgs 2:12). His mission is to show against the heathen *baals*—personifications of the powers of nature—that Yahweh, the God of Israel, is not a part of this creation but its Lord.

Elijah and Elisha

The name *Elijahu,* "Yahweh is the only God," is already a profession of faith. His whole personality reflects the power of the Lord of heaven and earth. "He stood up like a fire, and his word burned like a torch" (Sir 48:1).

On the great day of decision on Mount Carmel Elijah's calm and quiet confidence in the God of Abraham, Isaac, and Israel triumphs over the frenzy of the prophets of Baal (18:17-46). God's fatherly hand then takes Elijah and brings him from the height of victory on Mount Carmel—which means "garden of fruit trees"—into the desert, to taste the bitterness of exile and defeat. Utterly exhausted, he sits down under a broom tree and prays that he might die.

"It is enough; now, O Lord, take away my life; for I am no better than my fathers" (19:4). The titanic personality of Elijah must go through the "valley of death" to receive on Mount Horeb the great revelation of God's mercy. Standing on the rock where Moses once saw the "goodness of the Lord" (Ex 33:19) after the incident of the golden calf, Elijah sees the Lord passing by.

"And a great and strong wind rent the mountains, and broke in pieces the rocks before the Lord, but the Lord was not in the wind; and after the wind an earthquake, but the Lord was not in the earthquake; and after the earthquake a fire, but the Lord was not in the fire; and after the fire a still, small voice of silence" (19:9-12). Thus the prophet of divine wrath, the "chariots of Israel and the horsemen thereof," is initiated into the secret of God's love.

Centuries later we find Moses and Elijah listening again to the "still, small voice of silence" when Christ is glorified on Mount Tabor. "They spoke of his departure which he was to go through at Jerusalem" (Lk 9:31). The "voice of silence" is the Lamb of God, who opens not his mouth when he is crushed for our iniquities (see Is 53:5-7). It is the "voice of silence" that rebukes James and John when they suggest that the Lord should send fire from heaven and consume the Samaritans, "even as Elijah did": "The Son of man has not come to destroy men's lives, but to save them" (Lk 9:54-56).

The God of Israel shows his superiority over the heathen gods of fertility, animal growth, and sexual love not by destroying his enemies but by sending his Son to become a sacrifice for their sins. The resurrection and the ascension of the crucified Christ is the final triumph over the powers of nature. In the same way, the historical mission of the great antagonist of the *baals* ends with his assumption into heaven (2 Kgs 2:11).

"When Elijah was sheltered by the whirlwind, Elisha was filled with his spirit" (Sir 48:12). Elijah's spiritual son continues his work (2 Kgs 2:1–13:21). His name, "God has helped," is again an indication of his mission. He is the healer and helper whose numerous miracles foreshadow the Good Physician, who will come and heal the multitude (Lk 6:17-19) to show that he is the Saviour.

When the son of the Shunammite dies, Elisha sends Gehazi to put his staff on his dead body, but the boy does not come to life again. So Elisha goes himself. He prays and lies upon the child; he puts his mouth upon his mouth, and his eyes upon his eyes, and his hands upon his hands. The child's flesh grows warm, and he opens his eyes (see 2 Kgs 4:8-37). The whole history of our salvation is depicted in this scene, from the rod of the Old Testament to the incarnation of the Son of God and the sacrament of baptism. With another "symbol" of baptism—a man's corpse being thrown into the prophet's sepulchre and coming to life when it touches Elisha's bones—the story of Elisha ends (13:21).

The last part of 2 Kings (18:1–25:26) describes the history of the kingdom of Judah, which survives the Assyrian flood—in which Israel has perished—because Sennacherib of Assyria is forced by a pestilence to give up the siege of Jerusalem (19:35). After the fall of Assyria (622 B.C.), Judah follows a policy of shifting alliances between the two big powers, Egypt and Babylon. Eventually Judah is crushed by Nebuchadnezzar of Babylon.

Jerusalem is destroyed in 586 B.C., and the last of the sons of David, Jehoiachin, is deported into captivity. The history of the house of David does not end, however, with the destruction of the temple that Solomon built but with the report of the release from prison of Jehoiachin and of his exaltation by the king of Babylon (25:27-30), a striking prophecy of the resurrection of the last of the sons of David, Jesus Christ.

God's promise to David concerning his son, "I will be to him a father and he will be to me a son; and if he commit any iniquity, I will correct him with the rod of men; but my mercy shall not depart from him" (2 Sm 7:14-15), is thus fulfilled.

TWELVE

Tobit, Judith, and Esther

After the capture and destruction of Jerusalem by Nebuchadnezzar, king of Babylon, the chosen people cease to exist as a political entity; but the spirit of Israel continues to live in the more intimate circle of the Jewish family. Here the fire of faith is kept burning, not only through the study of the Law and the prophets and the sages but also through little stories, light and attractive, that appeal to the imagination and are circulated by word of mouth. These stories are not pure fiction. They grow around a historical event, but their authors show no intention of retaining historical accuracy in their details.

That Tobit, Judith, and Esther belong to this kind of literature can be inferred from the fact that they have come down to us in a great many versions—some more developed, some abridged, some in Greek, some in Aramaic or another form of "vernacular." The free use of historical names, as for example those of "Arphaxad king of the Medes" and "Nebuchadnezzar king of the Assyrians" in the Book of Judith, inaccuracies of geographical and historical detail, and the use of oriental legends, as in the Book of Tobit, point in the same direction. It is probably on account of this, their "romantic" character, that Tobit and Judith are not considered canonical by the Jews, and that the Book of Esther found its way into the Jewish canon only after a prolonged controversy.[1]

That the Catholic Church has declared the three books to form part of the inspired Word of God is not prejudicial to their literary character. It simply reflects a realization that the Holy Spirit can use the peculiar manner and intentions of the authors to serve the purposes of divine revelation. Even a superficial study of the books shows that they are indeed full of the light of divine truth and that each of them fulfills a specific function in the living organism of Holy Scripture.

Tobit evidently is the book of the family. It reveals one of the most central of all Christian mysteries: the relation of father, son, and bride, reflecting the intimate communion of life that exists in the bosom of the Holy Trinity and proceeds from the Father through the Son to the Church.

Judith, on the other hand, is the book of the woman. It shows the role God has assigned to the woman in the dispensation of his grace.

Esther, finally, is the book of the nation. It is the key to one of the most burning questions of all times, that of antisemitism and the relationship between Jews and gentiles.

Tobit

The Book of Tobit—the name means "Yahweh is good"—tells the lovely story of two venerable couples who with their two only children live in exile in Persia. Tobit is a pious man of the tribe of Naphtali who helps his fellow countrymen in selfless charity. When he becomes blind he sends his only son Tobias to Rages in Media to collect a debt.

On this journey young Tobias is accompanied by a guide, who later reveals himself as the angel Raphael, "one of the seven who stand before the Lord" (12:15). They stop at the house of Raguel, a near kinsman of old Tobit, who has an only daughter, Sarah by name. She is a widow but still a virgin, because each of her seven successive husbands has been slain on his wedding day by the evil spirit Asmodeus.

At the angel's instigation, young Tobias marries Sarah. To avoid the fate of his predecessors, he follows Raphael's advice: He burns the liver of a fish that he caught in the River Tigris and used for food on the journey. This puts the evil spirit to flight. He returns with his wife to his home and cures his father's blindness using the gall of the fish. They all live in peace to a ripe old age, seeing their children and their children's children.

The little book is filled with that good family spirit that always has been the precious heritage of the chosen people. The history of salvation during the time of the Old Testament is the history of families. When God orders Moses to "take the sum of all the congregation of the children of Israel," he adds "by their families" (Num 1:2). The Israelites do not exist as individuals but as sons, because it is the "Son of Abraham," the Messiah, in whom their destiny is fulfilled.

The history of the Old Covenant culminates in the holy family of Nazareth. The family of Tobit is an image of that family, where Jesus is the only begotten Son.

Right at the beginning of the book we find Tobit's little family gathered together at the good dinner that has been prepared in his house at a festival of the Lord (2:1). The father sends the son to invite the poor to share the joy of the family. It is an old ordinance in Israel: "With your son, your daughter, your male and female servants, the Levite living in your community, the stranger, the orphan and the widow who are in your community, you are to rejoice before the Lord your God" (Dt 16:11).

We can see already how young Tobias takes on a similarity to the Son of God, sent by his Father to invite the poor into the kingdom of God (Lk 4:18) and to pour out his Spirit upon sons and daughters, upon servants and handmaids (Acts 2:17). What an invitation, at the same time, to a Christian family to celebrate the feasts of the New Testament at their home in the same spirit of all-embracing charity!

Another aspect of the true family spirit is shown in Tobit's beautiful admonitions to his son (chapter 4). There he really fulfills the office of the father, whose function it is not only to take care of the physical needs of the family but to teach, to become a father by laying his words of wisdom as a foundation in the heart of the son. In this the earthly father imitates his heavenly prototype, the eternal Father whose word is his Son; while the son who reverently receives the father's word to hand it down to his own children represents the Son of God made man, who says: "What the Father has taught me I speak" (Jn 8:28).

The heart of the matter, however, is reached in young Tobias' marriage with Sarah (chapters 6–8). The Old Testament gives to the relationship between husband and wife a deeply spiritual meaning, lifting it up to be a sign of the union between God and his people. God cannot be shut out from human wedlock, because the love that urges a man to leave father and mother and to cleave to his wife (Gn 2:24) is an image of the love that causes the Son of God to leave his Father's glory to become one flesh with his bride, the Church (Eph 5:31-34).

The story of young Tobias' wedding with Sarah is really a prophecy of the messianic marriage between Christ and his Church. Who else can the seven former husbands be but those who love mankind in the selfish spirit of this world, and thus deliver themselves up to the deadly power of the prince of this world? The seemingly superstitious manipulation with the entrails of the fish receives a completely new and spiritual meaning when we remember that the fish is the symbol of Christ in his life-giving passion and death. The heart, liver, and gall are Old Testament symbols of the innermost life and emotions. The liver and the heart of the fish burnt on coal symbolize the sacrifice of Christ, who on the cross gives up his spirit into the hands of his Father and thus destroys the dominion of the devil.

We read that Raguel and his servants dig a grave for Tobias, and a maid is sent in the early morning to the young couple's chambers. When she finds them safe and sound, she hurries to bring the good news to the parents (8:11-14). This reminds us of the empty tomb on Easter morning and of the women who, when the sun is rising, receive the glad tidings of the Resurrection and bring them to the apostles.

Tobias and Sarah's return to Tobit's home reads like a prophecy of the final reunion between the Church of the gentiles and the Jewish people, whose blindness will be healed by the light that radiates from the sacrificial love of Christ, represented symbolically in the gall of the fish (11:13). In the light of this faith old Tobit sees the glory of the New Jerusalem and hears the eternal Alleluia sung in its streets (13:16-18).

The depth of spiritual meaning hidden in the Book of Tobit should not make us overlook, however, the wealth of practical wisdom it has to offer to this present day and age, in which we witness such an appalling disintegration of family life. The deeply religious character of matrimony naturally requires spiritual kinship in the unity of faith between husband and wife (4:12; 6:18), with God himself joining them together and fulfilling his blessing in them. At the same time this supernatural bond requires a sound natural foundation through a written agreement about the juridical and financial rights of husband and wife (7:13).

"And afterwards they made merry, blessing God" (7:14). A marriage blessed by God has nothing puritanic about it. It is the lovely flower of true humanity, which makes the husband the saviour of his wife (6:18), enthrones the wife in his care and protection (10:13), gives honor and peace to the parents (10:12), and fuller praise to God in children (13:13). Tobias' little dog, the family pet who follows him on his journey (6:2; 11:4), fits into this happy picture like the dot on the i.

Judith

The theme of Judith is "God has given salvation into the hand of a woman." Woman appears in Scripture as God's natural ally in his struggle against a selfish world. She is made to receive new life, to rear it patiently, to suffer that it may prosper, to decrease that it may increase. In this she represents the love described in the New

Testament, love that "seeks not its own" (1 Cor 13:5).

The emnity that God set between the woman and the serpent after the Fall (Gn 3:15) represents the struggle between the human order of selfishness and tyranny and the divine order of grace and charity. The victory is won when Mary the virgin, "full of grace," gives to God's call the answer that only a woman can give: "Behold the handmaid of the Lord: be it done to me according to your word" (Lk 1:38). The whole history of the chosen people, the "virgin daughter of Israel," has been a constant preparation for this, its fulfillment in Mary. It is the Book of Judith, however, that singles out this aspect of sacred history and lifts it into the sphere of sacred types.

The very name *Judith* (Jewess) is typical. The widow of Bethulia represents the virgin daughter of Israel. The clash between heathenism and God's people appears as the clash between "man's world" and "woman's world."

The former is depicted in the first chapters of the book as a world of power, tremendous fortresses, immense armies, vast empires, and mighty rulers, who are constantly scheming to overthrow one another. These men hate liberty and independence. The use of power makes them thirsty for more power. The rights of others they consider insults to themselves. Using the cowardly submissiveness and adulation in those who are subject to their rule, they build up gigantic war machines, which like irresistible steamrollers crush all resistance in their path (2:11-18).

At the moment of crisis, however, all this power may suddenly come to naught. Because the whole system is built on the absolute power of one leader, it is unable to work without him. Then all the boastfulness turns into panic, and of those who once marched to conquer the world, each now runs to save his own skin (15:1).

Against the power of man Judith rises in the totally different strength of the woman. Her strength is her faith, and her faith is trust in the mercy of God. "For God will not threaten like man, nor be inflamed in anger like the son of man: let us seek God with tears, that according to his will he would show mercy to us: that as our heart is troubled by their pride so we also may glorify him in our humility" (8:15-17). Because God is love, "his power is not in a multitude, nor is his pleasure in the strength of horses, nor from the beginning have the proud been acceptable to him, but the prayer of the humble and the meek has always pleased him" (9:11). Therefore the Lord decides that the mighty Holofernes will not fall by young men or by tall giants but by the hand of a woman (16:6). The triumph of Judith is the triumph of the Lord, who "puts an end to wars" (16:2).

For Christian readers one important detail in the story of Judith reminds us that we are still in the Old Testament: the sword of Holofernes in the hand of the woman. With all her fasting, her tears, her prayers, and her humility, Judith remains a "daughter of Simeon" (8:1). Simeon was that son of Jacob who, together with his brother Levi, killed the Schechemites to avenge the rape of their sister Dinah (Gn 34:25-26). Judith prays to the Lord, God of her father Simeon, who gave him a sword to execute vengeance against strangers (9:2).

Esther

Simeon and his "daughter" Judith represent the militant Jewish nationalism that also fills the Book of Esther. Reading the story of Esther, one gets the impression that the only solution to problems between gentiles and Jews is either the gentiles' slaughtering the Jews or the Jews' slaughtering the gentiles (9:5). In the center of the story stands the "great beam," a gibbet, fifty cubits high (5:14). The whole question is, Who shall hang on it: Mordecai the Jew or Haman the gentile?

Mordecai is, so we are told (2:5), the son of Kish, of the tribe of Benjamin, of the family of Saul (1 Sm 9:2). Haman is of the race of

Agag, king of the Amalekites, whom Saul spared (1 Sm 15:8). This genealogy of the two opponents clearly indicates the problem of the book. The tribe of Benjamin, the only son of Jacob born in the Holy Land (Gn 35:16), is always inclined toward extreme nationalism. Haman, on the other hand, is the typical antisemite. When he feels insulted by Mordecai, he is not satisfied to lay his hands on him alone. Hearing that his offender is a Jew, he wants to destroy all the nation of the Jews (3:6).

In Haman's words to the king we hear the antisemite of our days speaking: "There is a people scattered through all the provinces of your kingdom, who keep separated from everybody, use their own laws and ceremonies, despite the king's ordinances, and imperil by their insolence the authority of the state" (3:8). The old struggle between Jacob and Esau degenerates in the Book of Esther into a political struggle between two races.

The Feast of Purim, at which Esther is read, is not one of the great "feasts of the Lord" but a day for making fun of the people's enemies. Jewish wit, irony, and sarcasm mock the kings, dictators, and other mighty ones who, like the strutting little peacock Haman, fall into the pit they prepared for the Jews. "Turning of the tables" would probably be the best translation of Purim.

If the slaughtering of the gentiles were the only solution to antisemitism recommended by Esther, we could rightly ask why the book has found a place in the canon of Holy Scripture. It is of great importance, however, to know that the spirit of Jewish nationalism is not approved of by Old Testament revelation. Jacob solemnly disowned Simeon and Levi's deed: "Simeon and Levi, brethren, vessels of iniquity, waging war,... cursed by their fury, because it was self-willed, and their wrath because it was cruel" (Gn 49:7).

For this reason the Book of Esther would not be complete without the additional sections of the book that are not included in the Hebrew canon but are found in the Septuagint and have been accepted as canonical by the Catholic Church. They include the dream of Mordecai (10:4-13; 11:2-12), in which Mordecai and Haman, Jewish nationalism and antisemitism, appear as two dragons fighting each other. During their struggle a little fountain appears and grows into a river, which turns into light and into the sun (11:10). It is Esther (10:6), the personification of the Church.

Then antagonism of the two archenemies is overcome when the little fountain springs from the heart of Jesus pierced on the cross. Guided by the fanatic will to save people and country (Jn 11:50), Jewish nationalism becomes guilty by delivering the "King of the Jews" into the hands of the gentiles. The latter become guilty by killing Jesus in their hatred of the Jews. Haman's gibbet is replaced by the cross, and on it hangs not the Jew, not the gentile, but the Son of God made man. He dies for both, "killing the enemies in himself and reconciling both to God in one body" (Eph 2:16). Through him Jews and gentiles have access in one Spirit to the Father.

Esther approaches the king in a spirit of complete surrender ("If I perish, I perish!" 4:16), supported by faith and followed by charity holding her flowing train (15:5-7). Her humility and her beauty overcome the king's wrath. He leaps from his throne, lays his golden scep-tre upon her neck, and kisses her.

The Church incorporated this scene into the canon of holy writ for good reason. It represents the final triumph of the Church in the love of Jesus. The golden sceptre is the symbol of the cross. Those who touch it in faith find peace in the embrace of their heavenly Father. They may be Jew or gentile, if only they know that they are "prodigal sons."

THIRTEEN

The First and Second Books of Maccabees

The books of Tobit, Judith, and Esther show how, during the night of the Babylonian exile, the light of faith is kept burning in the intimate circle of the Jewish family through the constancy of the Jewish woman. With the Books of Maccabees, we enter into a completely different world. The very name Maccabees, the "hammerers," indicates that here we are in the world of man.

"Maccabeus" is the name first given to Judas and then also to his brothers, the sons of Mattathias, champions of the Jewish struggle for religious and political liberty against the kings of Syria in the second century B.C. The name is extended to all those valiant guerilla fighters who take part in the heroic struggle against the overwhelming superiority of men and material that the Syrian generals muster against them. They are a brotherhood of true comrades in arms, animated by a deep love for the law of God and bitter hatred against the sacrileges of the heathen and against the quislings in their own nation.

What they despise most is compromise. In supreme disregard of their personal welfare, they are ready at any moment to lay down their lives for the way of life that the law of Moses has prescribed. The Books of Maccabees sing the virtues of soldiers who fight for the salvation of their souls, for their brothers, and for the glory of their God. They celebrate the fortitude of the martyr.

The Jews in Exile

What a change has taken place in the spirit of the Jewish nation, since we left Jeremiah on the ruins of Jerusalem mourning over the apostasy of the people and its kings! The great trial of the Babylonian exile evidently has left an indelible mark on those who survived it. A Jewish story tells us:

> When Israel was led into captivity, away from his homeland, God spoke to his people:
>
> "Whom do you want to have with you? The fathers of old, Adam, Noah, or Shem? If you do, I shall raise them from their tombs and put them over you. Or do you want to have Abraham, Isaac, and Jacob, the patriarchs, or do you want to be led by Moses? I shall raise them up from their tombs and put them over you. Or if you would like to have David and Solomon again as your kings, I shall raise them up and give them to you."
>
> But Israel answered: "We do not want a patriarch, nor a leader like Moses, nor a king, but only thee. Thou art our Father. Abraham does not know us, Israel has forgotten us. Thou alone art our Father and our Saviour; thy name is of eternity."
>
> Then the Lord answered: "Because you talk to me this way I shall go with you to Babylonia in exile."[1]

There is no better illustration of the spiritual change the Exile brought about. Deprived of everything that can distract their attention as a nation to the outside world—deprived of the glory of their kings, of the absorbing interests of a state and a country—the will of the people is directed inward, toward the spiritual center of their lives. There they find the light that for generations has been the guiding star of their destiny, the divine name that was revealed to Moses at the burning bush: "I am who I am" (Ex 3:14). Although surrounded with the protecting wall of silence and kept in reverent secrecy, its meaning now penetrates deeply into the heart of the people and forms every phase of its life.

"I am who I am" is the name of a God whose most striking characteristic is his uniqueness. "I am who I am" means "There is no one like me." It also reveals an infinite depth of personal life and an absolute truth. "I am who I am" will be a rock to the one whom he takes into his confidence. His promises stand. Those who belong to him, the Only One, will be separated from the rest of the world and will become so absorbed in him that they will say: "Whom have I in the heavens but you? And having you I wish nought else on earth" (Ps 73:25).

Deprived of all other support and thrown on him alone, the Jews of the Exile go to the school of the divine name and learn to be holy as he is holy. As the Only One is "separated" *(parush)*, so they too become *perushim*, separated ones. "Only if ye separate yourselves from the nations are ye mine," said Simeon ben Yohai, the disciple of Rabbi Akiba.[2]

This separation, however, serves the one purpose of building up and maintaining the life of a community of saints. The preservation of the strict purity and cohesion of the Jewish community in the midst of the "filthiness of the nations" is the goal of those zealots for the Law who later become known under the name of Pharisee (from *perushim*). Their task is to erect and defend the *Seyag la-Torah,* the protective fence around the religion. This fence consists of numerous precepts not contained in the Law of Moses but aiming to produce saintliness by separation from the nations.

The Pharisees are opposed by the Sadducees, a name probably derived from Sadoc, who was made high priest by Solomon and whose descendants ever afterward held this office. The Sadducees become, after the return from exile, the ruling class in Jerusalem. They are conservative insofar as they acknowledge the Mosaic Law exclusively, disregarding later traditions, and progressive inasmuch as they are inclined to play ball with the foreign powers and, at the time of the Maccabees, to compromise with Hellenistic civilization.

During the Babylonian exile a community is formed for the first time in history that, without the support of a state, constitutes itself a spiritually independent group in the name of religion. Its symbol is the synagogue, the house of worship. The synagogue shapes the congregation. Here a new form of divine service appears, consisting of prayer, the reading of passages from the Scriptures, and the explanation of the Scriptures. This takes the place of the elaborate ceremonial of the temple sacrifices. Through public reading and study, especially on the Sabbath, the Bible becomes the book of the people. It takes the place of the altar; and the scribe, or scholar of the law, replaces the priest.

The whole development is well summarized in an old explanation of Numbers 18:20: "There are three crowns: the crown of the Torah, the crown of the priesthood, the crown of the kingdom.... The crown of the Torah is offered to everyone, and he who has won it stands before God as though all three had been offered him, and he had won them all."[3]

Reconstruction

During the Exile a great winnowing takes place; out of it emerges a remnant of those who are determined to remain faithful. They are certain of the unique character of their religion and their chosenness, and this very certainty gives them an absolute determination to survive and an abiding hope in their future.

When the dawn of a new day seems to arise with the downfall of Babylon, and Cyrus, king of Persia, ends the Babylonian exile in 537 B.C. through a decree allowing the Jews to return to their homeland, forty thousand are ready. Under the leadership of Zerubbabel, a prince of the house of David, as governor, and Jeshua, son of Josadak, as high priest, they set out to rebuild the temple and the city. After long years of rivalries, intrigues, and open hostilities on the part of the neighboring tribes, the second temple is finished and dedicated in the year 516 B.C. (Ezr 6:15-17).

When the attacks from the outside do not cease, Nehemiah, a high official of Jewish blood at the Persian court, is sent to rebuild the walls of Jerusalem. Despite determined opposition on the part of Israel's enemies, this task is carried out successfully. "With one hand they did the work, and with the other they held the sword" (Neh 4:17). In 445 B.C. the walls are completed (Neh 6:15).

Now the last and most important step in this whole work of reconstruction is taken by Ezra, the scribe. He is a man of the book. He represents all that Israel has learned in the school of the exile. When he arrives in Jerusalem, all the people assemble as one man in the open square in front of the Water Gate. There a wooden platform is raised for Ezra.

Erza opens the book in the sight of all the people, and all the people stand up. Thereupon Ezra blesses the Lord, and all the people answer, "Amen, Amen," with uplifted hands as they bowed their faces to the ground and worship the Lord. Thus Ezra reads from the book of the Law of Moses. All the people are overcome with holy fear. They weep when they hear the words of the Law. But Ezra says to them: "Go your way, eat fat meats and drink sweet wine and be not sad, for the joy of the Lord is your strength" (Neh 8:1-10).

Now all the essential factors that are going to determine this period of Jewish history are set up: the temple with its ritual and its leading official, the high priest; the walls of Jerusalem under the guardianship of the governor; the Law, entrusted to the scribes. Divine Providence is now leading the chosen people into the last phase of preparation for the coming of the Messiah Jesus, and he arranges the course of events so that all the Jewish hopes in these three things come to nought.

The temple with its treasures and the high priests with their enormous revenues become objects for foreign powers to plunder or buy. The walls of Jerusalem, the symbol of political power, conquered after bloody battles by Judas Maccabeus, are held thereafter by Jewish kings, until "the sceptre is taken away from Judah" (Gn 49:10) by Herod, the Idumaean. The "fence" that the Pharisees have built around the religion finally eclipses the Law of Moses, so that when the Messiah comes he can say to the scribes: "You make void the commandment of God that you may keep your own traditions" (Mk 7:9). The entire period of reconstruction that follows the Babylonian exile is designed to make it clear that this temple, this Jerusalem, and these doctors of the Law are not the fulfillment of the glorious promises God has made through Isaiah and Jeremiah about the new covenant he will make with his people.

This is also the tragedy of the Maccabees. With all their valor and all their heroism, their restoration of the temple and of the Jewish state is never wholly successful. In the eyes of orthodox Jews they remain usurpers, and for this reason the two books that tell of their great deeds are never received into the Jewish canon of Holy Scripture.

For us Christians, however, these books are of greatest importance, because they give us a picture of the conflict between Judaism and Hellenism that developed in the third and second centuries B.C. This is a consequence of the invasion by Greek civilization that takes place in the wake of Alexander's conquest of the Persian empire. After the victory over Darius at Issus (333 B.C.) the great Macedonian, a disciple of Aristotle, led his armies in triumph down to Egypt and planted Greek colonies all along the eastern shore of the Mediterranean. Greek language, art, manners, thought, and law spread everywhere. Even in Jerusalem, in the immediate vicinity of the temple, a gymnasium was erected, and it is reported (2 Mc 4:14) that the priests neglected the sacrifices to assist at the games.

The process of Hellenization might well be capable of going much further, but Antiochus Epiphanes of Syria changes the situation when he attempts to substitute pagan worship for Jewish. Following in the footsteps of the kings of Assyria and of Babylon, he decrees that in his kingdom "all the people shall be one: and everyone shall leave his own law" (1 Mc 1:41-42). This brings about the Maccabean revolt recounted in the Books of Maccabees.

The First Book

The introductory section of the First Book of Maccabees (chapters 1-2) pictures the general situation in Palestine after the conquest of the country by Alexander and briefly records the insurrection and death of Mattathias, father of the Maccabean brothers. The first main part (3:1–9:22) gives an account of the fight of Judas Maccabeus against the generals of Antiochus. A master of guerilla warfare, he defeats several of them. Faith in God supplies what he lacks in military strength, numbers, and equipment. "The success of war is not in the multitude of the army, but strength comes from heaven" is his principle (3:19). In 165 B.C., three years after the temple's desecration by Antiochus, Judas is able to purify and rededicate it (4:41-59).

In memory of this event the Jews still celebrate in December the "Feast of the Lights" or Hanukkah. Hanukkah is dedicated to the memory of Judas Maccabeus, who throughout his career never betrays a trace of selfishness or vainglory, and to the lamp he kindles again in the temple (4:50), which becomes a symbol of the light of faith which no external force is ever able to extinguish. Jesus uses this feast to reveal himself as the Good Shepherd and as the Christ, the lamp of God's anointed (Jn 10:27-30).

In the following years Judas defends his achievements against attacks from the neighboring tribes (chapter 5) and from the generals of Antiochus Eupator, the successor of Antiochus Ephiphanes. His greatest victory is that over Nicanor, who hates Israel bitterly (7:26) and is the first to fall in the battle (7:43).

At the news of Nicanor's death the king sends Bacchides against Judas. This time Judas' men lose heart and "slip away." When Judas sees that he has only eight hundred men left, he realizes that he has lost, but he refuses to flee. "I will never do this thing and flee from them; and if our time has come, let us die bravely for our brothers, and not leave a stain upon our honor" (9:10). So he dies truly the death of the good shepherd.

The third part of the book (9:23–12:52) is devoted to the deeds of Judas' brother Jonathan. He is not so much a fighter as a diplomat. He knows how to take advantage of the intrigues and rivalries between the various pretenders to the crown of Syria in order to extend and strengthen the young Jewish state (chapter 10). With the consent of Syria he becomes high priest in 153 B.C. (10:21). A year later Jerusalem and her territory are declared free (10:31), and Jonathan receives the princely purple and is recognized as governor (10:65).

When Jonathan is killed in 142 B.C. (12:48), the last of the Maccabean brothers, Simon, assumes leadership as high priest and prince of the Jews (12:53–16:24). He is a wise statesman who gains complete political independence and procures for his people an era of peace and prosperity. "And the land of Judah was at peace as long as Simon lived: he sought the good of his nation; his rule and renown pleased them all his life" (14:4).

This peace does not extend to his own kin, however. Ptolemy, his son-in-law and governor of Jericho, invites Simon and two of his sons to a banquet, where he murders them in cold blood (16:16). Fortunately another son, John Hyrcanus, escapes to become his father's successor. In this way the dynasty of the Hasmonaeans is established. With the title of king of the Jews they assume the pomp and power of secular rulers until they are overcome by Herod the Great, who is not a Jew but an Idumaean. With Herod the scepter departs from Judah. This happens immediately before the coming of Christ.

The Second Book

The Second Book of Maccabees, which presents itself as an abridgement of five volumes that a certain Jason of Cyrene wrote (2:23), covers nearly the same period as 1 Maccabees. As introduction (1:1–2:18) the author gives two letters from the Jews in Jerusalem to the Jews in Egypt, recommending the celebration of the dedication of the temple (Hanukkah). The main part of the book is divided into two sections, each of which ends in the institution of an anniversary feast: the dedication of the temple (10:5-8) and Nicanor's day in memory of Judas' greatest victory (15:35-36).

Each of the two sections is again divided into two, each of these treating one of the kings of Syria who persecuted the Jews: Seleucus IV, who sends Heliodorus to seize the treasures of the temple (3:1–4:6); Antiochus Epiphanes, who tries to force the Jews to leave the law of their fathers (4:7–10:9); Antiochus Eupator, who sends the generals Gorgias and Lysias against Judas but finally seeks peace (10:10–13:26); and Demetrius Soter, who sends Nicanor (14:1–15:37) to confront Judas.

The author of 2 Maccabees evidently stresses the practical and devotional aspects of the valiant struggle of Judas Maccabeus. Of greatest importance to him is the story of the fire, which is given from heaven to the second temple under Nehemiah to show that it equals the tabernacle as well as the temple of Solomon, both of which were dedicated through heavenly fire (1:22; 2:10). The fire descending from heaven is symbolic of "the manifestations that came from heaven to them that behaved manfully on behalf of the Jews, so that, being but a few, they made themselves masters of the whole country, and recovered again the most renowned temple, and delivered the city and restored the laws that were abolished, the Lord with all clemency showing mercy to them" (2:21-22).

This fire from heaven triumphs over bodily pains in Eleazar, "one of the leading scribes, advanced in years," who groaning under the stripes of the executioners prays to God: "O Lord, you know I endure dreadful pains in my body, but in my heart I am glad to suffer this because I fear you" (6:30). This fire burns in the hearts of the seven brothers who with their mother suffer martyrdom for the Law (chapter 7). It gives courage to Judas and his followers in the face of overwhelming odds.

"They trust in their arms and daring, but we trust in the almighty God, for he is able with a mere nod to strike down not only our enemies but the whole world" (8:18). With these words Judas characterizes the spirit in which he conquers. In this spirit he prepares his soldiers for battle through prayer, fasting, and the reading of God's Word (13:12; 11:9; 8:23). In this spirit they sing hymns of thanksgiving after victory is won (10:38) and share the spoils with orphans and widows (8:28).

"The help of God" (8:23) and "the victory of God" (13:15) are their watchwords. So "fighting with their hands, but praying to the Lord with their hearts" (15:27), they overcome the rage of the kings, their armor and their elephants, under the leadership of Judas, who is "altogether ready, in body and mind, to die for his countrymen" (15:30).

The Faithful Martyr

In the Books of Maccabees the opposition between Judaism and Hellenism reaches its climax, but these books also point to the eventual absorption of both Judaism and Hellenism into the unity of the far higher Christian revelation. Hellenism cultivated the idea of harmony between beauty and goodness through equal development of mind and body, but it scoffed at the idea of the resurrection of the flesh (see Acts 17:32) and thus rejected what would have been its own last fulfillment.

The ideals of Judaism, on the other hand, transcended this visible world to such a degree that the human body really did not seem to matter much. The Books of Maccabees put before us the ideal of the martyr. He reaches the unity of mind and body by completely surrendering both of these as a sacrifice to God for the redemption of the people (7:37). In martyrdom the spirit of God's selfless love takes absolute possession of the body and therefore leads to the resurrection of the flesh (7:9, 11, 14, 23, 36).

The story of the Maccabean brothers points to the "faithful martyr" (Rv 1:5), Jesus Christ, who judges Hellenism when he says: "Whoever loves his life [that is, the whole man, mind and body] will lose it; whoever hates his life in this world, will keep it for eternal life" (Jn 12:25). Through his passion and glorification the Word of God made flesh fulfills the ultimate aims both of Judaism and of Hellenism. The latter rejects the idea of the resurrection of the flesh because it does not know the omnipotence of the Creator. Judaism does not understand how God can become man and die for sinners, because it has not grasped the fullness of his love. Christianity accepts both in the risen Christ, who lives in every member of his mystical body.

The Maccabees live and die for the temple and for the Law. Ultimately their struggle ends in failure, because the Jews show themselves unable to reconcile the two. The bitter antagonism between the men of the temple—the Sadducees and the high priests—and the men of the Law—the scribes and Pharisees—contributes much to the final destruction of the temple by the Romans in A.D. 70.

In the meantime temple and Law, body and mind, have found their true unity in the Word of God made man. With the coming of the reality the shadows vanish. Judaism is fulfilled in Christ. In the martyrs of the Books of Maccabees it touches the very heart of Christianity, the Resurrection. By the fact that the Church numbers these heroes of Judaism among her saints, celebrating their anniversary on the first of August, she shows that she is the heir of Judaism.

The lights of Hanukkah are now burning Christmas night when the Church announces the glad tidings that the life that was with the Father from the beginning has appeared to us and has fulfilled the most noble aspirations of Hellenism. Christ brought that peace between Judaism and Hellenism that the heroism of the Maccabees was not able to achieve.

FOURTEEN

The Book of Job

Those who, after passing through the instruction of the wisdom books, enter with the Church upon a study of the Book of Job, will find themselves on familiar ground. It is evident that the author and the acting personalities of the book belong to the class of the "wise"—those versed in the literary arts, in the knowledge of nature, ethics, and diplomacy—who were to be found all through the countries of the Near East, especially at the courts of the princes. Their function was to hand down from generation to generation the traditional wisdom of the ages.

Job is one of the wise, and so are his three friends who come to mourn with him. The topic of their conversation, the question of the sufferings of the just, is often treated in the books of wisdom. The two speeches of God in which the whole book culminates praise the divine wisdom in lines of great poetic beauty. The Book of Job, however, claims our interest not only because of its wisdom and its extraordinary artistic beauty but foremost because it is the most human and the most "modern" among the books of the Old Testament.

The modern reader, who on the whole is not too fond of dogmatism, will be surprised and delighted to find in the Bible a spiritual drama in which the smug representatives of a narrow-minded, old-fashioned "orthodoxy" receive a crushing verdict from God, who at the same time pronounces himself in favor of a man who has passed through the depth of doubt and bitterness of soul until he finds that "his Vindicator lives" (19:25). Who would suspect that five hundred years before Christ a "play" could be written (and later received into the canon of Holy Scripture) in which the self-righteous representatives of tradition, who ride comfortably along the well-known paths of orthodox thinking, are exposed as unwittingly defending the cause of Satan?

A Modern Man

In Job himself we find "a man whose way is hidden, and God has surrounded him with darkness" (3:23). After his traditional faith has been shattered by overwhelming adversities, he battles his way to a larger conception of God and a deeper understanding of his own personal relation to him. This Job is a "modern man"; in fact, he is modern to *all* times. He is not a member of the chosen people but an Edomite, one of the sons of Esau. Pictured as having lived before the covenant with Moses was established, Job does not live in the light of the special revelation of God on Mount Sinai. He is an "outsider," one of the vast mass of the *hoi polloi* who do not belong to the approved "church" yet have God as their Creator.

Job is just a man. He does not invoke the "God of Abraham, of Isaac, and of Jacob," but he pleads with his Maker. He revolts against the idea that God should have taken such great delight in forming man from clay, only to punish him severely at the slightest transgression (10:7-22).

Job is not a pious model hero wearing a custom-made suit of new Sunday clothes. He is a man of flesh and blood—and a miserable, sick, crushed man at that. He loves life with his whole heart. He is not patient and detached by nature. He longs above all for understanding in the extreme anguish of soul that has befallen him.

Job is supreme in the art of skillfully pleading his cause, but right in the middle of it he breaks down and cries out: "Have pity on me, have pity on me, O you my friends, for the hand of God has struck me!" (19:21). What Job is really looking for is not so much an answer to a theological problem as a friend. The wonderful "actuality" of the Book of Job consists precisely in this: Without insisting on an intellectual solution to the problem of the suffering of the just, it leads Job through a maze of philosophical argumentation, only to let him find his real self deeply anchored in the love of God, which surpasses all understanding.

Not many people are aware of the "modernity" of the Book of Job. This is partly due to the popular misconception that Job, a man smitten with leprosy and sitting upon a dung heap, is the saddest of all men who pours out his misery in endless complaints against God, leading nowhere. In reality Job is plunged into the depths of human misery only to reach the rock bottom of unshakable faith in God's goodness. It is the story of one who rises above his fate in the power of faith and humbly rejoices in the assurance that God is on his side.

The Question

Another difficulty in appreciating the Book of Job is the overemphasis given to the intellectual result of the debate between Job and his three friends. How meager this result is can be seen from the summary one commentator gives of it:

1. The suffering of the just is not the result of sins of ignorance or inadvertence. This follows from Yahweh's judgment on the merits of the debate (dialogue and epilogue).
2. The suffering of the just must not be attributed to injustice on the part of God (Elihu).
3. The suffering of the just must not be attributed to want of wisdom and power on the part of God (Yahweh).
4. No positive solution of the problem is attempted. The motive

of God's action in an individual case is a mystery. In the case of Job, the writer lifts the veil in the prologue, and reveals the real cause of his misfortunes; but this has been done to provide the setting for the debate, and is not of general application.[1]

If it were the whole aim and purpose of the book to reach this conclusion, we could rightly wonder why so much art is wasted on proving so little. Actually the question around which the whole drama of Job revolves is not an abstract problem at all but the very concrete one that Satan asks in the prologue: "Does Job fear God for nothing?" (1:9). The Satan of the Book of Job is not identical with the "prince of this world" of the New Testament, who has been cast out of heaven for his rebellion against God. That Satan, the devil, has set up an "independent" dominion and, for the purpose of extending his evil power, seeks to accomplish the spiritual ruin of mankind by tempting it to sin.

The Satan of Job, however, occupies rank and place at the heavenly court. As his name "adversary" or "accuser" suggests, he is a sort of "prosecuting attorney" of the kingdom of God. He is "roaming the earth, walking to and fro therein" (1:7) to find out its hidden faults. He would win his case against God if he could prove that there is no selfless love of God among men.

The universe, created by God for his glory, will prove to be a failure if men and women love God only for selfish reasons. The glory of God shines only in the hearts of those who, forgetful of their earthly happiness, sing: "We give you thanks, O Lord, for your great glory." We realize immediately that if God's justice consisted in his rewarding the just with earthly happiness and punishing the wicked with earthly misfortune, he could never prove that men love him for his own sake and not for selfish reasons.

When, therefore, God points out Job to Satan as a man "perfect and righteous, who fears God and shuns wickedness" (1:8), the latter has only a sarcastic smile: "Have you not hedged him round about, and his house and all that belongs to him, blessed the works of his hands, and his wealth has spread abroad in the land?" (1:10). So he obtains permission from God to strip Job of all his possessions.

The adversities that strike Job in quick succession are not able, however, to silence the voice of thanksgiving in his heart: "The Lord gave and the Lord has taken away. Blessed be the name of the Lord" (1:21). Even when his flesh, the stronghold of selfishness in man, is smitten with the most hideous of all diseases, black leprosy, and his wife tempts him, as Eve once tempted Adam, to curse God and die, he upbraids her as a "foolish woman" who does not know God. His answer—"Should we receive good from God and not receive evil?" (2:10)—shows that he loves God more than all earthly goods. Sitting on the dung heap, Job remains a faithful witness to the glory of God.

The Debate

At this point the friends appear on the scene (2:11). They come to condole with Job and to comfort him. But when they find him smitten with leprosy, they believe they see the unmistakable proof of God's displeasure. Instead of showing sympathy, "they rend their garments, and they sprinkle dust over their heads by casting it heavenwards" (2:12). By this strange performance they mean to express not so much grief on Job's account as solicitude on their own. They seek to ward off the danger of becoming affected themselves with the curse they believe has befallen Job.

The latter understands the significance of the friends' behavior, and this knowledge cuts him to the quick. The loss of his property and even his bodily affliction is nothing in comparison to the mental anguish now caused by the fear that he might indeed be forsaken by God. After seven days and seven nights of complete darkness of soul, without a word of consolation from his friends, Job curses his day (chapter 3).

His moving lamentation is the outcry of a man who cannot live without God. It reveals the impenetrable gloom that accompanies the suffering of the innocent. Like Jeremiah—of whose famous complaint (Jer 20:14-18) this chapter is only a poetic enlargement—and like our Lord exclaiming on the cross, "My God, my God, why hast thou foresaken me?" (Mt 27:46)—unable to see in his sufferings the mark of God's justice—Job only feels that God has withdrawn from him.

The debate between Job and his friends (chapters 4–31) is not a logical development of pro and con with regard to the problem of the suffering of the just but the drama of Job's faith, which rises like the day star out of the night of his supreme temptation. It is arranged in three rounds of discourses, during which each of the friends states his argument and Job replies.

The friends explain the traditional doctrine of retribution, according to which men are divided into two classes—the just, who are the happy ones because God blesses them with all kinds of material blessings, and the wicked, who are the unfortunate ones because God punishes them. Consequently everyone who suffers must have committed sin, either wittingly or unwittingly, because God is just and will not punish the innocent. They therefore exhort Job to submit to his sufferings as to a divine chastisement, that he may regain his former prosperity. Without knowing it the friends are playing Satan's part; if Job would yield to them, God would lose his case.

As it is, Job's sufferings surpass all human standards of retributive justice to such a degree that they simply do not fit the small pattern into which his bourgeois friends try to press God and the world. Job seeks their hearts, but they hide the emptiness of their souls behind a facade of pious arithmetic, falsifying the facts that they may fit their accounts.

In deep disappointment Job appeals from the tribunal of human justice to God the friend. One abyss calls to the other. The depth of Job's heart probes into the depth of the heart of God. The very darkness of his soul fills him with the one great desire to see God. He reaches beyond the cheap identity of righteousness and earthly happiness into the only region where human bliss and divine glory become one: the beatific vision.

Round One

During the first of the three rounds, the friends treat Job with some consideration. Especially Eliphaz, the oldest one of them, tries hard to be very tactful. He veils his hint to Job in the form of a dream, during which he hears a mysterious something speaking with a gentle voice: "Can a mortal be righteous before God, or a man be pure before his Maker?" (4:17). "If I were you," he continues, "I would seek for God, and to God I would state my case" (5:8).

This idea Job will take up later. In Eliphaz' mouth it is only a polite and roundabout way of inviting Job to submit to his sufferings as to a divine chastisement, which would make everything fine (5:17-26). Because he is not too sure of himself in all this Eliphaz adds an emphatic appeal to authority: "There it is! We have investigated it; It is so! Hear it and know it for your very self!" (5:27).

No, Eliphaz does not know a thing about Job's very self. This is what Job in his reply tries to make clear. Eliphaz has no idea of the immense burden of calamity weighing on Job's shoulders; he does not realize that the arrows of the Almighty are planted in Job, that the terrors of God are besetting him so that his only hope is that God might crush him completely (6:2-13).

In a masterful way the inspired author uses the psychology of the sick to lead immediately into the very heart of the whole debate. The sick man is not looking for principles but for understanding. Job does not find it with his friends (6:14-17), nor with the God of his friends, who seems to be like a policeman without a heart (7:20).

In his answer to Bildad, who only repeats in a cruder way what Eliphaz has already suggested (chapter 8), Job complains that, in front of a God who is absolute power and nothing else, he has no chance even to explain his case. Since God is not a man like himself, there is no common ground where they can meet.

Job, therefore, calls for an umpire, who can lay his hands on both God and him to mediate between them. Because there is none, Job in a most pathetic gesture, tells in a moving monologue (chapter 10) what he would say to God if he were not afraid of him. Why has God created him, why has he preserved Job's life with so much solicitude, if he has only been waiting for Job's first trespass to destroy him? (10:18). Deeply discouraged, Job sinks into the darkest gloom.

Zophar, the youngest of the friends and the most inconsiderate and dogmatic of them, impatiently bursts into the debate. He belongs to those defenders of the faith who, in order to convert people, start off by offending them (chapter 11). He admonishes Job not to let perversity dwell in his tent and promises that if Job would heed this advice he would soon forget all his trouble (11:14).

His platitudes arouse Job's most bitter sarcasm. "No doubt but you are the people, and wisdom will die with you!" (12:2). What a heartless world it is in which they live, where "Contempt for the unfortunate!" is the motto of the prosperous. "A kick for those whose feet are slipping!" (12:5).

Job himself has enough experience to know that the world as it really is does not justify any cheap optimism. Look at human politics: "God takes away the intelligence of the leaders of the people of the earth, and makes them wander in a pathless waste. They grope in darkness with no light, and he makes them stagger like a drunken man" (12:24-25).

Disgusted with the lack of sincerity on the part of mankind (13:1-13), Job, in the depth of despair, is ready with "his flesh in his teeth, and his life in his hands" (13:14) to appear before God and to hurl the whole weight of his innocence into the face of God's wrath (13:15-27). But at the last moment strength and courage leave him, and instead of boldly defending his case, he pours out his tired soul in a moving elegy on the nothingness of man (chapter 14). When the high wave of his indignation breaks on the rock of God's power, Job stretches out the hands of his heart to find God as his friend: "O that you would hide me in Sheol [the realm of the dead], that you would conceal me until your wrath turn, that you would set me a time and remember me!" (14:13).

Round Two

The first round of the debate has led to a climax in which Job catches the first glimmer of a possible life after death with God as his friend. During the second cycle of speeches (chapters 15–21) the friends become more bitter and personal and openly accuse Job of arrogance.

Eliphaz' picture of the proud man's fight against God (15:25-29) evokes in Job's excited imagination the terrifying features of God as his enemy, running upon him like a warrior, seizing him by the neck, smashing him, splitting his kidneys without mercy, and breaking him with breach upon breach (16:12-15). But out of the depths of Job's good conscience rises triumphantly his faith in another God, who is his witness in the heavens and who will testify for him. In a magnificent paradox Job appeals from God to God, from the God of human justice to One who is higher (16:19-21). Job does not know his name, but we know it: Jesus Christ, the Mediator between God the Father and his children.

In his reply to Bildad (chapter 19) Job sees Christ standing beyond the grave in the land of the living to champion Job's cause. "Would that my words were hewn in the rock forever! As for me I know that

my Vindicator lives, and that at last he will appear on earth. After my
skin is stripped off, did I but see him; without my flesh were I to
behold God, he whom I would see would be on my side, and he
whom my eyes would behold would not be an enemy" (19:25-27).

Job's faith in God as his friend leads him to the very gates of the
Resurrection. The Old Testament did not have a clear and definite
doctrine concerning the fate of the soul after death, because it linked
the life of the soul so closely to the life of the body that the two were
almost identical. The existence of the soul after its separation from the
body was considered a state closer to death than to life (see Job 10:21-
22). This dark picture of the hereafter is the main reason Job's friends
insist that divine justice must find its fulfillment on this side of the
grave. Job, however, gropes around in the dark until he suddenly finds
the door that opens to him the land where God is eternally humanity's friend.

With this solemn profession of faith Job's personal problem has
found its solution; but the question of retributive justice in general has
not yet been solved. Job answers Zophar's wrong generalization of the
happiness of the just and the misfortune of the wicked (chapter 20)
with the opposite picture of God "storing up trouble for his sons"
(21:19) and of the wicked being spared in the day of disaster (21:30).

Round Three

In the third round of speeches (chapters 22–31) the friends answer
Job's arguments with personal invectives, accusing Job openly of grave
sin (22:5) and evidently resorting to calumny (22:6-11). Against this
dark backdrop, however, the true greatness of Job reveals itself more
and more, until his full stature shines forth in his magnificent confession (chapters 29–31). This he closes by solemnly affixing his signature
(31:35), an act that receives its full significance when we remember

that in those ancient days the signature consisted in the sign of the cross.

After Job has silenced the three wise "friends," a younger teacher ushers himself upon the scene, assuming, bold, and supercilious. Elihu stands there, with his long-winded speeches, as an empty shadow between the discourses of Job and the address of the supreme Judge, whose actual appearance shows the nothingness of Elihu and causes the shadow to vanish.

Appearing suddenly with overpowering magnificence, God disregards Elihu, passes by the friends who have presumed to be his advocates, and directs his words to Job. He does not give an intellectual solution to the problem of the suffering of the just, nor does he make known to Job his reasons for subjecting him to trial. Instead he reveals the hidden depth of his personality as it appears in his works (chapters 38–41).

In majestic words God makes himself known as the great Father of all, who laid the cornerstones of the earth, when the morning stars sang together and all the heavenly beings shouted for joy (38:7); who covered the sea at its birth with the swaddling cloth of the clouds (38:9); who provides its prey for the raven, when his young cry unto God and wander for lack of meat (38:41); who gives his strength to the horse and clothes his neck with power (39:19). In true humility of heart Job repents in dust and ashes, because his eye has seen God's glory (42:5-6).

The glory of God is definitely vindicated when Job asks God's forgiveness for the friends who have maligned him (42:8). Here lies the true key to the interpretation of Job. The innocent sufferer of the Old Testament points to God's Son, who will one day answer for all mankind the question of selfless piety by sacrificing himself for the glory of his Father and for his friends' salvation.

On Jesus' way to Golgotha he rebukes Peter as a satan for suggesting that the innocent one should not drink the cup of suffering. "You think the thoughts of men and not of God" (Mt 16:23), he says, because it is God's eternal privilege to think in terms of selfless love (see Job 10:5). With the question of Job on his lips—"My God, my God, why have you forsaken me?"—the Saviour dies. But the Father vindicates him, raises him from the dead, and gives him the power to intercede for men.

Thus Job's longing for an "umpire" is fulfilled in Christ. God has appeared on earth as the friend of humanity. The sufferings of the just have been shown to be the means by which God establishes the kingdom of his love. "You have heard of the patience of Job and what the Lord brought out of it: the Lord is merciful and is a lover of men" (Jas 5:11). It is not God's absolute power that answers the question of the innocent sufferer—"Why have you forsaken me?"—but his absolute love, which surpasses all understanding and transforms the suffering of the just into a fountain of salvation.

FIFTEEN

The Book of Psalms

In our study of the Scriptures we have on several occasions come across certain basic ideas that form in their repeated occurrence pathways of understanding. These make us realize the marvelous unity of scope and spirit in the vast forest of God's Word. Because the Scriptures are the progressive revelation of God's love for us, and because love drives out fear, it is only natural that one of the most important of these pathways is formed by the idea of delight, the "delight of the Lord" (Ps 27:4). It is in wandering along this path that we find the Psalms.

The Lord God, after he created man, took him and "put him into the paradise of pleasure, to dress it and to keep it" (Gn 2:15). The meaning of this passage becomes clearer when we try to render the shades of meaning suggested by the Hebrew text: "The Lord God took man gently by the hand, and set him free and at rest in the garden of delight to serve it and to keep it."[1] God did not create Adam in Paradise, but after he had formed him from the dust of the earth, he showed his fatherly love for his firstborn in a new and special way by initiating him into the mystery and the life in the garden of delight.

The Paradise of Genesis has nothing to do with the "dreamland" of our fairy tales. It is not the land of plenty with idleness. It is a sanctuary, the place of God's loving presence, where God himself does the work of the gardener and plants the trees (Gn 2:8); it is a prophecy, pointing to "the year of the Lord's good pleasure when all that mourn in Zion shall be called terebinths of righteousness, the planting of the Lord where he will be glorified" (Is 61:3).

199

In this garden the man is free and at rest to do what is the function of the priests and Levites in the temple: to serve and to guard. Adam is priest and Levite in one. As a priest he has to guard what is God's and keep it undefiled. As a Levite he has to serve—the Hebrew text suggests that it is the delight rather than the garden which he is to serve,[2] if the two can be separated at all.

The delight of Paradise is not merely the pleasure of the senses. It is primarily spiritual. The trees that God planted there are first of all "beautiful to behold" and only then "good to eat" (Gn 2:9). It is the "delight of the Lord"—the reflection, in the heart of man, of God's loving presence—that Adam is to serve. In God's sanctuary there is no room for the glorification of self but only for the services of God's glory. As a Jewish commentary states: "The glory of God cannot rest in man except in joy."[3]

Delight is the bond that unites the Lord and his servant in the garden, the delight of contemplation and praise. The "garden of delight" is the first temple where mankind is set free and at rest to praise the glory of God.

Because God used delight as the incentive for the man to serve him, Satan makes of it a bait to draw the man away from his Creator (see Gn 3:6). The Fall deprives the man of delight. He is able to serve only through the sweat and toil of work and the anguish and labor of birth. Lust replaces delight, and soon lust turns into cruelty (see Gn 4:23-24).

However, God's mercy, which took Adam and set him free and at rest in the garden of delight, is not dead. Another "Adam" is created: God's chosen people. Out of Egypt God calls his firstborn son (Hos 11:1), and after leading him gently through the desert, he brings him into the Promised Land, "a good land, a land of brooks of water, of fountains and depths, a land of wheat and barley, of vines and fig trees and pomegranates, a land of olive trees and honey" (Dt 8:7).

The Promised Land was not like the land of Egypt, where man was the gardener, "where when the seed is sown, waters are brought in to water it." Rather, it is a land of hills and plains, expecting rain from heaven. And the Lord God does always visit it, and his eyes are on it from the beginning of the year unto the end thereof" (Dt 11:10-11). In this garden of delight Israel is set free and at rest through David, in whom God finds a man for his service.

The Psalmist

Unlike Adam, David and his people enter into their "rest" after the fall of mankind has made Satan the prince of the world. Therefore, the "rest" cannot be achieved without battle and conquest. How infinitely significant it is, however, that David enters upon the scene of history with the harp in his hands, fighting, with the sweet melodies of his songs, the evil spirit of depression that is upon Saul (1 Sm 16:23).

David certainly does not shun battle. As a true soldier he takes up the challenge of Goliath: "In the name of the Lord of hosts, the God of the armies of Israel, that all the earth may know that there is a God in Israel, and all this assembly may know that the Lord saves not with sword and spear; for the battle is the Lord's, and he will give you into our hand" (1 Sm 17:45-47).

It should be noted that these first words of David are nothing but an explanation of the word "Israel," which means "God fights the battle." David is the ideal "Israelite," who knows that God fights his battle for him. With absolute trust and confidence in God he sees in his victories only God glorified before his people and before all mankind.

David is the true servant of God. He is God's soldier and God's singer, and he is both of these because he is the anointed one upon whom the spirit of God rests (1 Sm 16:13). His soul is like a pure mirror, drinking in the rays of God's mercy in confidence and radiating them in praise. Every event in his life—his struggles, his sorrows, his triumphs, every tear, and every joy—become a song on his lips. This he sings not for his own sake but that God's kingdom might be established in the hearts of his people. His kingdom is a kingdom of hearts, not an attempt to control the minds of his subjects.

We have only to read Deuteronomy 17:14-20 to realize that the institution of the king in Israel has nothing to do with a totalitarian system of government. In Israel the king is not the legislator for his people, for the law has been given by God, and the judges and the priests are in charge of its interpretation and application. Neither is he the military leader, for God himself is his people's shield.

Israel's king is the ideal Israelite. His function is to lead the nation in the specific task assigned to it by God—namely, to realize the kingdom of God on earth and, as a priestly nation, to lead the rest of the world to the recognition of God's universal rule. The king is enthroned after the land has been seized and peace has been established. He is warned not to glory in horses and treasures. But he is advised, as soon as he has taken his seat on his royal throne, to make a copy of the Law and to peruse it all the days of his life (Dt 17:19).

The Psalms form an essential part of this program. Through them David enthrones God on the hymns of his people (see Ps 22:3) and of all mankind. "With his whole heart he praised the Lord, and loved God that made him.... And he set singers before the altar, and by their voices he made sweet melody. And to the festivals he added beauty, and set in order the solemn times even to the end of his life, that they should praise the holy name of the Lord, and magnify the holiness of God in the morning" (Sir 47:10-12).

David's son Solomon completes his father's work by building the temple for the glory of God to dwell in. "And he carved all the walls of the house round about with carved figures of cherubim and palm trees and open flowers" (1 Kgs 6:29). The temple is the "garden of delight" where the divine Bridegroom promises "his eyes and his heart to be perpetually" (1 Kgs 9:3), to dwell with his bride Israel, and to sing with her the canticle of their eternal love.

However, the prince of this world succeeds once more in drawing human beings away from the delight of the Lord through the pleasure of the senses; and again lust degenerates into tyranny and cruelty. Solomon loves many foreign women, who turn his heart to follow their gods, and he makes the yoke of the people heavy (1 Kgs 11:1-2; 12:4). As a result, the disintegration of Israel begins right after his death.

The True Rest

This son of David, and his temple, are only a shadow. The reality comes when the true Son of David rebuilds the temple of his body by rising from the dead. On Easter morning he appears to Mary Magdalen as the gardener (Jn 20:15), to indicate that now the "year of the Lord's good pleasure has come, when all that mourn in Zion will receive a crown for ashes, the oil of joy for mourning, the mantle of praise for the spirit of grief, that they might be called 'terebinths of righteousness' to glorify God" (Is 61:2-3; see also Lk 4:21).

The risen Christ sets his disciples free and at rest in the garden of the Church. His Spirit fills the hearts of the disciples, makes them praise the "wonderful works of God" (Acts 2:11), and lets the whole mighty organ of David's Psalter resound on the lips of the faithful. These speak to one another "in psalms and hymns and spiritual canticles, making melody in their hearts to God, giving thanks always for all things, in the name of the Lord Jesus Christ, to God the Father" (Eph 5:19-20).

The Psalms have remained the voice with which the "new Adam," Christ and his body, glorifies the Father. Our present Psalter contains 150 psalms, seventy-three of which have the superscription "of

David." This does not always mean "written by David" but at times "concerning David" or "in the style of David." The headings ascribe also one psalm to Moses (90), two to Solomon (72; 127), twelve to Asaph (50; 73–83), and eleven to the "sons of Korah" (42; 44–49; 84–85; 87–88). There are several other distinctive groups or collections, such as the "songs of ascent" or "gradual canticles" (120–134), and the Alleluia psalms (106; 111–114; 116–118; 135–136; 146; 148–150). It is evident that the Psalter did not come into being at once but grew over a long period of time, until by the middle of the first century B.C. it had assumed its present form.

As happens so often in the Old Testament, authorship of the Psalms serves as a means of classification rather than of origin. To recognize to what type or family a psalm belongs is of great importance for its interpretation. To have stressed this in our days is the merit of Hermann Gunkel,[4] whose line of thought has been followed further by Sigmund Mowinckel[5] and Hans Schmidt.[6] The fruits of these studies have been brought within the reach of the general reader by E.A. Leslie.[7]

Trying to penetrate behind the literature to the life that created it, Gunkel realized that the origin of a great many of the psalms is to be found in the organized public worship of the chosen people. More than a century ago the great J.G. Herder had already pointed to this in words that still deserve to be quoted:

Three times in the year, at the great national festivals, there was a general assembling of the people. They came together not to hear sermons or Mass for seven days, but to rejoice together in their community of privileges, and to feel that, as the people of God, they were one people. All their three great festivals were national, and associated with liberty. The passover was a memorial of the day which made them a free people; the feast of Pentecost, of the law by which that freedom was confirmed; and the feast of tabernacles, of its enjoyment in their first simple dwellings and unrestrained family intercourse.

All the festivals abounded in sacrificial feasts, in music, songs and dances. The people of God in the presence of their invisible Lord, and before the tabernacle, in which his law was deposited, could not but be a rejoicing people. By these assemblages their ... delight in the Lord, the fraternal relationship of the several tribes, who all had but one Lord, one invisible king, one law, one temple, were awakened and cherished, and by their social participation of the feast and song, the origin of the nation, the history and memorials of their patriarchs, were preserved, and remained always fresh in their minds....

If we consider the spirit of social union and friendship that animates the national poetry and songs, when all ranks of free people come together mutually to excite and congratulate each other, in prosperity, in joy, and in successful well-doing, or to condole with each other respecting national misfortunes, we shall find in most of the psalms more beauty and interest.[8]

The Psalms became the prayer book of the Church—not because of their poetic beauty; not because they voice the whole scale of human emotions, from the shout of the triumphant conqueror to the wailing of the bereaved and oppressed; not even because they are inspired, and in them "God has praised himself, that he may be praised well by men"[9]—rather because of their liturgical character.

Worship the Lord

In its public worship the Israelite people were lifted up above the level of everyday life and became conscious of its divine destiny. The whole meaning of its existence crystallized in the ritual. Past and future, beginning and end, met in the "today" of the feast. The yearly celebration of the Passover commemorated the past deliverance of the people from Egypt and anticipated the future great deliverance to be brought about by the Messiah. The New Year feast in the autumn saw in the beginning of the new year the mystery of the first beginning of creation renewed.

Not only did events compenetrate each other in liturgical worship, but also persons. The individual merged into the common spirit of the whole people. The "fathers" of the past, the leaders of the present, grew together in the perspective of the future Messiah.

It is this twofold compenetration of events and of people that found in the Psalms its most perfect expression and that enables them to be as "actual" on the lips of the Christians as on the lips of the Jews. In the person of Christ all persons and peoples, and the whole of mankind, compenetrate one another; his work of redemption, his death and resurrection, heads all events that make the history of the chosen people. The compenetration of events gives a Christian meaning to the whole Psalter, and not only to some "messianic psalms," by turning them toward the central event of Christ's pasch. The compenetration of persons makes it possible, without distorting the literal sense, to hear in the Psalms the voice of Christ addressing his Father, or the voice of the Church directed to Christ and through him to the Father.

Psalm 3, for instance, is, according to the heading, "a psalm of David when he fled from Absalom his son." It became part of the Psalter because the fate of David is the fate of the people, and the fate of the people is fulfilled in Christ, whose voice we therefore hear in the psalm. The decisive "event" on which the song hinges is described in verse 6: "I lie down, and I sleep; I awake, for the Lord sustains me." Helpless as he is, surrounded by his enemies, David falls asleep, and while he sleeps the Lord renews his strength.

This "event" is not an isolated, negligible detail. It happened to Adam when Eve was made from his side. It happened to Jacob when he slept on the stone. It happened to Elijah when he had to flee from Jezebel. It was fulfilled in Christ's death and resurrection. It is repeated sacramentally in every baptism and gives supernatural meaning to the rising in the morning of every Christian. For this reason the psalm was chosen by St. Benedict to be sung at the beginning of the monastic vigils (matins). By saying this psalm as his morning prayer, every Christian can make his rising in the morning an image of the Resurrection and thus merge his life into that of Christ.

The compenetration of persons and of events that we find expressed in the Psalms makes them a means of bringing the entire range of human life—its sorrows and its joys, in fact the whole of God's creation—into the presence of God. A great number of the psalms are hymns of praise. The Hebrew word for praise, *tehillim*, became the name for the entire Psalter in the Hebrew Bible.

The praise of the Psalms, however, is far more than the external acknowledgment of God's glory by the assembly of worshipers. It is the throne of his presence. The word *tehillim* comes from *hallal*, which not only means "to praise" but primarily means "to radiate" or "to reflect." The famous acclamation "Hallelujah," therefore, does not only mean "praise the Lord" but "radiate the Lord."

We cannot praise God with our lips only. We have to praise him with our soul (146:1), with our heart (138:1), with our inmost being (103:1). Then our whole being becomes the throne of God's glory, and the praise itself becomes God's work (compare St. Benedict's expression *opus Dei*).

Jewish teaching pointed out long ago that the reason the *Alleluia* is so highly valued in worship is that it joins together, in one unity of concept and of action, the human activity—*hallelu*, "praise ye"—and the divine name—*Yah*, "the Lord."[10] The heart that radiates God's glory in praise becomes itself "glory."

The medieval Jewish poet Jehuda Halevi expressed beautifully the spirit of the Psalter when he said: "Look on the glories of God, and awaken the glory in thee." He alluded to verses 7-8 of Psalm 57: "My heart is ready, O God, my heart is ready. I will sing, yea, I will sing praises. Awake, my glory, awake, psaltery and harp!"

The "glory" of which the psalm speaks is man's "higher soul" (see Ps 7:5; 16:9; 30:12),[11] where God and man meet in the most intimate way. In the light of the New Testament it is the spirit of the risen Christ in the soul of the baptized. The last sentence of the Psalter, "Let all that has spirit praise the Lord!" is fulfilled only in the Church, which "sings with the spirit" (1 Cor 14:15).

As glory penetrates into the last depth of the human heart, so it also expands, reaching out to the very end of time and extending over the entire universe. The praises of the Psalms are universal and eschatological. They are the "new canticle," an expression that occurs frequently in the Psalter (33:3; 40:3; 96:1; 98:1; 144:9; 149:1) and that designates a psalm pertaining "to the new age," when God's kingdom has come. This eschatological character of many psalms predestined them to become the songs of the new Israel in the age of Christ.

Cry to God

The same sense of divine reality that characterizes the psalms of praise is also evident in the songs of petition (tephillot). They are penetrated by a profound confidence in God (25; 27; 31), which leads to the certainty of being heard (6:9; 7:12; 63:5-11) and to immediate thanksgiving (79:13). The psalmist takes refuge under "the wings of God" (17:8; 36:7; 57:1; 61:4; 63:7; 91:4), an expression that reveals its whole meaning when Christ extends his arms on the cross. Covered by the wings of Christ's sacrificial love, we are certain to be heard. "Therefore I say to you: whatever you ask in prayer, believe that you have received and it will come to you" (Mk 11:24).

The unique combination of the crying need of the poor and the certainty of divine help that we find in the psalms of petition is evidently the work of the Holy Spirit, who is also responsible for the union of the two most fundamental ideas of the Psalter: the defeat of God's enemies, yet the sufferings of God's people.[12] By praying Psalm 22 while he was hanging on the cross, our Lord has shown that the triumph over God's enemies is the fruit of the sufferings of God's Son.

All those passages in the Psalms that seem to be "unchristian" have to be interpreted in the light of the Cross. The enemies of God, over whose fall the psalmist rejoices, are the enemies of the cross, those who have rejected the love of Christ, the unrepentant sinners. The "hatred" of the Psalms and their "curses" (see 137:9) are not essentially different from the attitude in which Christ says to those at his left, "Depart from me, you cursed, into everlasting fire!" (Mt 25:41).

The psalmist does what Adam was supposed to do: He serves the delight of the Lord, and he guards it against those who defile it. The Church will have to do the same, until "there shall be no curse any more" (Rv 22:3). But those who serve in the garden, at the river of the water of life, with the tree of life bearing twelve fruits, before the throne of God and of the Lamb, will sing the new canticle: Give thanks to the Lord of lords, for his mercy endures forever!

SIXTEEN

The Books of Wisdom

We read in the book of the prophet Jeremiah: "The law shall not perish from the priest, nor counsel from the wise, nor the word from the prophet" (18:18). Three kinds of revelation are mentioned in this sentence: the Law, the word, and the counsel.

The Law is the divinely revealed foundation of the community life of the chosen people, contained in the five books of Moses. The word is a divine directive, revealed now and then to the prophets and intended to show to the people the course God wants them to follow on their way through history. It is recorded not only in those books of the Old Testament that we call prophetic (Isaiah, Jeremiah, and so on), but also in the historical books, beginning with the Book of Joshua and including the Books of Samuel and Kings.

The counsel is different again both from the Law and the word. It concerned the spiritual life of the individual and is used by the "wise men" or sages for the instruction of their disciples. It is this counsel that we read in the books of Wisdom.

The sapiential books used to be quoted in our missals simply under the one name of *Liber Sapientiae* or *Sapientia*. In reality there are four different books that belong to this group: the Proverbs of Solomon, Qoheleth or Ecclesiastes, Wisdom, and Sirach or Ecclesiasticus.

The Book of Proverbs is the oldest of the group. Solomon is designated as the author in 1:1 as well as in 10:1 and 25:1. In 1 Kings 4:29 it is said that "God gave to Solomon wisdom and understanding exceeding much," so that he was "wiser than all men" and "spoke three thousand proverbs" (4:31–32). Solomon, therefore, was certainly the author of many proverbs.

The Book of Proverbs, however, is evidently composed of various collections, partly attributed in the text itself to authors other than Solomon (see 30:1; 31:1) and in part showing a much later style (see 30:15-33; 31:10-31). Two collections, which stand out as evidently older than the rest (10:1–22:16 and 25:1–29:27), are the only sections that might actually have a Solomonic origin. The entire collection was named for Solomon, however, because he was considered *the* sage of Israel. In the same way, David was considered *the* singer, and therefore the Psalms were gathered around his name.

The Book of Ecclesiastes is no longer regarded as having been composed by Solomon. In its present form it goes back only to the third or fourth century B.C. The language of the book is not that of the golden age of Hebrew literature but shows everywhere the influence of the Aramaic dialect.

The same is true of the Book of Wisdom, which in its form is strongly influenced by Greek civilization and cannot have been composed before 200 B.C. Ecclesiasticus must have been written between 190 and 170 B.C. by Jesus, son of Sirach, as we can see from the Greek translation that his son made in about 120 B.C.

Solomon

The modern mind is much concerned about questions of authorship and, from the point of view of historical exactness, rightly so. However, in Hebrew literature, as in Oriental literature in general, authorship is used very often for the sake of classification rather than for historical identification. The name of an author often does not stand for an historical person but for a type.

Solomon, in the Old Testament, is more than an historical person. He is the representative of a certain stage in the spiritual development of the chosen people. Solomon is the king par excellence. The institution of the kingdom in Israel is indicative of that spiritual maturity which makes possible the inner union of the heart between God and mankind.

The Law is the form of revelation that corresponds to Israel's childhood. The word of the prophets is like the rod of the teacher, used in the days of boyhood and adolescence. The counsel of the wise is different; it is the ripe fruit of lifelong experience, the result of much searching and thinking on the part of the wise. The Law is written upon tablets of stone and kept in the ark as "a witness against a stiff-necked people." The word comes and goes. But wisdom makes her abode in the heart of the wise. Therefore the king, the representative and guaranty of the stable union of the heart between God and man, is the wise man par excellence. He participates in the wisdom with which God rules the universe.

We have to put the emphasis on the word *universe*. Wisdom is essentially cosmopolitan. She is the law that is not confined to one nation only but reaches from one end of the earth to the other. The king is, for that same reason, part of a supernatural order. He deals with other nations. His outlook reaches far beyond the narrow borders of his own country.

Solomon's wisdom is not confined to particular customs or traditions of his own people. It exceeds that of the Egyptians and Babylonians, but it also incorporates much of the wisdom found among the nations of the world. Proverbs 22:17-24 shows some affinity with the Egyptian wisdom book called "The Teaching of Amenemope." Lemuel, who is mentioned as author of some of the sayings in the Book of Proverbs (31:1-9), was not of Jewish origin. This only goes to show that the sapiential books belong to that stage of spiritual maturity in which Israel stretches out her arms to bring the spiritual wealth of the nations, the "gold of the Egyptians," home to God.

Solomon prefigures the gloriously reigning Christ, who will restore all things under him as the head. When, therefore, Jesus was born at Bethlehem in Judah, "wise men from the East arrived at Jerusalem and asked: 'Where is the newly born king of the Jews? For we have seen his star rise in the east, and we have come to adore him'" (Mt 2:1-2). The wisdom of the nations recognized its author.

There can be no doubt, however, that the wisdom that has been incorporated into the canon of Holy Scripture is not the invention of the human spirit or of human ingenuity left to itself. Solomon prayed for wisdom (1 Kgs 3:9). In answer to his prayers he received an "understanding and listening heart." This means that wisdom, unlike the prophetic word put into the prophet's mouth, is an abiding virtue, an inner disposition of the very center of the human person.

In the Old Testament the heart is not considered the seat of the emotions or feelings. Rather it is the most noble, the central, part of man, from which thinking and acting receive their directions. It brings about unity, coherence, and consistency in all the various activities of the human person. The heart, therefore, is the seat of wisdom, because wisdom is the power that coordinates and gives unification of purpose and harmony to all things.

Consequently, Solomon does not receive this or that specific counsel from God, but he receives a listening heart. Out of this heart there springs, as from a living fountain, the counsel—and not only one but thousands of them, because wisdom is never niggardly.

The true wisdom given by God to the heart of man as an abiding virtue is a reflection of that divine wisdom that constitutes the very "heart of God." It enables man to decipher the signs God's wisdom has formed there in this visible world. "God set his eyes upon men's hearts to show them the greatness of his works" (Sir 17:8). The wise man can read "in between the lines" of the book of creation and is able to penetrate into its deepest meaning. "It is the glory of God to conceal a thing, but the glory of kings is to search out a matter" (Prv 25:2). For that purpose God has "set the world in man's heart" (Eccl 3:11), and the extent of Solomon's wisdom is "large as the sand on the seashore" (1 Kgs 4:29).

Here lies the great danger for the wise: They may be caught in the snare of the world, as was Solomon. Hence, the one and fundamental root out of which all true wisdom must grow is the fear of the Lord (Prv 1:7). It forms a "fence" (Ex 19:12) around the mountain of God's majesty and excludes all wrong and presumptuous intimacy with God on the part of the wise.

A Matter of the Heart

However, to fear God, in the Old Testament, does not mean to be afraid of him but to be devoted to him. "In the fear of the Lord a man has strong confidence.... The fear of the Lord is the fountain of life" (Prv 14:26-27). The wisdom that grows out of this fear of the Lord is, therefore, a progressive transformation of the heart.

The observance of the letter of the Law does not admit of degrees. The meeting between the word and the prophet is an instantaneous thing. Wisdom, on the contrary, is a matter of education. "For the fear of the Lord is wisdom and education" (Sir 1:24). Education is a matter of the heart. "My son, give me thy heart" (Prv 23:26) is the constantly repeated invitation that wisdom extends to man. Wisdom invites; it does not command.

Wisdom has built her house. She has hewn out her seven pillars. She has prepared her meat; she has mixed her wine; she has also furnished her table. She has sent forth her maidens; she calls from the highest places of the city: Whosoever is thoughtless, let him turn thither. As for him that lacks understanding, she says to him: Come, eat of my bread and drink of the wine which I have mixed.

PROVERBS 9:1-5

This invitation wisdom directs to the crowds of the thoughtless in the marketplace. "Wisdom cries aloud in the streets, she lifts up her voice in the squares; at the head of noisy thoroughfares she calls, at the openings of the city gates she utters her words" (Prv 1:20-21). She tries to rouse the busybodies out of their absorption in worldly affairs. She raises a bugle call to penetrate hearts and bring men to conversion.

These exhortations or warnings form a central part of all wisdom literature. I venture to say that within the group of sapiential writings preserved in the Old Testament, the Book of Ecclesiastes constitutes such an exhortation.

St. Jerome, in his commentary on Ecclesiastes, points out that Solomon has three different names in holy Scripture: Jedidiah which means "God's darling" (2 Sm 12:25), Solomon, which means "peaceable," and Qoheleth, which we translate as "Ecclesiastes" or "preacher." These three names correspond to the three books attributed to Solomon in the Old Testament.

"God's darling," the name of love and union, corresponds to the Song of Solomon, which reveals the mystery of love and of union between God and man, or between Christ and his Church. The Book of Proverbs (and Wisdom) is a guide that establishes peace in the minds of the faithful by bringing them into contact with the light of that divine Wisdom that rules the world gently and peacefully. It corresponds, therefore, to Solomon, the peaceable.

The name *Qoheleth* is related to *qahal,* the Hebrew word for public assembly. Qoheleth or Ecclesiastes is the "public speaker" or "preacher" who addresses himself to the crowds to wake them up and upset their false security, to fill them with doubts and problems. He wants to show how questionable the accepted standards of the world are in order to draw people away from the marketplace into quiet seclusion, where they may close their ears to the vanities of the world and sit down instead at the feet of the wise, who are able to guide them on the way of light and of life.

We see that the three books form a definite spiritual pattern, in fact the basic pattern of all spiritual life: the purgative, illuminative, and unitive ways.

As soon as we look at the teaching of Ecclesiastes as a call to conversion, as an invitation to the *via purgativa*, we realize that the author's "skepticism" has a deeper meaning than is at first obvious. It is not a case of pessimism creeping illegitimately into the sacred precincts of Holy Scripture. What the preacher ridicules and condemns are the worries and the toil, the sweat and the labors, of men who are lost in themselves and therefore go around in circles all the time, with their own dear "ego" as the empty center.

Self-love in all its forms is like the wind, "which goes toward the south, and turns about unto the north; it turns about continually on its circuit, and returns again to its circles" (1:6). As long as we think that everything in life depends exclusively on ourselves, all things turn into weariness. Learning becomes futile, "for with more wisdom is more worry, and increase of knowledge is increase of sorrow" (1:18). Neither pleasure (chapter 2) nor riches (chapter 4) are able to keep their glittering promise. They fade into vanity and striving for the wind.

The Way of the Wise

From this negative part of his book the author leads, in the second part (7:2–12:7), to the positive conclusion that it is true wisdom to stop searching and worrying and trying to find out whether one is wise or not, whether one is good or not; for if one tries, one must say in the end: "I do not know." True wisdom is to lay up in one's heart knowledge that "the righteous and wise and their works are in the hands of God" (9:1). Whoever comes to this conclusion should then follow the invitation: "Go your way, eat your bread with joy, and drink your wine with a merry heart: for God has already accepted your works. Let your garment be always white, and let your head lack no oil" (9:7-8).

The last utterance of Ecclesiastes, "the end of the matter, after everything has been said," is "Fear God and keep his commandments, for this is the whole man" (12:13). The fear of the Lord, the keeping of the commandments, the right way of life—this is the object of the other sapiential books: Proverbs, Wisdom, and Ecclesiasticus. They are written for the instruction of beginners.

The Church of old always recommended that the reader of Holy Scripture start with these books because they are so easy to understand. Unfortunately there are too many people in our days who apply to Holy Scripture the rule that to read a book properly one must start from the beginning. They forget that the Bible is more like a library of many books, from which we may choose what suits us best.

The sapiential books offer beginners the advantage of being composed not of long doctrinal treatises, nor of complicated historical development, but of short sentences that are easy to grasp. Many of them are similes and parables. Others contrast the way and fate of the righteous with that of the wicked (Prv 10:1–15:9). Wisdom and folly are opposed to each other as life and death (Prv 8:35-36).

It is the Way, the Truth, and the Life (Jn 14:6) who speaks in these proverbs. His charity is foreshadowed in the love of the poor, which we find so often in the sapiential books: "He who is kind to the poor lends to the Lord, and he will repay him his deed" (Prv 19:17; 17:5; 23:10-11). The simplicity and humility of the Our Father shines in this beautiful prayer:

Two things I ask of thee,
Deny them not to me before I die:
Put falsehood and lying far from me,
Give me neither poverty nor riches—
Provide me with bread sufficient for my needs—

Lest I be full and disown thee,
Saying: "Who is the Lord?"
Or lest I be in want and steal
And profane the name of my God.

PROVERBS 30:7-9

Contemplation

Beyond all the good common sense they contain, the sapiential books reach the most sublime heights of contemplation. Wisdom was with her Father when he established the heavens, and when he set a circle upon the face of the deep, and when he appointed the foundations of the earth (Prv 8:22-31). Therefore Wisdom opens to the eyes of men the divine meaning of this visible creation.

"Has not the Lord made the saints to declare all his wonderful works, which the Lord almighty has firmly settled to be established for his glory?" asks Sirach (42:17). Then he sets forth to describe the beauty of creation in a magnificent hymn: the majesty of the burning sun, the changing moon as marker of seasons and festivals, the armies of the stars, which at the command of the Holy One never fail in their watches.

"We may say more, but we will not reach the end, but the sum of our words is: 'He is all'" (43:28). It is indeed the essence of man that God "set his eyes upon their hearts to show them the greatness of his works" (17:7) and to confess, in the end, that he is all.

The most wonderful field for contemplation is, however, the way in which God led his chosen people through the vicissitudes of history. The Book of Wisdom (chapters 10–19), as well as Sirach (chapters 44–50), reviews the course of Jewish history to praise the magnitude of God's mercy, in which he delivered Israel, his firstborn, out of the hands of those who sought his life. There is no better way to a deeper understanding of the Scripture than the passages of Wisdom that refer the whole history of the patriarchs to the constant presence of wisdom in God's chosen ones.

A few words are sufficient, for example, to put Noah in the full light of God's eternal designs fulfilled in Christ: "When the deluge destroyed the earth, wisdom healed it again, steering the course of the just one with contemptible wood" (10:4). When Wisdom throws her light on the great fathers of the chosen people, they begin to shine as the images of him in whom they were all fulfilled.

Sirach is a master at the art of painting, with a few strokes, a faithful picture of the great spiritual leaders of Israel, and in their portraits we recognize the features of Christ: in Abraham, the father of many nations (44:19); in Moses, the friend of God and men (45:1); in Aaron, the priest "blessed in glory" (45:7); in Joshua, valiant in war and great in saving God's elect (46:1).

The greatest picture of them all, however, is that of Simon, the high priest, with whom the whole series closes (50:1-21). In him the beauty of all creation is concentrated. The enthusiastic description of the solemn temple service at which he celebrates makes it clear that the wisdom of the Old Testament is looking forward to the glorification of God through his people in the heavenly sanctuary, under the glorified high priest Jesus at the end and fulfillment of human history.

The Breath of God's Power

The teaching of the sapiential books would not be complete, however, without the revelation of two other great mysteries, which represent in some way the beginning and the end of God's ways: the mystery of the divine personality of the Word of God and that of the eternal life of the just. Wisdom is not a mental image or an abstract thought or a guiding principle. It is a divine person.

The Lord possessed me in the beginning of his ways, before he made anything from the beginning. I was set up from eternity and of old before the earth was made. I was with him in forming all things: and was delighted every day, playing before him at all times, playing in the world, and my delights were to be with the children of men.

PROVERBS 8:22-31

It is the inner nature of wisdom to be the true, substantial image of the Father's glory. "For she is the breath of the power of God, and a pure emanation of his almighty glory, a reflection of the everlasting light and a spotless mirror of God's majesty, and the image of his goodness" (Wis 7:25-26). These words are used in the Letter to the Hebrews (1:3) to describe the only begotten Son of God.

If Wisdom were only a personification of the Law, she would be dead. Only as a divine person can she become a source of life. "Though she is one she can do all things, and while remaining in herself she makes everything new" (Wis 7:27). This is shown in the beginning of creation, and still more gloriously at the end. The last triumph of wisdom is the Last Judgment, which will bring eternal life to the just. In the earlier periods of the Old Testament revelation, the immortality of the soul was shrouded in mystery. Now it enters into the full light of faith. "The souls of the just are in the hands of God, and the torment of death shall not touch them. In the eyes of the unwise they seemed to die, but they are in peace" (Wis 3:1-2).

From the beginning to the end the universal rule of Wisdom has been established. Nevertheless, those whose eyes have been opened in baptism to the light of Christ will realize that the teaching of Solomon lacks one thing: the "foolishness of God," Christ crucified. Wisdom is to be more than a guide to the wise, more than eternal life for the just, more, even, than the beginning of creation. She is to become the Lamb who will not only expose but take away the sin of the world.

The Wisdom of Solomon preaches reward to the virtuous and death to those who hate her. But more than Solomon is here, where Christ Jesus becomes unto us sinners "wisdom and justice and sanctification, and redemption" (1 Cor 1:30) through the foolishness of the cross.

SEVENTEEN

The Prophecy of Isaiah

The word *advent* had for the people of old a magic sound. It put before their eyes the glorious scene of a king's return from a victorious war. Preceded and followed by the might of his arms, carrying with him the spoils of victory, the hosts of his captives, the treasures of the enemy, he stands on his chariot, vested in the purple of triumph, the golden wreath of victory on his head. The whole city is in a delirium of joy. The festive throngs of the citizens line the streets. They greet their king with the "royal shout," acclaiming him "saviour" and "kyrios" with incense and hymns. In the evening thousands of lights appear on windows and doorways, on temples, gates and palaces, for the light is come, and the glory of the king is risen upon the city.

The advent of our ecclesiastical year does not celebrate the triumphant entry of an earthly king into his capital, but it sees the King of Kings, whose might covers the earth like a cloud, returning to the world he left because of its sin. He comes to crush his enemies, extirpate sin, and establish a kingdom of peace for those who believe in him. This is the divine action of salvation that constitutes the real meaning of history, although it may take centuries and centuries to be accomplished.

That the birth of Mary's little babe in the humble manger of Bethlehem is the beginning of this glorious advent would be hidden from the eyes of men, had the glad tidings not been announced from heaven and had the Holy Spirit not spoken in times past to the fathers by the prophets. It is really the "vision" of the prophets that opens the eyes of the faithful to see beneath the humble form of man the glory of God and to realize that Christ's first coming in patience and charity is the beginning of the Day of Judgment, which will see the Son of Man coming on the clouds of heaven to receive the eternal kingdom from the hands of the Father. It is the unique gift of the prophets to see "sign" and "reality," the human and the divine, the present and the future, in their compenetration. Therefore, they "rendered service not so much to themselves but to us" (1 Pt 1:12), who celebrate the advent of God in that incomparable compenetration of visible sign and divine reality that is the liturgy of the Church.

The prophets are the voice of the Church's mysteries. There is none among them who has experienced more deeply the joy of the Lord's coming to his city than Isaiah. He is a true child of Jerusalem by birth and training, a member of the nobility and a counselor to her kings.

> The city of David is to Isaiah the center and return of all his thoughts, the hinge of the history of his time, the one thing worth preserving amidst its disasters, the summit of those brilliant hopes with which he fills the future.... It is for her defense he battles through fifty years of statesmanship, and all his prophecy may be said to travail in anguish for her new birth. He was never away from her walls, but not even the psalms of the captives by the rivers of Babylon, with the desire of exile upon them, exhibit more beauty and pathos than the lamentations which Isaiah poured upon Jerusalem's sufferings or the visions in which he described her future solemnity and peace.[1]

With the eyes of the glory of God, the prophet penetrates the dark clouds of disaster which have gathered over his beloved city, and he sees the day when her light has come and the glory of the Lord has risen upon her (60:1).

The Historical Background

Isaiah lives in an age that witnesses the first attempt by a single nation to achieve world domination. Tiglath-Pileser, greatest of the Assyrian kings, ascends the throne of Nineveh, capital of Assyria, in the year 745 B.C. He spends the first years of his reign consolidating his power and organizing an army, which for more than a century keeps the people of Asia under its sway.

The Assyrians specialize in developing machines to take and destroy fortified places. By this means they loot practically the entire Near East. Their policy is to kill off all who can bear arms; the rest of the conquered populations they deport to other parts of their vast empire. In this way they try to abolish the local gods of various nationalities and countries and to establish the lordship of their god Assur over an amorphous mass of uprooted peoples, materially and spiritually at the mercy of the conquerors.

In 738 B.C. Tiglath-Pileser begins his assault on Syria and Palestine. Rezin, the king of Damascus, and Pekah, the king of Samaria (capital of Israel), makes an alliance against Assyria. When Ahaz, king of Judah, refuses to join this coalition, the two kings march against Jerusalem to depose him and replace him with a puppet-king of their own choice (chapter 7). At this time Isaiah gives Ahaz the sign of the virgin and her child. Jerusalem and Ahaz are saved, because Tiglath-Pileser takes Damascus and invades Israel.

At the peace settlement Tiglath-Pileser slices off the northern part of Israel and organizes it into an Assyrian province. For the first time in history, a part of the Promised Land comes under the domination of a foreign power. This same region receives from Isaiah the promise that its inhabitants will be the first to see the Saviour. "As in days gone by he brought contempt upon the land of Zebulun and the land of Naphtali, so in the time to come will he bring glory, upon the land along the Sea Road, beyond the

Jordan, the Galilee of the gentiles" (9:1; see Mt 4:12-16).

At the death of Tiglath-Pileser in 727 B.C., Israel revolts against Assyrian domination. But the new king, Sargon, invades the country once more and this time (722 B.C.) takes Samaria, deporting most of its inhabitants to Assyria (28:1-4). The vacant territory is then appropriated by foreign settlers.

Under Sennacherib, Sargon's successor, the Assyrian tide sweeps southward into the kingdom of Judah. Sennacherib has left his own account of the campaign in an inscription which reads: "Hezekiah, the Jew, I shut up like a bird in a cage." Isaiah himself gives us a description of the siege of Jerusalem and how the city is summoned to surrender (chapter 36).

But King Hezekiah has the faith that Ahaz lacked, and therefore God saves the city "for his own sake and for the sake of his servant David" (2 Kgs 19:34). He "put a hook into Sennacherib's nose and a bridle between his lips, and caused him to return by the way by which he came" (Is 37:29). A remnant survives in Jerusalem, to strike root again and bear fruit under the pious King Josiah.

It is, however, only a brief respite for the kingdom of Judah during the period of Assyria's decline. When Nineveh falls into the hands of the Chaldeans in 612 B.C., their king, Nebuchadnezzar, takes over the conqueror's role. He set about recovering the territories Assyria has lost and soon invades Judah. In 597 B.C. Jerusalem surrenders for the first time, and the Babylonian exile begins. This ends only about sixty years later when Cyrus, the king of Persia, takes Babylon and gives the Jewish exiles permission to return to Jerusalem.

These events form the historical background of the Book of Isaiah. In reading it we should bear in mind that it represents a collection of various sermons and utterances of the prophet, arranged and edited by his disciples. Our present division into chapters and verses is, as in all of Holy Scripture, a later arrangement, which very often does not correspond to the content of the book.

Three main groupings of material can easily be distinguished. The first part, called "Book of Commination" (that is, threats), comprises prophecies that have mainly the struggle against Assyria as their historical background (chapters 1–35). The interlude that follows, describing the siege of Jerusalem by Sennacherib (chapters 36–39), is mostly taken from 2 Kings 18–20. The third part, called "Book of Consolation," refers to the Babylonian exile and to the return of the "remnant" to Jerusalem (chapters 40–66).[2]

The Way of Salvation

Isaiah sees these historical events in the light of revelation. The king of Assyria is to him the representative of that spirit of pride and self-glorification that, all through history, tries to organize human power against God and against his people.

> By the strength of my hand I have done it, and by my wisdom, for I have understanding. I have removed the boundaries of the peoples, and I have plundered their treasures. I brought down the inhabitants to the dust. My hand has seized like a nest the wealth of the peoples. And as one gathers eggs that are left, all the earth have I gathered, and there was none that moved a wing, or opened the mouth, or chirped.
>
> ISAIAH 10:13-14

The multitude of the Assyrian army is like another flood: "Behold the Lord is bringing upon them the waters of the river, mighty and many, even the king of Assyria and all his glory. And it shall rise above all its channels, and shall pass over its banks, and shall sweep on to Judah in an overwhelming flood, and shall reach as high as the neck" (8:7-8).

Jerusalem is like an island surrounded by a raging sea. "Ah, the surging of many peoples, that roar like the roaring of seas; and the surging of the nations that surge like the billowing of many waters. The nations may surge like the surging of many waters, but he will rebuke them, and they will flee far away. At eventide—lo, terror; before morning—it is gone" (17:12-14).

The people who are threatened by the Assyrian flood find themselves in the same situation as their fathers, caught hopelessly between Pharaoh and the deep sea. As the latter were warned by Moses, "Only keep still, and the Lord will fight for you" (Ex 14:14), so Isaiah exhorts his own generation: "It is through conversion and calmness that you will be saved. In silence and in confidence shall be your strength" (Is 30:15).

However, Jerusalem "spurns the waters of Shiloh that flow gently" (8:6), and when Ahaz hears that the first wave of invasion is surging against Jerusalem, "his heart and the heart of the people 'shake' as the trees of the forest shake before the wind" (7:2). At this fateful moment Isaiah goes to the king and warns him: "If you do not believe, you shall not subsist" (7:9). These words represent the very heart of Isaiah's message. Only faith can make the chosen people a firm rock in the swirling waters of the world. The substance of this faith is contained in these words:

> I, I am the Lord, and there is no saviour beside me.... When you pass through the waters I will be with you; and through the rivers, they shall not overwhelm you; when you walk through the fire you shall not be scorched, or through the flame, it will not burn you; for I the Lord am your God, I the Holy One of Israel am your Saviour.
>
> ISAIAH 43:11, 2-3

The Two Great Signs

The prophet himself is a living "sign" of this faith. His name, *Jeshajahu,* means "Saviour is the Lord alone." He has been sent by God to manifest to his people the two great "signs" upon which this faith in God the Saviour rests. One shines quietly like a star in the dark sky, high above the surging waves of the Assyrian flood: the virgin and the child Emmanuel. The other "sign" rises from the grave of the Babylonian exile as the sure hope of new life: the suffering servant.

The Virgin and Child

In sharp contrast to the brutal masculinity of the Assyrian kings—whose bearded statues with their martial look are a lasting memorial of a thing which is alive in every stage of human history, our own century not excluded—the mother and the child are by their very nature a beautiful sign of mercy, of love, and of the peace that the world is evidently unable to give. Let a soldier in his foxhole take a look at a picture of his wife and his little child, and all the tenderness of the human heart blossoms forth in him and makes the bloody, damnable business in which he sees himself engaged the more disgusting to him.

The sign of the mother and the child is a crushing verdict against the brutal methods with which mankind tries to solve its problems. In Isaiah's days it condemns the ruthless king Sennacherib, "shaking his fist at the mount of the daughter of Sion, the hill of Jerusalem" (10:32). The mother and the child will always be a sign that love is stronger than violence.

Isaiah's sign, however, is not only the mother but the virgin who will conceive and bring forth a son (7:14). The virgin-mother represents "salvation from God alone," because her child is not born of the will of the flesh nor the will of man but of God. "That which is conceived in her is of the Holy Spirit" (Mt 1:20). Her child, the Emmanuel—God with us—is "salvation from God alone." In him God and humanity meet in perfect harmony. He springs as a shoot from the root of Jesse, David's father, and the Spirit of God descends and rests upon him (11:1).

The names given to him show that he is God: Wonderful Counselor, God Almighty, Father of the age to come, Prince of Peace (9:6). The sevenfold fullness of the Spirit of God makes him a ruler who establishes the kingdom of God's descending love, where the poor and the needy enjoy peace, and where brutal force has lost its power, so that the calf and the young lion graze together and a little child leads them (11:6). It is evident that these prophecies of the Emmanuel find their fulfillment in the Son of God born of the virgin Mary, who is to be given the throne of his father David (Lk 1:32). The name he received from God explains his identity: Jesus—"the Lord is Saviour."

The Suffering Servant

At the time of the Assyrian flood Jerusalem is saved through the faith of Hezekiah, of the house of David. When about a hundred years later the Chaldeans invade the country, Jerusalem is taken, the temple is destroyed, and the king with the flower of the people is taken captive. This time the son of David, together with his people, has been swallowed up by "Leviathan" (Is 27:1).

On the dark backdrop of the Babylonian captivity another sign of faith in God the Saviour is shown by Isaiah: the suffering servant who dies and rises again. Like the virgin birth, the resurrection is a sign of "salvation from God alone," because God alone "brings down to the land of the dead and raises up again" (1 Sm 2:6).

When Isaiah is about to reveal this sign he cries out: "Who will believe what we have heard? And the arm of the Lord—to whom has it been revealed?" (53:1). That God's chosen one should be wounded for our transgressions and be crushed for our iniquities, that the Lord would burden him with the guilt of us all (53:5-6), is indeed nonsense to those who are on the way to destruction; but to those who are to be saved, it means all the power of God (1 Cor 1:18), because the vicarious sufferings of the servant end in the Resurrection. "The fruit of his suffering shall he see, and be satisfied" (53:11).

This prophecy may point to Jehoiachin, the last of the kings of the house of David, who languishes for years in the dungeons of Babylon, until he is released and "his throne is set above the throne of the kings who are with him in Babylon" (2 Kgs 25:28). It may point also to the deliverance of the people from the Babylonian captivity. This sign of the suffering servant is fulfilled only, however, in the Lamb of God who removes the world's sin (Jn 1:29), in Jesus Christ, who is pointed out by Philip as the One of whom the prophet spoke (Acts 8:34-35).

The whole aim and purpose of the incarnation, passion, and resurrection of the Messiah, described so vividly by the "evangelist of the Old Testament," is the new birth of Jerusalem, image of the Church. Isaiah's prophecy culminates in the description of her glory. For a small moment God has forsaken her, but with great compassion he will gather her. In a little wrath he hid his face from her for a moment, but with everlasting kindness he will have compassion on her and return to "the wife of his youth."

God will come to his city not like a conqueror, not like a judge, but as the bridegroom comes to the bride. "As a young man marries a maiden, so shall your builder marry you; and as a bridegroom rejoices over his bride, so shall your God rejoice over you" (62:5). Jerusalem, the barren one who has borne no children, will break into singing because God's grace bestows upon her the joys of motherhood (54:1). Her children will rejoice with their beloved mother. They will suck to their fill from the breasts of her consolation and drink deeply with delight of the abundance of her glory. Her sucklings shall be dandled on her knees. "Like one whom his mother comforts, so will I comfort you—through Jerusalem shall you be comforted" (66:12-13). It is the sun of God's charity which, in the end, breaks through all the clouds of wrath and justice and descends upon her as an unfailing light (60:19).

Make Way for the Lord

The visions Isaiah has seen over Judah and Jerusalem are the visions of all those whose eyes the Spirit of Christ has opened to see the signs of the times. That "the foundations of the earth tremble," that "the earth breaks asunder, reels like a drunkard and sways like a hammock," that "rebellion lies heavily upon it," that "joy has reached its eventide, and the mirth of the world has gone," is as true today as it was in Isaiah's time. The inhabitants of the earth have broken the everlasting covenant. Therefore a curse is devouring the earth, and its inhabitants are paying the penalty (24:1-20).

Go to war-torn areas, and you will see these people as Isaiah saw them in his day: "They pass through the land, hard pressed and hungry, and in their hunger they become mad with rage. They curse their king and their God, and look upon the heavens and down again to the earth, but lo! nought but distress and darkness, the gloom of anguish and impenetrable murk" (8:21-22). The unsuccessful attempts that the "well-meaning people" of our day make to cope with this situation, especially the interminable discussions between nations that are evidently not united, that speak of peace when they put their real trust in bombs, remind us of the words of Isaiah:

See! the Lord's arm is not too short to save, nor his ear too dull to hear; but your iniquities have been a barrier between you and your God, and your sins have hidden his face, so that he could not hear you. For your hands are stained with blood,... your lips have spoken lies. There is none who sues honestly, none who pleads his case truthfully, but each one trusts in vanities and speaks lies, conceives wrong and brings forth iniquity. Vipers' eggs they hatch, and spiders' webs they weave. He who eats of their eggs will die. Their webs are useless for clothing,... and deeds of violence are in their hands.... The way of peace they know not, and no justice is in their tracks....

We look for light, but lo! darkness; for the rays of dawn, but we walk in gloom. We grope like blind men along a wall, like men without eyes we grope. We stumble at noonday as in the twilight, in the strength of manhood we are like the dead. All of us growl like bears, and sadly moan like doves; we look for redress, but it comes not, for salvation, but it remains far from us.

ISAIAH 59:1-6, 8–11

There is only one way to see the light again rising over Jerusalem, and that is to break down the barrier between us and our God, to build the bridge of faith that Isaiah has preached, faith in God who through the incarnation and the resurrection of the Emmanuel proved to be our only Saviour. It is to clear the way of the Lord through penance, which raises up the valleys of guile and brings low the mountains of pride (40:3-4). It is to open the heavens with prayer: "Drop down dew, O heavens, from above, and let the clouds rain the just one, let the earth open her womb, and bring forth the saviour" (45:8).

If we do not believe, the world cannot subsist. If we do not open the road for God's coming, the light will not arise over Jerusalem. But those who "love his advent" (2 Tm 4:8) will not be afraid of the surging waves. They will remember Isaiah's word: "Take knowledge, you peoples afar; gird yourselves and be dumbfounded! Plan a plan—it shall come to nought! Speak a word—it shall not stand! For— Emmanuel (God with us)!" (8:9-10).

EIGHTEEN

The Prophecy of Jeremiah

During Holy Week the Church enters into a period devoted mainly to the commemoration of our Lord's blessed passion. She has appointed the prophet Jeremiah to be read during this time, because in his message he is the most ardent preacher of penance to his people, a fearless and scathing denouncer of their sin. In his life he is the most faithful picture of the suffering Christ that exists in the Old Testament.

The Book of Jeremiah is clearly divided into three main parts. The first part contains poems and addresses of the prophet (chapters 1–25). The second part is a report, probably written by Jeremiah's secretary Baruch, describing the activities of the prophet from the time of his famous temple address (609 B.C.) to the exile in Egypt (chapters 26–45). The third part is a collection of prophecies against foreign nations (chapters 46–51). Chapter 52 is a kind of historical appendix, quoted from 2 Kings, chapter 25.

To read Jeremiah is no easy matter and sometimes even a penance. The sadness and gloom poured out on page after page have a depressing effect. Moreover the book itself, resembling the time in which it was written, is evidently very much out of order and therefore apt to confuse the reader.

The best way to approach Jeremiah is to read first the Second Book of Kings, chapters 21–25. Here the historical background of Jeremiah's prophecies is described. After the northern kingdom of Samaria (Israel) has been annexed to the Assyrian Empire (722 B.C.), the southern kingdom, Judah, becomes an Assyrian vassal state. Under the kings Manasseh and Amon, Assyrian religious practices are officially encouraged.

However, when an unexpected new invader, the Scythians, appears on the scene, the star of Assyria began to decline. Coming from the north, the Scythians overrun the whole Mediterranean coast and even reach Egypt.

During this time the saintly Josiah is king of Jerusalem. The disintegration of Assyria gives him a breathing spell of independence, during which he tries to reform the life and worship of his people along the lines of Deuteronomy, the fifth book of Moses, which has been discovered in the temple in 621 B.C. In a vain attempt to stop the Egyptians who have come to the aid of the Assyrians, Josiah meets his death in 609 B.C. at Megiddo (see 2 Kgs 23:29-30; 2 Chr 35:20-25). The Egyptians make Josiah's son, Jehoiakim, their puppet king in Jerusalem.

The capture of Nineveh, capital of Assyria, by the allied Medes and Chaldeans in 612 B.C. leaves only two powers to contend for world domination, Egypt to the south and the so-called Neo-Babylonian Empire of the Chaldeans to the north. In 605 B.C., during the reign of Jehoiakim, the Egyptians are defeated by the Chaldeans under Nebuchadnezzar in the battle of Carchemish (see Jer 46). Judah is now at the mercy of the king of Babylon.

A True Prophet

Jeremiah receives his call to the prophetic ministry in 627 B.C., when Josiah is still reigning in Jerusalem. He is at that time a youth of twenty years of age, son of a priest who lived at Anathoth in the land of Benjamin (1:1). During the first period of his prophetic career he tries to call Israel to repentance. He begins by denouncing the apostasy of the people and inviting them to return to the Lord (2:1–4:4). Realizing that his invitation is going unheeded, he threatens them with punishment through the foe from the north, the Scythians (4:5–6:30).

When Josiah, in the course of his reform, abolishes the local sanctuaries and centers the worship of the nation on the temple in Jerusalem, Jeremiah leaves Anathoth and goes to the capital. There he realizes that Josiah's reform, ordered from above, has not changed the hearts of the people (8:8).

After the death of Josiah, in the beginning of the reign of Jehoiakim, Jeremiah enters into a new phase of his mission. He warns the people not to put their trust in external institutions. In his famous "temple address" (chapters 7 and 26) he denounces those who would rely on the temple as a pledge that all will be good. When Jeremiah foretells that the temple will be destroyed if the people do not amend their ways, the priests and the prophets lay hold of him, saying: "You shall die!" Centuries later Jesus is tried on the charge that he had spoken of the destruction of the temple (Mk 14:58).

Jeremiah goes a step further in his "pottery sermons." He sees a potter engaged in work on the wheels. Whenever the vessel at which he is working becomes marred, as clay is apt to do in the potter's hand, he turns it into another vessel, such as seemed suitable in the potter's eyes (18:3-4). Watching him, Jeremiah receives the word of the Lord: "Cannot I deal with you like this potter, O house of Israel? As the clay in the potter's hand, so are you in my hand, O house of Israel!" (18:6).

The conviction rises in Jeremiah's heart that only complete destruction, not only of the temple but of the nation, can bring about salvation. He goes to the entrance of the Potsherd Gate, and there, before the eyes of the elders and priests, he throws an earthen bottle on the refuse heap so that it breaks into pieces. "As the potter's vessel is broken and cannot be mended again, so will I break this people and this city!" (19:11).

From now on Jeremiah's way is clear. Convinced that "the sin of Judah is written with an iron pen, and is engraved with the point of a diamond on the tablet of their heart" (17:1), he announces God's irrevocable decision: "I have set my face against this city for evil and not for good. It shall be given into the hands of the king of Babylon, who shall burn it" (21:10). Jeremiah himself suffers agony under the burden of his mission: "Cursed be the day on which I was born! The day on which my mother bore me—let it not be blessed.... Why came I out of the womb, to see trouble and sorrow, that my days should be consumed with shame!" (20:14, 18; see 6:19-20).

The inner sufferings of the prophet are deepened by persecution from his enemies. King Jehoiakim burns the scroll containing Jeremiah's prophecies. The author and his scribe Baruch must go into hiding (chapter 36).

The word of the Lord, however, is fulfilled. Jehoiakim's rebellion against Nebuchadnezzar ends in the former's ignominious death (22:13-19). His successor, Jehoiachin (also called Coniah), is deported to Babylon, together with the best part of the population (13:18–19:24). This is the beginning of the Babylonian captivity (597 B.C.), which according to the prophecy of Jeremiah will last for seventy years (25:12; 29:10).

Nebuchadnezzar makes Zedekiah king of Judah. He is a weak man, who after much vascillating from one to the other finally sides with the false prophets of Israel's national glory (chapter 21 and 23:9-40) and rises against Nebuchadnezzar. This brings the Chaldeans to the gates of Jerusalem in the second siege of the city, in 588 B.C. The record of the siege is contained in chapters 21, 32–34, 37, and 38.

Jeremiah's struggle rises to its pitch. He reiterates his counsel to surrender and is thrown into a cistern as a defeatist. An Ethiopian eunuch rescues him.

When in July 586 the city falls, the king is taken captive and blinded. The city and the temple are burned to the ground (chapter 39). Jeremiah is treated with great respect by the conquerors and is allowed to go where he pleases.

Promise of a New Covenant

Jeremiah stays with the remnant of the people. The word of the Lord has been fulfilled. The earthen vessel was broken. The dawn of a new day seems to be rising.

Gedallah, a nobleman whose father and grandfather were friends of Jeremiah, is made governor. Chapters 30–31, and 39–44 record the history of this period. They contain some of the most beautiful and most consoling of Jeremiah's prophecies. He sees in the spirit the age of a new covenant approaching.

Gazing at the long train of refugees leaving the ruins of the city to find a new home, he exclaims: "The people that escaped from the sword shall find grace in the wilderness. When Israel goes to seek rest, the Lord from afar shall appear to him. With an everlasting love have I loved you, therefore with affection will I draw you to me. Again I will build you, and you shall be built, O virgin Israel" (31:2-4).

In Ramah, where the scattered groups of refugees gather in great sadness, like Rachel weeping for her children (31:15), Jeremiah hears the voice of the Lord: "Restrain your voice from weeping, and your eyes from tears, for your labor shall have its reward. Is Ephraim my precious son? Is he my darling child? For as often as I speak of him I cherish his memory still. Therefore my heart yearns for him, I must have pity on him" (31:16, 20). Then follows the solemn pronouncement, and a landmark in the history of salvation, that after the old law has shown its impotence in the ill-fated reform of Josiah, and after the walls of the Holy City have been broken, and the temple has been burned to the ground, a new covenant will be made:

> Not like the covenant which I made with their fathers on the day that I took them by the hand to lead them out of the land of Egypt—that covenant of mine which they broke, so that I had to reject them—but this is the covenant which I will make with

the house of Israel after those days: I will put the law within them and will write it on their hearts, for I will pardon their guilt and their sin will I remember no more.

JEREMIAH 31:31-34

This prophecy, the climax in the prophetic career of Jeremiah, is not fulfilled in his days. Gedallah is killed by fanatics (chapters 40 and 41). In fear of the wrath of Nebuchadnezzar, the hapless remnant of the Jews flee into Egypt, again despite the warnings of Jeremiah (chapter 42). In a pathetic last appeal the prophet tries to prevent them from sacrificing to the "queen of heaven" (chapter 44). Their answer shows that the whole work of Jeremiah has been in vain. Their religion still was a "prosperity religion," a means to obtain earthly security:

As to the word that you have spoken to us in the name of the Lord, we will not listen to you. But we will certainly perform every word that is gone forth out of our own mouth, by offering sacrifices to the queen of heaven, and by pouring libations to her, as we did, both we and our fathers, our kings and our princes, in the cities of Judah and in the streets of Jerusalem. For then we had plenty to eat and were well and met with no trouble; but since we gave up offering sacrifices to the queen of heaven and pouring libations to her, we have been destitute of all things, and have been consumed by sword and famine.

JEREMIAH 44:16-18

The chalice of Jeremiah is filled to the brim. According to a very probable tradition, his countrymen stone him to death. It is the death of a true martyr, an unflinching witness to the word of God.

Shortly after, the last of Jeremiah's prophecies is fulfilled: Egypt falls into the hands of Nebuchadnezzar. The heartrending tragedy of Jewish national pride, fighting in vain against the word of God—which is so clearly the word of the cross—has drawn to its close:

> O Jerusalem, Jerusalem! murdering the prophets and stoning those who are sent to you, how often have I longed to gather your children around me, as a hen gathers her brood under her wings, and you refused! Behold, now your house is left desolate!
> MATTHEW 23:37-38

Wholly God's

If we ask what the Book of Jeremiah means to us today, we hear very often that Jeremiah initiates a new period in Old Testament piety that frees the individual from the bonds of community life, that he is the first to record faithfully his innermost religious feelings, and that he is one of the great fighters in the battle for liberty of the spirit against the tyranny of dead ceremonials. Looked at in this light Jeremiah would automatically become one of the "great liberals," and that would mean one of us.

In reality Jeremiah is wholly God's. God takes possession of him before he is born (1:5). During his life the word of God is his one and overwhelming passion. Abraham receives the promise; Jacob, the blessing; Moses, the staff. David is anointed. Isaiah has his lips cleansed with burning coal. Ezekiel has to eat the scroll. As for Jeremiah, the Lord stretches forth his hand and touches his mouth, saying: "I am with you, I put my words into your mouth. This day I give you authority over the nations and kingdoms, to root and pull down, to wreck and to ruin, to build and to plant" (1:9-10).

It is the Emmanuel (God with us), the God of the Word made flesh, who takes possession of Jeremiah. In no other prophet is the union between the prophet's heart and the word of God as intimate and as deep as in Jeremiah. The word is his strength and his cross. It makes him, a youth of twenty years and by nature a timid man, a "fortified city, an iron pillar, and a bronze wall against the whole land" (1:18).

"The word of the Lord," he exclaims, "is in my heart like a burning fire, shut up in my bones. I weary myself to hold it in, but cannot" (20:9). "As for me," he cries out, "your word is my joy and my delight, for I bear your name, Lord, Lord of hosts!" (15:16). He never mixes the word of God with purely human dreams and desires, as the false prophets do (23:16). The word of God in his mouth is "like a hammer that smashes the rock into pieces" (23:29).

The words of the Letter to the Hebrews must be applied to Jeremiah's preaching: "For the message of God is a living and active force, sharper than any double-edged sword, piercing through soul and spirit, and joints and marrow, and keen in judging the thoughts and purposes of the mind" (4:12).

Jeremiah's message is judgment. He does not say what people like to hear. "An awful and appalling thing has happened in the land! The prophets prophesy falsely, and the priests make profit through them; and my people love to have it so. But what will you do when the end comes?" (5:31).

Jeremiah knows the human heart: "Deep beyond sounding is the heart, and sick beyond cure, who can know it?" (17:9). Mercilessly he denounces its main sickness, adultery and pride:

> When I had fed them to the full they committed adultery, and assembled themselves in troops at the harlots' houses. They were as fed horses roaming at large, everyone neighed after his neighbor's wife. Shall I not visit for these things, and be avenged upon such a nation as this?
>
> JEREMIAH 5:7-9

Hear and give ear and be not proud, for the Lord has spoken. Give the Lord, your God, the glory, ere it grow dark; before your feet stumble in darkening mountains, and you wait for light, but darkness is there, and he turns it into gloom. In secret my soul shall weep because of your pride, and my eyes run down with tears, for the Lord's flock is led captive.

JEREMIAH 13:15-17

Death and chaos are fruits of sin, and nobody has described them as vividly as Jeremiah:

I looked at the earth, and lo! it was chaos; at the heavens, and their light was gone. I looked at the mountains, and lo! they were quaking; and all the hills swayed to and fro. I looked, and lo! there was no man, and all the birds of the air had flown. I looked, and lo! the garden land was desert, and all its cities were sacked before the Lord, before his fierce anger.

JEREMIAH 4:23-26

The Innocent Lamb

If Jeremiah is of great importance to us as a trumpet of divine judgment calling to repentance and conversion, he is still closer to us as an image of the Suffering Servant, who redeems us through his death and resurrection. His words, "I was like an innocent lamb, that is led to the slaughter" (11:19), are, in the mind of the Church, the key to understanding the prophet's life and mission. There can be no doubt that this expression alludes to the paschal lamb that the Israelites offered and ate the night of their deliverance.

The paschal lamb is a symbol of the chosen people and of their destiny. It shows that the price God asks for their deliverance is their willingness to live as a "priestly nation," ready to serve God in his work of salvation. The Promised Land is given to them not as a political domain but as an altar upon which to offer themselves in obedience to God's will. As the symbol of this readiness, a lamb is offered in the temple every morning and every evening.

Jeremiah clearly understands and accepts his mission as the innocent lamb. His advice to surrender to the king of Babylon is not the fruit of considerations, nor is it the result of discouragement and defeatism. His motive is exclusively religious. He accepts the chalice of God's punishment. He is willing to suffer for the sins of the people, he who was sanctified in his mother's womb and who was always faithful to God's word. For the same reason it is he, the only one in Israel who has kept himself free from the general spirit of apostasy, who longingly sings, "O that I had in the desert a wayfarer's lodge! For fain would I leave my people, and go clean away!" (9:2). It is he who stays with his people to the bitter end. He foreshadows the Lamb of God, who empties himself to take upon himself our sins.

Exposed to the persecutions of his enemies, treated as a public criminal, put into the stocks, thrown into the pit, Jeremiah nevertheless again and again prefigures the Resurrection. After a day he is released from the stocks. An Ethiopian eunuch saves him from the pit, indicating that, when the time is fulfilled, the gospel will pass from the Jews to the gentiles. Shortly after the destruction of Jerusalem he buys a field (chapter 32) to show that he believes in the future of the Promised Land and its people. The destruction of the walls of Jerusalem indicates to him the extension of the kingdom of God's love over the hearts of all mankind in the new covenant (chapter 32). He is the "prophet of the gentiles," like St. Paul, with whom he has so much in common.

It is for this reason that the Book of Jeremiah ends with the little chapter about Jehoiachin, who is released from prison and reinstalled to his royal dignity (chapter 52). Modern critics think that this appendix is "of little importance to the whole." Such a verdict only goes to show that they have not understood the meaning of the whole book, which aims to point out that God's everlasting love (31:3) exalts the "son of David" who has humbled himself. Jeremiah is not the "man of tears" of popular conception. He is the great fighter for freedom of the heart under God, and therefore his book closes with a "resurrection."

The Lamentations

Jeremiah's message would scarcely be complete without the Lamentations. Here the acid, bitter denunciation that prevails in his prophecies is changed into the freely flowing tears of motherly sorrow and compassion. Jeremiah is not only the innocent lamb led to the slaughter; he is also the mother who weeps over her children. To make him a real "mediator," both hearts had to be in him: the burning heart of the Saviour and the sorrowful heart of the mother, pierced by the sword of compassion.

The Lamentations are sung during the Vigils of Holy Thursday, Good Friday, and Holy Saturday. They are the voice of mother Church. The groups of verses are adapted to the day for which they are chosen.

In the Lamentations of Holy Thursday, the day of reconciliation of the penitents, the accent is on repentance. The verses culminate in a moving confession: "The Lord has delivered me into a hand out of which I am not able to rise." Only the hand of the Saviour is able to lift up Jerusalem from the dust. On Good Friday the Lamentations express the idea that the death of the Man of Sorrows is the real destruction of Jerusalem.

On Holy Saturday the Lamentations cease to be exclusively songs of sorrow. The light of hope arises. "The mercies of the Lord are new every morning." We see that Jeremiah's tears are not those of the sorrow for the world, which works death, but of the sorrow that is according to God, which works repentance (see 2 Cor 7:10).

May this sorrow become ours. May we follow the invitation that, in this most critical hour, God's everlasting love extends to us through the mouth of Jeremiah: "Jerusalem, Jerusalem, be converted to the Lord your God!"

NINETEEN

The Prophecy of Ezekiel

Among all the prophets of judgment, penance, conversion, and hope, Ezekiel certainly is the most dramatic and the most picturesque. His whole prophecy is distinguished by a peculiar combination of word and symbolic action. In fact, the two are so closely knit together that in reading this book we cannot help thinking of the Word of God, which has been made flesh in order to redeem us, not only by its message but by its saving action on the cross.

That Ezekiel is indeed a type of Christ is evident from his very name, which means "God strengthens" or "power of God." The name of his father was Buzi, the "despised one" or "the lowly one." The son of the "lowly one" who becomes "power of God" has the divine mission to make it clear to the chosen people that their complete political annihilation, the destruction of their temple and of their city, and their present lowly state in exile are God's way of working in them a new beginning in the power of the Spirit. Thus Ezekiel is inspired to predict the coming of Christ, the despised one, who through the destruction of the temple of his body on Golgotha becomes the strong one, the Lord and head of a new generation.

Not without reason is Ezekiel the only prophet whom God consistently addresses as "son of man" or "son of Adam." He is indeed the spiritual father of a new generation, which he sees cleansed by the clean water of the Spirit of God, endowed with a new heart and a new spirit (36:25-27). He sees the new Israel rising out of the graveyard of the old (chapter 37), gathered around the shepherd David in an everlasting covenant of peace (37:24). He sees the new temple and the new country (chapters 40–48), watered by the ever deepening river of the Spirit of God (chapter 47). Ezekiel represents the new Israel, which rises like a new man out of the tomb of the exile. He is the head of a new creation. For this reason he shares with Christ the title "son of Adam."

The entire prophetic message that Ezekiel preaches to his people and to the whole of mankind is contained in the sublime vision of the glory of God with which the book opens (chapter 1). The fact that Ezekiel sees the glory of God far away from Jerusalem at the River Chebar shows that the holy presence is not bound to the temple, that God is with his people, and that he will be to them a "little sanctuary in the countries wherever they are scattered" (11:16).

The storm in which the vision draws near symbolizes the power of God's wrath and of his judgment, which the prophet reveals in the first (chapters 4–24) and second parts (chapters 25–32) of his prophecy. The cloud with the fire is the *shekinah,* the symbol of God's merciful presence among the people of the covenant. The chariot with the four living beings and the four wheels is the symbol of God's absolute dominion over the whole universe. In antiquity "four" always signifies the entirety of the visible world in its four directions. The wheels with eyes, moving wherever the Spirit directs them, indicate the omnipresence and omniscience of almighty God, whose providence directs the course of human history.

The four faces of the living beings have given rise to various explanations, the most widely known being the application to the four evangelists. The fact that different writers see them in various ways shows, however, that such explanations move on rather shaky ground. The four living beings, or *cherubim,* guard and support the glory.

The form of a man, which appears in the center of the inaccessible light, has been interpreted as a prophetic allusion to the mystery of the Incarnation. The rainbow that surrounds the likeness of a man on the throne (1:28) is the sign of peace between God and his creation (Gn 9:13). In Christian art this vision has become the standard representation of the gloriously reigning Lord *(Kyrios)*.

It is indeed the mystery of the Easter Christ that Ezekiel, son of Buzi, sees in the country of the heathen. His *Yahweh Adonai*—the name he uses for God throughout his prophecy and which means God as the one who in judgment manifests his love—is none other than the risen Saviour, who will come on the clouds of heaven to judge the living and the dead.

Prophet of the Exile

Ezekiel is the son of a priest and therefore belongs to the aristocracy, which, together with King Jehoiachin, is deported into exile after Jerusalem surrenders to the Babylonians in 597 B.C. He is always the "prophet of the exile." This gives him great importance for the Jews living in the dispersion, as it does for us Christians who are "refugees" as long as we live on this earth.

Ezekiel reveals to his fellow exiles the divine meaning of the calamity which has befallen them. Like Jeremiah, he warns them not to think of it in terms of power politics, nor to plan a political revolution to recover their national independence by physical force. Any such attempt would focus the attention of the people on material things and thus only prevent them from realizing the spiritual cause of their defeat, their sins.

To wake the people up to the gravity of their sins is the first and fundamental task of the prophet, which Ezekiel discharges in the first part of his book (chapters 4–24). The glory of God has not been expelled from the temple of Jerusalem by the Babylonian army; it was forced to leave the sanctuary because of the abominations through which Israel had desecrated it (chapters 8–11). In chapter after chapter Ezekiel unfolds the dark picture of Israel's sins as a mirror in which his contemporaries should contemplate their true selves. Ruthlessly he exposes the false prophets, who prophesy "out of their own heart" (chapter 13). With an indignation that only love is able to inspire, he upbraids Jerusalem as God's faithless wife (chapter 16). All these accusations and threats of punishment serve only the one purpose of leading the people to repentance. God does not want the death of sinners, but that they be converted and live. Ezekiel does not address himself only to the people as a whole. He realizes that penance and conversion are first of all the work of the individual. Every single soul is God's, and God judges it according to its deserts. No one, therefore, may hide his personal responsibility behind the shield of the community. God, who through his judgment manifests his love, turns to each man personally when he says, "Be converted and live" (18:32). Ezekiel is the first spiritual director in Israel.

In keeping with his name of "son of man," Ezekiel directs his message of judgment, punishment, and repentance not only to the house of Israel but to all nations. The second part of his book contains his prophecies over the gentiles (chapters 25–32). The defeat of Israel is by no means a triumph of heathen gods. As the nations are only instruments through which God judges his people, so they in turn will be judged by the God of Israel.

We would, however, completely misunderstand the true spirit of Ezekiel if we considered these prophecies as the outpourings of a nationalistic "spirit of revenge." The same Yahweh Adonai who "desires not the death of the sinner, but that he should be converted from his ways and live" (18:23) is also the judge of the nations. It is only a reflection of the spirit of mercy and compassion of his God that we find in the dirges of the prophet over the defeated nations (see chapters 27 and 32). As the judgment over Jerusalem is like a fire that destroys everything unclean and in the end restores the city to her original purity (chapter 24), so God's judgment over the gentiles is not for their utter destruction but for their "return to their ancient state" (16:55), when they will know that the God of Israel is also their God (28:26).

Prophet of Hope

To this positive part of his message Ezekiel turns in chapters 33–48, the last and most important section of the book. Chapter 33 forms the transition. The prophet tells of the day when a fugitive from Jerusalem arrives with the news, "The city is smitten" (33:21). In vain has Ezekiel preached against any attempt to restore by force the political independence of Judah before a real and decisive conversion has given the Jewish nation a "new heart." King Zedekiah, who has been installed in Jerusalem by Nebuchadnezzar as Jehoiachin's successor, rises against the Babylonian occupation. Nebuchadnezzar takes Jerusalem by storm, puts Zedekiah to death, and destroys the temple and the city.

Ezekiel's prophecies of doom have been fulfilled. The kingdom is destroyed. The people are deprived of any political power. Now the new age of the spirit can begin.

Ezekiel becomes a prophet of hope. Chapter 33 repeats his demand for conversion as the fundamental condition of any spiritual revival. In the following chapters, however, he develops the picture of Israel's rebirth. It begins with God's setting up the messianic shepherd (chapter 34), who feeds his flock "on fat pastures upon the mountains of Israel" (34:14). This exaltation of Mount Zion means judgment over Mount Seir, or Edom, the kingdom of this world (chapter 35).

In a solemn oath God pledges himself to change the heart of the house of Israel through a baptism of the Spirit, a prophecy that clearly points to the sacrament of baptism as the initiation into the new covenant (36:25-27). The vision of the dry bones in the following chapter shows that the rebirth of Israel is the work of the Spirit of God.

It should be noted that each of these beautiful chapters ends with a universal outlook, all the nations taking part in the spiritual renewal of Israel (36:37-38; 37:28).

This universal aspect of the history of salvation is explicitly developed in the two chapters on God's judgment upon Gog. The name *Gog* means "firm roof" or "gable." Gog, leader of the last universal onslaught against God and his people, represents that part of mankind that wants to protect and secure itself because it lives in enmity with the rest of the world and does not trust in God and his grace.

The people of God, on the contrary, live in "tabernacles,"—that is, huts, which are built with little effort and do not offer security. Huts are the dwellings of people who trust their neighbors and have no intention of fighting with them, because they know that God covers them with his pinions (Ps 91:4). The Israelite people lived in huts when God was their shield and their protection on their journey through the desert. They celebrated, year after year, the Feast of the Tabernacles as an expression of the joyful peace that they found in their trust in God.

Against them Gog plans "on that day" a mischievous scheme, saying: "I will march against this land of open villages; I will fall upon this quiet people who live in security, all of them undefended by wall or bar or gates" (38:11; compare Rv 20:8). "That day," however, "all hedges and walls fall to the ground" (38:20) through the power of God, and the history of mankind will end with the celebration, "by all that are left of all the nations," of the Feast of the Tabernacles (Zec 14:16).

Thus will be fulfilled the prophecy that stands at the very beginning of world history, that "Japheth will dwell in the tabernacles of Shem" (Gn 9:27). *Shem* means "name." Those who dwell in the tabernacles of Shem are those who know the name of God. "And they shall know that I am Yahweh Adonai" is the burden of Ezekiel's prophecy.

The Law of the House

After revealing the power that will bring about the rebirth of Israel and depicting the struggles that will accompany it, the prophet turns to a description of the new community (chapters 40–48). St. Jerome, the first among the fathers of the Church to explain these difficult chapters, calls them "a labyrinth of mysteries." It is certain that the various details, such as the ground plan and the measurements of the temple and the partition of the country, represent "teachings" or norms of spiritual perfection. God reveals the true form of the house (temple) to the house of Israel through the prophet, "that they may be ashamed of their iniquities" (43:10).

Unable to penetrate the maze of details in this short introduction, we have to be satisfied with the understanding of the fundamental "law of the house," which is revealed by the prophet in 43:12: "This is the law of the house: upon the top of the mountain the whole country! Round about in every direction is the holy of holies!" The law of the old Israel was, "They have set their thresholds next to my threshold, and their posts next to my posts, and there was a wall between me and them" (43:8). This separation of profane and holy will be abolished in the new Israel. There the whole life of man will be brought up to the level of the holy mountain, and the Holy of Holies will be really worthy of its name, because it will consecrate the entire universe.

The name "Holy of Holies" does not mean "a very small place set apart to be absolutely holy" but "center of holiness radiating sanctity in every direction." Ever since the veil that separated the Holy of Holies from the outside world was rent at the death of Christ, the architecture of Christian churches has reflected this new principle by admitting the entire congregation into the immediate presence of Christ in the celebration of the holy Eucharist. The full realization of this principle, however, will only take place in the New Jerusalem, in which there is no temple, "for the Lord God almighty and the Lamb are its temple" (Rv 21:22).

This fundamental "law of the house" is indicated everywhere in the picture that Ezekiel gives us of the new Israel. There is no strict line of demarcation between temple and city and country. The city is only an extension of the temple, the country only an extension of the city; both, city as well as country, are watered by the river that issues from under the threshold of the temple (47:1).

This river immediately turns toward the east, which in the symbolic language of the Old Testament stands for a practical realization in life of the divine commandments. Rather than drying up, the river becomes deeper and deeper the farther it moves from its source, until finally no man is able to cross it except by swimming (47:3-5). Unfortunately the Vulgate translation of 47:5 does not render accurately the Hebrew term for "waters in which you have to swim." The Hebrew word for "to swim" also means "to prostrate oneself" (where there is firm ground); the fundamental meaning of the root is "to surrender completely with your whole being."

In our days, when the earth is covered by the flood of salvation that issued from the heart of Jesus when it was pierced by the soldier's lance, we should not try to stand on our own feet. We should throw ourselves into the water and trust that it will bear us up. To swim means really to believe. True faith in God assures his presence. It takes the place of the country and forms the foundation on which is built the city whose name is "The Lord is there" (48:35). This, the last word of his prophecy, shows that the prophet of the exile has found his home.

TWENTY

The Prophecy of Daniel

Ezekiel is sent to the children of the house of Israel to show them the divine meaning of their defeat and exile. His words and visions make it clear that the destruction of the temple and the dispersion of the chosen people are not only God's way of bringing about the spiritual rebirth of Israel but also of preparing for the conversion of the nations to the one true God. The exile of Israel is intended to pave the way for the homecoming of the gentiles. The Jews are to carry the light of the true faith into the darkness of the pagan world.

The prophet who discharges this task of giving testimony of the majesty of the God of Israel to the heathen is Daniel. He comes to Babylon when he is a child of four. Remaining absolutely loyal to the faith of his fathers, he nevertheless enters into intimate contact with the life and the civilization of that great empire. He becomes an official at the court of Nebuchadnezzar and his successors. In the palace of the king he witnesses to the majesty of his God as the true ruler of the universe.

The Book of Daniel is divided into two main parts: a "historical" section (chapters 1–6) recording five episodes from the life of Daniel that show the power of Yahweh over the king of Babylon, and a "prophetic" part (chapters 7–12) containing four visions that reveal the superiority of God over the empires of the world. Two additional stories, that of Susanna (13:1-64) and that of Bel and the Dragon (14:1-42), are added; they should be inserted after chapters two and six respectively.

The fact that the book is written partly in Hebrew and partly in

Chaldean indicates its supernational character, which becomes still more evident when we examine the contents of the prophecy. The book is not concerned with the fate of the chosen people, of Jerusalem, and of the temple but with the fate of the gentile nations. Daniel emphasizes the universality of the messianic kingdom. He sees the "stone cut without hands"—Christ born of the virgin Mary—smashes the statue of the king and becomes a "great mountain which fills the whole earth"—the universal Church (chapter 2).

A similar idea is expressed in the vision of the four empires (chapter 7). This vision culminates in the coming of the "son of man," who does not rise out of the sea, as the empires do, but descends from above on the clouds of heaven (7:13). A little further on this "son of man" is identified with "the people of the saints of the Most High," indicating that the Messiah and his people are one, as head and body form one individual (7:18, 27).

According to the interpretation of most of the Fathers, this vision also defines the time of the coming of Christ in world history. The first empire is usually considered to be the Assyro-Babylonian empire, which was conquered in 538 B.C. by Cyrus, the founder of the Medo-Persian empire. This empire in turn succumbed to the Greco-Macedonian empire of Alexander the Great in 331 B.C. The empire of Alexander, after his sudden death in 323, disintegrated into various rival kingdoms, until Rome took over the entire east. Rome is, therefore, the fourth empire of Daniel's vision, the one that sees the beginning of the kingdom of Christ.

The famous prophecy of the seventy weeks seems to determine the coming of the Messiah with still greater accuracy. The archangel Gabriel reveals to Daniel the true meaning of Jeremiah's prophecy that the captivity of the people would last seventy years (Jer 25:11-12). The seventy years, he says, stand for seventy weeks of years—that is, 490 years. This period is the final fourth of Jewish history, reaching from the building of the second temple to the advent of Christ, whose coming is announced to Mary by Gabriel (Lk 1:26).

The character of Daniel as "prophet of the gentiles" probably accounts for his popularity among the gentile Christians of the early Church. The walls of the catacombs are covered with Daniel. Susanna is represented, standing between two wolves. She is the symbol of the Church and of the soul before its judge. The wolves are the elders, the unbelieving Jews and gentiles. The garden is this world. The bath points to baptism. The two maids are faith and charity. Young Daniel stands for Christ, the deliverer.

Likewise the story of the three youths in the fiery furnace (3:1-24) was popular among the Christians of old, because they saw in them a likeness of themselves. Reborn in baptism, these Christians moved unharmed and free, in the presence of Christ (the angel), joyfully glorifying God amid the flames of the furnace of this world.

How often do we see in these works of art Daniel standing in the lions' den, with his hands uplifted in prayer! The pit represents "the world yonder"; the lions, the enemy spirits. Daniel is the departed soul, saved through prayer in the name of Christ. Sometimes Habakkuk brings the bread of holy viaticum (see 14:33-39).

Daniel in the lions' den is also a prophecy of Christ, his passion, and his resurrection. In Lent it refers to the faithful Christian, who through fasting and penitential works takes upon himself Christ's sufferings and is strengthened through the holy Eucharist. In turn he will one day share in the Resurrection.

Thus Daniel is in every way a representative of the new generation that grew up in the Exile. He points to that other new generation that has been born through Christ's death and resurrection. Unimpressed by the pomp of the world in which they live, they turn their backs to the kings and the empires and go up to the altar of Christ, who is the joy of their youth.

TWENTY-ONE

The Minor Prophets

The name "minor prophets," first used by St. Augustine, does not suggest that these twelve books are of minor importance, but only that they are much shorter than the "major prophets," Isaiah, Jeremiah, Ezekiel, and Daniel. In the third century B.C., when their number was complete, the scribes put them all on one scroll or "volume," in an order that probably was intended to be chronological. Thus originated the "book of the twelve," as the minor prophets are called in the Jewish Bible.

The book covers the whole prophetic era, a period of approximately five hundred years. Hosea, Amos, and Micah are contemporaries of Isaiah in the latter half of the eighth century, when Assyria starts on her career of conquest and destroys the kingdom of Israel with its capital, Samaria (722 B.C.). Nahum, Habakkuk, and Zephaniah live in the days of Jeremiah, in the second half of the seventh century B.C., in the course of which Assyria succumbs to the rising power of the new Babylonian Empire, whose king, Nebuchadnezzar, then conquers Judah and razes Jerusalem (586 B.C.). Haggai, Zechariah, and Malachi prophesy after the Babylonian captivity, at the end of the sixth century and the beginning of the fifth. Of the lives and times of Joel and Obadiah nothing definite is known.

Although the reason for their being grouped together is a technical one, the twelve nevertheless display an inner unity. Their number reminds us of the other twelve who accompany the Lord as his apostles. The "apostle" is the herald who is sent to announce the coming of the king. "He is at hand! Get ready to receive him!" is the message of the apostle.

It is also the message of the twelve of the Old Testament. Each of them announces in his own way the coming of the "Day of the Lord." They do so at a time when the power of great pagan empires seems to eclipse completely the glory of the God of Israel.

The five hundred years of the prophetic era are for the chosen people years of almost unbroken calamity and repeated defeat. The Jews lose their political independence and their home country and are deported into the "desert" of the gentile world. During this time the twelve stand like columns, upholding the roof of God's mercy over his people among the ruins with which human violence fills the stage of history.

Insofar as the word *prophet* is associated with the idea of foretelling the future, it is not an adequate rendering of the Hebrew *nabi*. The latter denotes a man who is like a spring out of which the word of God wells up as clear water, unadulterated by human "dreams." Coming from the depth of the heart of God, the word of the prophet penetrates through the surface of life and time to confront the listening soul with the eternal reality of the living God, who is ever ready to judge the sinner and to forgive those who repent. Listening to the message of the prophets we should, therefore, heed the warning that every day, at the beginning of vigils, resounds in our ears, "Today when you hear his voice, do not harden your hearts" (Ps 95:7-8).

Amos

Following the order of the Vulgate, the minor prophets start with Hosea; Joel follows; then Amos, Obadiah, and Jonah. For a proper understanding of their message, however, it is important to know that Amos and Hosea are closely connected with one another.

Amos precedes Hosea, preaching in the northern kingdom at the time of great material prosperity, while Hosea witnesses the downfall of Israel. Amos is taken by God "from behind the flock" (7:15). He is not a priest nor a professional prophet but a sheep farmer, a man of the people, in the poor and backward south of Palestine.

When Amos goes into the kingdom of Israel to announce its impending doom, he acts under an absolute inner necessity—"When the Lord God speaks, who will not prophesy?" (3:8). True to his name—"carrier of burdens"—Amos takes the heavy duty of God's stern justice and throws its crushing weight upon the responsible leaders of the people: priests, princes, and king. With supreme courage he denounces the sins of society:

- The oppression of the poor: "They have sold the innocent for silver, and the needy for a pair of shoes. They trample the head of the poor into the dust of the earth, and thrust aside the humble from the way" (2:6-7).
- The sensuality and worldliness of the ruling classes: "Hear this word, you cows of Bashan," he addresses the society ladies of Samaria, "who say to their men: 'Bring that we may drink!' The Lord God has sworn by his holiness, that there are days coming upon you when they will drag away what is left of you with fish hooks, and cast you on the refuse heap" (4:1-2; see 6:1-7).
- The hypocrisy of the state-licensed cult at the official sanctuaries: "Come to the Bethel, and transgress! Make pilgrimages to Gilgal, and multiply your sins!" (4:4).

In this state Israel has lost all privileges of a chosen people. The "Day of the Lord," which they expect to be a day of national triumph, will in reality be "darkness and not light, blackness with no brightness in it" (5:20). There is only one way to escape the approaching catastrophe: "Hate evil and love good, and establish justice at the gate; perhaps the Lord will be gracious" (5:15). This "perhaps the Lord will be gracious" is the meaning of the name John, given later to the Baptist, who is rightly called the Amos of the New Testament.

Amos is a trumpet of judgment, sent to wake up those who in care-less self-confidence dance into their ruin: "Woe to them that are at ease in Zion!" (6:1). Only a few years after his missionary journey through Israel, the catastrophe he announced takes place. After the death of Jeroboam II, Assyria invades the country, destroys Samaria, and deports the population. Israel literally vanishes from the earth.

Hosea

It is significant that the prophet who actually witnesses the downfall of the northern kingdom is called Hosea, which means "salvation," and that his message is one of pardoning love and of hope. In the midst of the dark clouds of God's wrath appears the glowing heart of divine love.

Hosea sees God as "the great lover," whose secret he discovers in his own heart as in a mirror (chapters 1–3). The love of the bridegroom for his bride and the love of the father for his son are the flowers of love in the heart of a man; in both Hosea is deeply disappointed, for his wife is unfaithful, and his son disobedient. His love, however, is too deep to be extinguished. It bends down to the harlot and is kindled in compassion for the prodigal son.

This personal experience reveals to him the secret of God's heart: It is too deep to be given to wrath forever. The denunciation of Israel's faithlessness is, therefore, followed by the solemn promise: "And I will betroth you to myself forever; I will betroth you to myself in right-eousness and justice, in love and compassion. And I will betroth you to myself in truth" (2:19-20).

God's complaint over the disobedience of his son ends in his mov-ing confession: "How can I give you up, Ephraim? How can I hand you over, Israel? My heart is turned within me, my compassion is kindled like a blaze. I will not carry out my fierce anger, nor will I again destroy Ephraim. For I am God and not man, the Holy One in the midst of you, and I will not destroy" (11:8-9).

These words represent a climax in the self-revelation of God in the Old Testament. The difference between God and man is not seen so much in terms of power and perfection; selfless *love (agape)*, which triumphs over wrath, is the essence of God. Hosea anticipates St. John's famous sentence, which is the very core of Christian revelation: "God is love" (1 Jn 4:8).

The revelation of his love through Hosea is God's answer to the state-supported "harlotry" of Israel with the *baalim*, the gods of vitality, fertility, and procreation. They are the lords of luck and prosperity (see 2:5). Their name, *baalim*, means violent, despotic masters; their image is the bull; their cult frequently consists in the offering of human sacrifices. This all shows that wherever earthly love dominates, the glory of God is changed into the image of a beast and man is degraded into slaves. Hosea stigmatizes the folly of the devotees of the *baalim* with the trenchant word, "They kill men and kiss bulls" (13:2).

In order to free the people from the worship of the gods of prosperity, God will strip Israel of all earthly power and lead her into the desert of the Exile to speak to her heart (2:14). This experience will renew in the hearts of the people the true love of God. Israel will call God "my husband" and not "my master" *(baal)* (2:16). Thus "the valley of desolation will become a door of hope" (2:15).

The course of history shows, however, that the Exile is not the final "baptism" that turns the wrath of God into love and gives a new heart to God's people. God's wrath is overcome only when the Father sends the Son of his love into the valley of the Passion to redeem those against whom his wrath is kindled. Hosea's message is fulfilled in Jesus.

Joel and Obadiah

Between Hosea and Amos the prophet Joel has been inserted. The name means "Yahweh is God." After an urgent call to repentance occasioned by a terrible invasion of locusts (1:2–2:7), his prophecy culminates in the proclamation of Yahweh's universal rule as God through the outpouring of his spirit over all flesh (2:18-32) and its consummation at the Last Judgment in the "valley of decision" (chapter 3).

The vivid and classical style of the book had a great influence on the writings of the New Testament, especially on St. Matthew and on the Book of Revelation. Joel, however, is known to us first of all as the prophet of Pentecost, whose word of the outpouring of the Spirit over all flesh St. Peter saw fulfilled when "a mighty wind filled the whole house where the apostles were sitting" (Acts 2:2).

The prophecy of Obadiah, which consists of only twenty-one verses, is the shortest book in the Old Testament. It is directed against the Edomites, the descendants of Jacob's brother Esau. These people are closely akin to the Israelites, but the two nations hate one another with the hatred of brothers.

The history of the chosen people is essentially prophetic. Peoples and countries involved in it represent spiritual principles. The significance of the Edomites is evident from the character of their ancestor Esau and from the country in which they live. From Esau, who was a "profane person" (Heb 12:16), the Edomites inherit the absence of a religious sensibility, the cruelty of the hunter, and a wisdom that—through its lack of faith, humility, and obedience—has become entirely worldly.

The Edomites live in the mountains of Seir, "the finest rock scenery in the world," perching high on inaccessible rocks, lying in wait to make their forays into the country of their brother-nation. Thus they become a symbol of the intellectual pride (v. 3) that leads the apostate to hate his former brothers.

The fathers of the Church applied Obadiah's prophecy to the heretic—the intellectual hunter who is unable to do constructive work in his father's house, lives on occasional spoils of truth, and watches for an opportunity to thrust the sword of his hatred into some weak spot of the Church he has deserted. We see the hatred of Edom living on in such apostates of modern times as the Nazis and Communists. God will continue what he has done in past centuries and is still doing in recent history. He will "bring them down" (v. 4) and "destroy the wise men out of Edom, and the understanding out of Mount Esau" (v. 8). The fire of faith burning on Mount Zion will burn the stubble of Edom (v. 18).

Jonah

The harsh judgment of apostasy is followed by a message of hope through repentance for the heathen who have never come in contact with the true faith. Jonah's prophecy shows that God's will to save is not limited to the chosen people but extends to the vast masses of heathen nations. The name Jonah means "dove," reminding us of the messenger of reconciliation that brought the olive branch to Noah at the end of the Flood. The way in which this reconciliation of the gentiles will come about is indicated in the "sign of Jonah." As his experience with the whale makes Jonah a preacher of repentance to Nineveh, so her exile, her being swallowed up in the belly of the pagan world, makes Israel a light of revelation for the heathen. Only in Jesus Christ, however, is the sign of Jonah fulfilled, because through his death and resurrection the whole world receives the Spirit of Pentecost (see Mt 12:39-41; 16:4).

Micah, Zephaniah, Nahum, and Habakkuk

Micah is, as St. Jerome says, the "heart" of the twelve, not only because he holds the center place but because of his message. A poor peasant, he bitterly denounces the two capital cities, Jerusalem and Samaria, for the ruling classes' maladministration of justice and their exploitation of the poor. The punishment for Israel's pride will be her utter humiliation.

But humiliation will be, at the same time, the cradle where the messianic king is born. The one "whose origins are from eternity" will come forth from Bethlehem, the smallest among the townships of Judah (5:2-3). Like a good shepherd, "he will gather together the lame and assemble the outcast and make them a chosen remnant" (4:6-7). He will teach them "the heart of the law": "Only to do justice, and to love kindness, and to walk humbly with their God" (6:8). God, who "delights in kindness," will "tread down their iniquities, and will cast into the depth of the sea all their sins" (7:19).

Zephaniah completes Micah's prophecy that the humility of the Messiah will transform the justice of God into love. Zephaniah means "one who knows the mastery of God." The great secret Zephaniah reveals is that for the "last day" the Lord "has prepared a victim, and has sanctified his guests" (1:7). He will "deliver the lame and gather the outcast" (3:19) and "renew them in his love" (3:17). "A people humble and poor" (3:12) will be called from all over the earth; "from beyond the rivers of Ethiopia to the farthest regions of the north they shall bring offerings to God" (3:10). The sacrifice of the cross and its eucharistic memorial are prophesied by the man "who knows the mystery of God."

In the order of the Scriptures, Nahum and Habakkuk separate Micah and Zephaniah. Nahum describes, in a style which for vividness and force has no parallel in the Old Testament, the sack of Nineveh, capital of Assyria (612 B.C.). The lion of Assyria perishes, true to the law of his origin, in an orgy of carnage and destruction. "Crack of whip—rumbling wheels—neighing horses—rattling chariots—charging horsemen—flashing sword and glittering spear—mass of slain, and no end of corpses!" (3:2-3). Over the ruins of earthly power rises the greater glory of God, who is "good to those that wait for him, a stronghold in the day of trouble, but with an overwhelming flood he will sweep away his adversaries" (1:7-8).

Habakkuk is the "prophet of faith." Out of the depth of doubt he cries: "How long, O Lord, must I cry for help, and you not hear? Call out to you 'Violence!' and you not save?" (1:2). His faith gives the answer: "Are you not from the beginning, O Lord, God, my Holy One? We shall not die!" (1:12).

Faith is the life of the soul: "The just man lives through faith" (2:4). St. Paul makes this sentence the keystone of his preaching (see Rom 1:17; Gal 3:11; Heb 10:38). He sees that Habakkuk's faith looks forward to its fulfillment in the risen Christ, whose glory the prophet sees in the magnificent psalm of chapter 3. Its end sums up the essence of faith in the beautiful words: "Though the fig tree flourish not, and there be no cattle in the stalls: yet will I exult in the Lord. I will rejoice in God my Saviour. The Lord God is my strength, and he makes my feet like the feet of harts. He leads me upon the high ways singing psalms" (3:17-19).

Haggai and Zechariah

Haggai and Zechariah are both among those who return to the Holy Land when the Babylonian exile ends with the edict of Cyrus. It is their mission to assure the people that the messianic promises, which seem to have been revoked when the "signs" of the temple and the house of David were destroyed, still hold.

Haggai prophesies that the future glory of the humble second temple will be greater than that of the first (2:9), as indeed it will be when the Son of God is brought to the temple on the arms of his mother (Lk 2:22). Haggai also foresees the restoration of the house of David in Zerubbabel, a prince of that house who acts as governor in Jerusalem. The prophetic expectation, however, that sees him as the seal ring on God's right hand (2:23; see Jer 22:24) is fulfilled only in his Son, Jesus Christ (Mt 1:13).

Zechariah is the prophet of the holy city, the symbol of the Church. The two parts of his book—the first of visions (1:7–6:15), the second of sermons (7:1–14:21)—both set forth the spirit of the New Jerusalem. God will be "a wall of fire round about her, and he will be splendor within her" (2:5). Her head will be the Messiah, the branch (3:8; 6:12), in whom the priestly and the kingly powers are united.

The priestly function of the Messiah is represented in the high priest Joshua (Jesus), who takes off the filthy clothes, the sins of the people, and receives the stone bearing the inscription: "I will remove the guilt of the land in one day" (chapter 3). The royal dignity of the Messiah is symbolized in the lamp and the olive tree and the keystone, which are brought in with jubilant shouts of "Grace, grace to it!" (chapter 4).

The motto of the messianic king is "Not by arms, not by force, but by my spirit, says the Lord of hosts" (4:6). He comes to his city "humble, and riding upon an ass" (9:9). For thirty pieces of silver, the price of a slave, he will be sold (11:12). The shepherd will be smitten, and his sheep will be scattered (13:7); but then the inhabitants of Jerusalem will receive the spirit of grace and of prayer, and "they shall look upon him whom they have pierced, and they shall mourn for him as one mourns for an only child" (12:10).

On that day a fountain will be opened to the inhabitants of Jerusalem for the cleansing of sin and uncleanness (13:1), and the house of Israel, which has been a curse among the nations, will become a blessing (8:13). Then, after the last great messianic trials (14:12-15), the rest of the nations will come up to Jerusalem to adore the King, the Lord of Hosts, and to keep the Feast of Tabernacles, the symbol of messianic peace and security (14:16).

Malachi

The last of the twelve is Malachi, whom the Jews rightly call "the seal of the prophets." He is indeed a résumé of all that the prophets have taught. At the same time, as his name ("the angel") indicates, he is the herald who precedes the coming of the Lord. "And suddenly to his temple shall come the Lord whom you are seeking, and the messenger of the covenant in whom you delight. Behold he comes, says the Lord of hosts" (3:1).

Like the other prophets, Malachi inveighs against the sins of the people, especially mixed marriages (2:11) and the lethargy of the priests (2:2). Angered by the externalism of the liturgy, he hears the voice of the Lord calling for an end to the Old Testament sacrifices: "O that there were one among you that would close the doors (of the temple), that you might not kindle fire on my altar in vain. I have no pleasure in you, and I will accept no offering from your hand" (1:10). But then his eyes are turned to a new and pure oblation: "From the rising of the sun even to its setting, my name is great among the nations; and in every place an offering is made, is presented to my name, a pure offering. For my name is great among the nations" (1:11).

Malachi looks forward to the new messianic era and its abundance of grace: "See if I will not open for you the windows of heaven and pour out for you a blessing that there shall not be room enough to receive" (3:10). That is the day when "the sun of justice will arise, with healing in its wings" (4:2). The twelfth of the twelve lifts his finger and points to the thirteenth who is about to come.

If we piece together the messages of the twelve, a complete picture of the "Day of the Lord" emerges. The justice of God (Amos) will be transformed into love (Hosea) through the humility of the messianic king (Micah and Zechariah), who will be offered as a victim, that through his sacrificial love he might renew the lame and the outcast (Zephaniah), who then will present a pure oblation to God all over the world (Malachi).

The Spirit of the Lord will be poured out over all flesh (Joel). He will cause the just to live in faith of the risen Christ (Habukkuk); he will destroy the rebellious wisdom of apostasy (Obadiah) and the brutal power of the prince of this world (Nahum), but he will save those who repent (Jonah). Thus the messianic promise will be fulfilled, the temple restored, the Son of David reenthroned (Haggai), the holy city (the Church) rebuilt, and its inhabitants filled with joy and peace (Zechariah).

Comparing the message of the twelve with its fulfillment in the Church and with the state of the world, it becomes evident that "we have the message of the prophets surer still. And we do well, therefore, to attend to it, as to a lamp shining in a dark place, until the day dawns and the morning star rises in our hearts" (1 Pt 1:19).

TWENTY-TWO

The Gospel According to St. Mark

One of the most impressive ceremonies of the Roman Lenten liturgy was the solemn handing over of the gospel to the catechumens; this was called *aperitio atiruim* or "opening of the ears." It took place on the Wednesday after the fourth Sunday in Lent, in the church of the great "teacher of the gentiles," St.-Paul-Outside-the-Walls.

After the chanters had sung the last words of the gradual, "Through the word of the Lord the heavens have been established, and all their host through the breath of his mouth," a solemn procession moved from the sacristy to the main altar. Four deacons, preceded by acolytes with candles and incense, each carried a gospel book, which they placed on the four corners of the altar. In a short address the presiding priest explained the general meaning of the Gospels. Thereupon the beginning of each of the Gospels was sung in turn by the deacons. These were interpreted briefly by the priest in the light of the famous vision of Ezekiel, in which the prophet saw the divine chariot with the four living creatures, which had "the face of a man and the face of a lion on the right side, and the face of an ox and the face of an eagle on the left side" (Ez 1:10).

Modern scholars may not put much store in the ancient thought of the Church, which interprets the four "living beings" as referring to the four evangelists. But what a deep sense of the *mystery* of the Gospels is revealed in this ceremony and this interpretation! The four Gospels on the four corners of the altar are the sacramental image of the four living beings who carry between them the throne of the Divine Presence. For they are indeed "living beings" who bear aloft through time and space the Word of God made man. All this is not poetic fancy but shows the very essence of the gospel, of that *god spell,* those "glad tidings" that proclaim the presence, in the midst of men, of the saving power of the risen Lord and his kingdom.

It is not the task of the apostles to give a dry record of facts about the "historical Jesus." They are "witnesses of the resurrection" (Acts 1:22). They are sent to announce that this Jesus of Nazareth who has been killed is the Lord, through whom all who believe might receive forgiveness of sins (Acts 10:38-43). This message is the "gospel" (1 Cor 15:11), as yet a single thing, the "gospel of the glory of Christ, who is the image of God" (2 Cor 4:4; see 1 Tim 1:11), the "good tidings of the unfathomable riches of Christ" (Eph 3:8), and "of peace to those who were afar off, and of peace to those who were near" (Eph 2:17).

The apostles who preach this gospel to the world act as "ambassadors for Christ" (2 Cor 5:20). Christ is present in them and speaks through them, as St. Paul says: "Out of God, before God, in Christ we speak" (2 Cor 2:17). Therefore, wherever the gospel is preached, Christ is present as the Lord who is establishing his kingdom. The gospel *is* Christ, according to the beautiful word of St. Ignatius of Antioch: "I take refuge in the gospel as in the body of Jesus."[1]

Sacred Messages

There can be no doubt that our present Gospels grew out of the apostolic preaching. They share its character as effective proclamations of the kingdom of Christ among men and perpetuate, as it were, its spiritual reality and power. As Christ himself is present in the preaching of the apostles, so it is he who speaks in the Gospels to the Church.

Christian writers of the first and second century quote the Old Testament with the words "It is written," but quotations from the Gospels are introduced by "The Lord says."[2] The Christian traveler Hegesippus, writing in the middle of the second century, summarizes his impressions of the various churches by saying that every bishop does things "as the law demands, and the prophets, and the Lord," evidently referring to the Gospels. The very fact that they do not bear the title "Life in Christ, written by ..." but "The Holy Gospel of Jesus (as the) Christ, according to ..." shows that they are not considered biographies but rather saving messages. They are "holy" because they contain "the Holy One of God" and have been written "in the power of the Lord, and of our God, Jesus Christ," as the Syriac version of the first Gospel says.

A crucial difficulty concerning the sacredness of the Gospels arises from the fact that "many took in hand to set forth in order a narrative of things that have been accomplished among us" (Lk 1:1). We still know the titles of about fifty of those "gospels," but the texts of only twenty are extant. Many of these are heretical, composed by men who, according to St. Jerome, "without the Spirit and grace of God attempted rather to weave a tale than to compile historical truth."

In order, therefore, that we may be sure that this Gospel ... was really dictated by the Holy Spirit, there must needs be the declaration and definition of the Church, which severs it from apocryphal writings, and pronounces it canonical.... Not because the authority of the Church is worthier, or of more weight than that of Holy Scripture—for Scripture is the word and the oracle of God himself—but because ... the Church has the Seal of God, even the Spirit himself, who was promised, and has been given to her, that he may abide with her forever. The Spirit recognizes his own handwriting. He it was who first dictated these four Gospels. And now he makes known to us, by the Church, that he did indite them.[3]

Toward the end of the second century the four Gospels—according to Matthew, Mark, Luke, and John—were universally recognized as canonical. St. Irenaeus[4] was the first to explain why there are precisely four Gospels, neither more nor less. This is not, he says, a matter of chance but of divine order, just as there are four points of the compass, four winds, four living beings with four faces in Ezekiel's vision of the divine chariot.

In the latter Irenaeus sees first of all a symbol of Christ himself, who has the face of a man because he was born of Mary the Virgin; the face of a bull because he died on the cross (the bull being the primary sacrificial animal of the Old Testament temple ritual); the face of a lion because he rose from the dead as the strong one; and the face of an eagle because he ascended to the right hand of the Father. The four mysteries of the Nativity, the Passion, the Resurrection, and the Ascension reflect the whole fullness of Christ—as man, as priest, as king, as God. It is exactly this fullness that is represented in the four Gospels.

One and the same Christ certainly is contained in the four Gospels, but each one emphasizes one of these fundamental aspects. St. Matthew begins his Gospel with the human genealogy of Christ, and throughout his book he stresses the teacher who showed mankind the way of life. St. Luke starts with the report of the sacrifice of Zechariah, the priest, in the temple. He focuses his narrative on the sacrificial love of Christ, the Lamb of God. St. John, "the disciple whom Jesus loved," who, lying upon the Lord's bosom, drank of the pure waters of mystical knowledge, soars aloft like an eagle from earth to heaven, beginning his Gospel with the sublime prologue that reveals the divine nature of the Word made flesh. John reduces the number of facts reported to a minimum, while he dwells at length on those aspects of the teaching of Christ that concern the inner life of the triune God and our union with him. St. Mark, the evangelist whose message we will explain more in detail on these pages, centers his Gospel around the mystery of Jesus as the Messiah-King.

Son of Peter

The tradition of the early Church attributes the second Gospel to John Mark of Jerusalem. His mother Mary occupied a fairly large house there (Acts 12:12), which was probably the scene of the Last Supper and of the descent of the Holy Spirit at Pentecost. To this house St. Peter turned his steps when released from prison.

Because Mark was a close relative of Barnabas (Col 4:10), it was natural that he should accompany Barnabas and Paul on their first missionary journey, in order to serve the two apostles (Acts 15:37). However, Paul was not satisfied with Mark (Acts 15:39). He refused to accept him as a companion on another voyage to Asia Minor, and Mark consequently sailed with Barnabas to Cyprus (Acts 15:40). A reconciliation with St. Paul took place later in Rome, where Mark found the latter a prisoner (Phlm 24).

More closely than to St. Paul, Mark was bound to St. Peter, who spoke of him as his son (1 Pt 5:13). One of the oldest and most trustworthy of Christian traditions (Papias, Clement, Irenaeus, Tertullian, Origen) represents Mark as St. Peter's secretary or interpreter and as the author of a collection of memoirs that gives the substance of

St. Peter's teaching and is our second Gospel.

In contrast to St. Matthew, who starts his Gospel with the human genealogy of Christ, "the son of David, the son of Abraham," and to St. Luke, who explains in his short preface that he intends to "write in order" the facts which he has most diligently obtained, St. Mark's Gospel keeps most faithfully the original character of the glad tidings of Christ as the Son of God and the Messiah. He writes not as a historian but as a preacher, recording faithfully what he has heard from St. Peter. In fact, St. Peter's address to the Roman colonel Cornelius (Acts 10:34-43) contains the outlines of St. Mark's Gospel.

This begins with "the baptism which John preached" and how "God anointed Jesus of Nazareth with the Holy Spirit, and with power" (Mk 1:1-13; Acts 10:37-38). The first main section describes Christ's ministry in Galilee (1:14–9:50), the "word which began in Galilee, about Jesus of Nazareth, who went about doing good, and healing all that were oppressed by the devil, for God was with him" (Acts 10:37-38). A brief survey (10:1–13:37) deals with "the things that he did in the land of the Jews (Judaea) and in Jerusalem" (Acts 10:39) and leads up to the second main section of the Gospel, which tells us how "they killed him, hanging him upon a tree," and how "God raised him up the third day, and gave him to be made manifest" (Acts 10:39-40; Mk 14:1–16:20).

The fact that St. Mark's narrative of the Lord's passion and resurrection is on a scale out of all proportion with the rest of the book indicates clearly that in the intention of the evangelist the person of the suffering and glorified Lord is the core and center of the glad tidings. Here is the key to the "mystery of the kingdom of God," which his Gospel proclaims. We need only read the first chapter of St. Mark's Gospel to realize that the mystery of the kingdom is the cross of the king.

This first chapter contains the "beginnings" of the entire Gospel.

The activity of the precursor is the "beginning" of Christ's work of salvation. As Christ reveals the mystery of the kingdom in his word and in his work, so does John preach repentance and administer baptism (1:2-8). Because the kingdom of God will not come in power and glory but in the self-sacrificing charity of the Son of God, only those can enter into it who "repent" or, better, "change their hearts" from the selfishness of the flesh to the selflessness of the Spirit.

The rite of baptism, through which the whole man is immersed in water and then rises, as it were, to a new life, foreshadows the work of salvation of the Messiah Jesus, who will be swallowed up in the waters of death to rise in the fullness of the Spirit. Rightly, therefore, does Christ begin his public life as Messiah by having himself baptized by John. He who never knew sin and does not need repentance has himself been made into sin for us, so that in him we might be turned into the holiness of God (see 2 Cor 5:21). His death is like another flood, drowning all that is earthly in man (see 1 Pt 3:21).

When he "comes up out of the water" (1:10), foreshadowing his resurrection, he is like another Noah, the favorite son of God (see Gn 6:8). Like Noah he receives the dove (Gn 8:9), the likeness of the Holy Spirit who descends upon this new Son of David (see Is 11:2; Ps 2:7; Is 42:1) to drive him like a captive into the desert (1:12-13). There he is "with the wild beasts." Exposed to the attack of the enemy, he remains victorious, so that after forty days and forty nights, which are symbolic of the "old age," the angels come and minister to him as the Lord of the new age. Through humiliation to exaltation, that is the way of the Messiah Jesus, who in his life repeats and fulfills the march of the chosen people from Egypt, through the Red Sea, into the desert, and ultimately to the Promised Land.

The Lord's Authority

Christ's baptism and his temptation are the "beginning" of the whole work of redemption. The rest of the first chapter gives the "beginnings" of the Lord's ministry in Galilee. The first beginning is the Word (1:14-21). Christ does not preach like the prophets, pointing into a distant future. With his coming the time is fulfilled. He announces the *presence* of God's kingdom. Teaching as one who has power (1:22), he demands faith in his gospel.

His call elicits immediate obedience (1:18) in the hearts of his first apostles, whom he makes "fishers of men" (1:17) to indicate that the days have come when God will send many fishers (Jer 16:16) to stand along the banks of the messianic torrent, in which there will be fish in abundance (Ez 47:10). In the light of this "beginning" we may go through the entire Gospel to see how Christ's teaching, far from being a systematic exposition of philosophical or theological truths, always leads his listeners into the presence of the kingdom of God, confronting them with judgment and salvation. Take, for instance, the parables of the kingdom in chapter four.

In his initial teaching Christ has set forth by word and exhibited by deed the kingdom of God, which he has come to give to all believers. He has shown his power over the demons (1:21-28). He has healed sickness (1:29-45). He has forgiven sins (2:1-17). He has announced openly that he is the Bridegroom who has come to celebrate the messianic wedding feast, that the new covenant has come (2:18-22), that he is the "Lord of the sabbath" (2:23-28; 3:1-6).

In the face of growing hostility he has set apart the twelve as the nucleus of the new Israel (3:7-19), which will develop as "God's family" (3:20-35). The children of the heavenly Father are brothers and sisters of Christ, because they do the will of the Father as Christ did it by drinking the chalice of the passion (14:36). The mystery of the kingdom cannot be revealed more clearly. The twelve have accepted it. The leaders of the people have rejected it (3:6). They tell the people that Christ's teaching and his actions are of satanic origin (3:22).

Consequently Jesus can preach the kingdom to the public only in parables (chapter 4), so that those to whom God has given ears to hear might enter into its mystery, and those who have not will not be able to touch it. The three parables of the sower (4:1-9), the growth (4:26-29), and the seed (4:30-32) constitute in their succession a perfect initiation into the mystery of the kingdom: It comes in the word; it is received in the heart; it grows through the Spirit; it fills the earth.

Closely connected with the words of Christ are his works. The Son of Man works on the Sabbath (1:21, 30). The Pharisees are scandalized, but what can they answer when he asks them: "Is it lawful to save life on the sabbath day?" (3:4). He himself is the Sabbath, the day of salvation. The six days of creation have come to an end, as it were. The Saviour begins his work, omnipotence is fulfilled by charity.

Two things Christ does on the first Sabbath in Capernaum: He drives out the unclean spirit (1:23-27), and he heals St. Peter's mother-in-law, going to her, lifting her up, taking her by the hand (1:31)—the good, loving, self-sacrificing physician of the poor! He conquers the demon with his power; he cures the sick woman with his charity. These are the two kinds of works he repeats again and again during his public life, between his childhood and his passion, which the Fathers used to call "the divinely ordained time of the miracles" (*kairos thaumaton*).

Conquering and healing are also the two basic aspects of Christ's chief work: his passing through death into life. From his pierced side water and blood flow into the chalice of the Church as a divine medicine to cure a sick world. In the power of God he rises as victorious king over death and Satan. Moved by the same compassion with which he gives his life on the cross for the remittance of our sins, he heals sick bodies, for the sake not of the body but of the soul. And the greatest of his miracles is the transformation of man through forgiveness of sins (2:10).

In the same power in which he will rise from the dead, he deals with the unclean spirits. Even in our days, in pagan countries, diabolical possession is a very common phenomenon, and magicians try to break the power of the evil spirits. But Christ does not act like a magician. The way he drives out the unclean spirits is so totally different from the long and complicated exorcisms the Jewish rabbis used to apply against them that the audience is amazed: "This man commands the unclean spirits, and they obey him" (1:27).

It is evident that Jesus acts as one in authority, and not as one who has concocted some recipe which he hopes will be effective. It is he himself, and not the formula, that has the power. But here we must add immediately: Christ also shows clearly that his power is not *his* power. He never takes on the role of a miracle worker wanting to build up his reputation. During his earthly life his power remains a "secret" (1:44). Whatever the Lord does, he does in prayer (1:35) as the Son, and as the Son of God made man.

Signs of the Mystery

The miracles of Christ are "signs," but not in the sense in which the Pharisees ask for a "sign from heaven," which causes the Lord, "sighing deeply in the spirit, to say: 'Why does this generation seek a sign? Amen, I say to you, a sign will not be given to this generation'" (8:12). Indeed, no sign will be given that will confirm their worldly ideas of a political kingdom. No sign will be given that can destroy the mystery of the kingdom of God. But to anybody with eyes to see, the miracles of Christ are signs pointing to the mystery of the Messiah Jesus. The four outstanding miracles that St. Mark reports in 4:36–5:43 show this clearly.

The stilling of the storm (4:36-40) reveals the power the risen Lord has to restore nature, which through the fall of Adam "has been made subject to vanity" (Rom 8:20). The storm is part of this "vanity." Therefore the Second Adam, rising out of his sleep on the low bench in the stern of the ship—where he has put down his head, weary, faint from hunger and exhaustion (4:38)—rising as it were out of his tomb, rebukes the wind, the symbol of the power of evil. He says "Peace" to the waves, the figure of the redeemed, as he will say "Peace" to his apostles and to his Church on Easter morning.

The healing of the demoniac of Gerasa (5:1-20) is a "sign" of the redemption of the pagan world through Christ. The region of Gerasa is pagan country and does not belong to the Holy Land. Pagan humanity, represented by the demoniac, is subject not only to one but to a legion of evil spirits. The Holy Spirit makes of those redeemed one heart and one soul, but the confusion of an incoherent multitude is the fate of those who rebel against God (see Gn 11:9).

The Saviour suffers the legion to enter into a herd of swine, which are "carried with great violence headlong into the sea" (5:13). What a weird scene, when we think of the Lord touching the shore of Gerasa late in the evening, when the moon is shedding her pale light over the cemetery where the wild demoniac lives like an animal among the tombs! What a picture of the world without God! With Christ, judgment enters into this world. The Spirit triumphs over the flesh. Indeed, the next morning finds the one who has been troubled with the "legion" clothed and mentally well, sitting peacefully at the feet of his Saviour like a neophyte (5:15).

The raising of the daughter of Jairus from the dead has always been understood by the Fathers as a "sign" of the final redemption of the Jewish people. The name of her father is mentioned by the evangelist because it is significant. *Jair* means "The Lord enlightens." In the heart of Jairus the light of faith in the resurrection has been kindled. While those who do not have this faith are put out of the room, Christ takes him and his wife, together with Peter, James, and John, to become witnesses of his power over death (5:40-41).

The whole material universe, the pagan world, and the Jewish people will all be restored to life and peace by the risen Saviour. On the way to his final victory, the conversion of the Jews, Christ meets the woman with the issue of blood. She is a touching picture of the Church as she walks now, after the first coming of Christ and before his final advent, in faith following her Saviour, touching his garment, symbol of the sacraments, through which she is healed because she believes (5:25-34).

Our Lord's public ministry was limited mainly to three regions: Galilee west of Lake Genesareth, the region of the Ten Towns (Decapolis) east of Lake Genesareth, and Judaea in the south. Each time his ministry in a district is brought to a close by a supper, a festive entertainment on his part. The first of these suppers is the feeding of the five thousand in Galilee, where his Jewish guests want to proclaim him Messiah-King (6:34-46). His ministry in the preponderantly gentile Decapolis closes with the provision for the four thousand, where Christ as the "Son of Man" gives food to those gentile multitudes who have been with him for three days (8:1-9).

Both these feasts lead up to the Last Supper, which marks the end of his ministry in Judaea (14:12-26). There Christ ends the divinely appointed time of the miracles and, as priest and sacrifice, feeds his own with the bread of life and the chalice of salvation, his own Body and Blood.

TWENTY-THREE

The Gospel According to St. Luke

In order to describe the inspiration of Holy Scripture, we usually compare the action of the Holy Spirit upon the human author with that of an artist using tools to produce a piece of art. It has to be understood, however, that the inspired writer is not a lifeless, mechanical instrument in the hand of God. The Holy Spirit, far from doing violence to the human author, lifts him up from within—illumining his mind, moving his will—because he is "all-powerful, all-comprehending, penetrating every spirit" (Wis 7:23). He does not suppress the personal characteristics of the writer but uses them to bring to light more clearly those aspects of divine revelation that correspond to his personality. This general law of inspiration is especially evident in St. Luke, the author of the third gospel.

When St. Luke sets out to write, he does not seem to be conscious of any direct influence of the Holy Spirit. "Forasmuch as many have taken in hand to set forth in order a narration of the things that have been fulfilled among us ... it seemed good to me also to put the story in writing for you exactly as it happened, having first traced it carefully from its beginnings" (1:1-3). Here speaks a man who is a historian by nature, eager to get to the facts and to present them with precision.

Although he is not an eyewitness of the events he relates, St. Luke has ample opportunity to get firsthand information. As he remarks himself (1:3), he has been a Christian "from the very first," probably one of the Greeks received into the Church at Antioch (Acts 11:20). Around the year A.D. 50 he joins St. Paul at Troas (Acts 16:8). Six years later he accompanies the apostle on his journey from Philippi to

Jerusalem (Acts 20:6). This is about twenty years after the death of Christ, when many of the eyewitnesses are still alive. St. Luke evidently owes much information to the women who belonged to the immediate company of the Lord (8:2-3). It is very probable that the Mother of Christ, who at this time would be in her seventies, is one of those with whom he has intimate contact.

As a faithful disciple of St. Paul, St. Luke shows us Christ as the Saviour of the entire human race, whom the Holy Spirit of God's love has sent "to preach the gospel to the poor, to heal the brokenhearted, to preach deliverance to the captives, and recovering of sight to the blind" (4:18). Nature has prepared St. Luke for this task, as a gentile and as a physician. As a gentile he is one of those who must be satisfied with the crumbs that fall from the table of the chosen people, one of the laborers called at the eleventh hour but who for this very reason has a special mission "to glorify God for his mercy" (Rom 15:9).

As a physician St. Luke is accustomed to the sight of human ills. He is familiar with the misery of man, and evidently his whole heart turns in compassion to those who suffer. We get an impression of his goodness from St. Paul's reference to him as "Luke, the well-beloved physician" (Col 4:14). We see it also in his Gospel: He is the friend of the poor, of the sinners, of the weak, of the women and the children. To all of them he becomes "the herald of Christ's meekness."[1]

Children of the Promise

St. Luke traces the gospel story, as he promises in the short preface (1:1-4), from its very beginnings. He starts with the narrative of the infancy of Christ, to which he adds that of St. John the Baptist because he wants to show that the lives of both serve one and the same divine plan. It is the mystery that from the beginning of the world has been hidden in God but now enters into history and is manifested to us as

God sends his only begotten Son into the world, that we might live through him.

Therefore an angel is sent to the parents of St. John (1:5-25) as well as to the Virgin Mother of the Messiah (1:26-38) as a messenger of God's great counsel. He comes to announce to them and to all mankind that the births and the lives of these two children are not just another episode in the vast pattern of human history but its very center, where all the threads of Divine Providence meet. The name of the angel is Gabriel, the same who once was sent to Daniel (Dn 9:24) to indicate to him the time when the Messiah would come: "Seventy weeks are determined upon your people and upon your holy city, to finish the transgression and to make an end of sins and to make reconciliation for iniquity, and to bring in everlasting justice, and to seal up the vision and prophecy, and to anoint the most Holy."

The new apparitions of Gabriel means that the seventieth week has come, that the acceptable time of the Lord has arrived. The angel is sent to a barren couple and to a virgin, because the two children that will be born are not "children of the flesh, but of the promise" (Rom 9:8), like Isaac (Gn 17), like Jacob (Gn 25:21), like Samuel (1 Sm 1:2). The births of the Saviour and of the forerunner do not depend on the will of man, but on the Holy Spirit.

Consequently their names are not chosen by men according to considerations of the flesh (1:61), but they are given by God (1:13, 31) to indicate the new order of divine grace beginning with these two children. John *(Johanan)* means "the Lord has mercy." Jesus is the Greek form of the Hebrew *Joshua,* or "the Lord saves," a name carried first by the victorious leader who conquered the Promised Land (Jos 1:1-3) and then appeared at the end of the exile as the name of the high priest who led the "remnant" of the people back to Jerusalem (Zec 3:1; Ezra 2:2).

The One who now bears this name is both king and priest. He is king because "the Lord God shall give to him the throne of his father

David" (1:32), and priest because "he shall save his people from their sins" (Mt 1:21). In Jesus-Joshua everything has been fulfilled that had been foreshadowed in the Old Testament, for he is the "Son of the Most High" (1:32).

God manifested himself to the chosen people under the name Yahweh (Ex 3:14; 6:3). When the term "Most High" occurs in the Old Testament, it signifies God as the Lord of all mankind, of Jews and gentiles alike (see Dt 31:8). Melchizedek, the king of Salem, is "priest of the Most High" (Gn 14:18). Jesus, born as son of Mary "by the power of the Most High" (1:35), is the true Melchizedek who will unite Jews and gentiles into one new Israel. His disciples are not Jews anymore and not gentiles, but "children of the Most High" (6:35), because with Christ begins the new priesthood "according to the order of Melchizedek" (Heb 5:10; 6:20). Zechariah, who represents the old priesthood of Aaron (1:5), is silenced, while the Virgin speaks the word that opens the gates of salvation to all mankind: "Behold the handmaid of the Lord. Be it done to me according to your word" (1:38).

The Annunciation is followed by the visitation (1:39-56). The Holy Spirit of God's love that has descended upon Mary urges her to serve. The higher goes to the lower; the Lord visits his prophet. As so often in the history of salvation, where not nature but grace is at work, the younger one is the greater one (see Gn 25:23; 48:14), and the elder serves the younger. Nothing could be more contrary to the spirit of selfless love than the proud motto: "I shall not serve" (Jer 2:20). The Holy Spirit, who fills her child, moves Elizabeth to greet the mother of Jesus as the "mother of my Lord" (1:43). Mary immediately refers the homage to the true source of all grace: *My soul doth magnify the Lord* (1:46-55).

The Four Songs

It is certainly not by mere coincidence that the entire Gospel of St. Luke is filled with the spirit of prayer and of glorification of God. As a faithful disciple of St. Paul, he knows that "the abundant grace should through the thanksgiving of many redound to the glory of God" (2 Cor 4:15). Again and again he shows what a central place prayer held in the life of our Lord (3:21; 5:16; 6:12; 9:18; 11:1; 22:32, 44; 23:34) and in that of his disciples (11:2; 18:1; 22:40). No less than four of the most beautiful hymns of the New Testament are contained in the history of the infancy of Christ and of the Baptist: the *Magnificat* of Mary, the *Benedictus* of Zechariah (1:68-79), the *Gloria* of the angels (2:14), and the *Nunc Dimittis* of Simeon (2:29-32). All these songs are incorporated into the hymn of praise that the Church offers day by day to her Lord in the celebration of the Divine Office and of the Eucharistic Sacrifice.

The song of Mary is the song of the mother of all mothers. It shows the work of the grace of God in the hearts of those who enter into the kingdom of the Messiah, first of all in Mary herself (1:46-49) and then in the new generation of God's children (1:50-53). The same divine love that once chose Israel, a small and weak and stiff-necked people (Dt 7:7), to be his servant—will now bring about a reassessment of all values. What has been bloated up by self-love will be deflated (1:51), and the poor will be exalted.

The message of the *Magnificat* is the message of the Christmas bells, which were heard for the first time in the song of Hannah, initiating the new age of David, the shepherd-king (1 Sm 2:8). It fills the starlit sky over the pastures of Bethlehem and resounds in the hearts of the shepherds (2:10-17). It rings in its full force in the "beatitudes" (6:20-23) and in the "woes" that follow them (6:24-26), and it continues through many of the most beautiful of the parables, those of the rich man and the beggar Lazarus (16:19-31), of the Prodigal Son

(15:11-32), of the Pharisee and the publican (18:9-14).

The Church has adopted the *Magnificat* as the crowning part of Vespers. At the end of the day, when the sun has lost its power, when man's energy is exhausted and the night brings all human activity to an end, then we sing the song of Mary in praise of the divine charity, which receives into its arms all those who labor and are burdened, to give them rest (see Mt 11:28).

The *Benedictus,* which Zechariah sings at the birth of his son (1:68-79), is inspired by the same Holy Spirit who overshadowed Mary (1:67). However, there is a marked difference between the two songs. The sentences of the *Benedictus* are longer and heavier. It is the song of a priest, a morning song. It celebrates the power and glory of the kingdom of God, who has "raised up a horn of salvation" (1:69).

"Horn" is used in the Old Testament as an expression for power, might. The "horn of salvation" is the saving power of the Messiah-King, who in the second part of the canticle, which refers directly to the child John (1:76-79), is called "the dayspring from on high" (1:78). The Greek translators of the Hebrew Scriptures render the word "shoot," which occurs frequently in the Old Testament as a title of the Messiah (see Nm 24:17; Jer 23:5; Zec 3:8; 6:12), as *anatole,* which can also mean "dayspring." The addition "from on high" marks the Messiah as descending from the "heart of mercy of our God" (1:78) to bring divine light and divine peace into this world of darkness and strife.

The real power of the Messiah is his selfless love. Therefore his kingdom is a spiritual kingdom, and the "enemies" from whose hands we will be saved (1:71) are not the political enemies of the Jewish people but the spiritual enemies of God's love.

The Benedictus forms part of the story of the nativity of the Baptist (1:57-80). St. Luke's description of the birth of Christ (2:1-20) is written in the hearts of generations and generations of Christians, because it tells so vividly the story of the God who once thundered on Mount

Sinai and did not redeem, but who in our days as a babe wept in the manger, and redeemed (St. Jerome). Bethlehem, "the smallest among the townships of Judah," sees the Son of God, "whose origins are from eternity" (Mi 5:2), wrapped in swaddling clothes and laid in a manger because there is no room for him among his own (2:7). The newborn Messiah is a king, but his people are not the priests in the temple of Jerusalem nor the mighty ones in their palaces. He "gathers together the lame, and assembles the outcast, and makes them a chosen remnant" (Mi 5:6-7). This prophecy of Micah is fulfilled that Christmas night in the fields of Bethlehem, when the shepherds, who are considered outcasts, hear the glad tidings of great joy from the angel, "and the glory of the Lord" shines around them (2:9). There could be no more glorious picture of the new kingdom that the child in the manger is establishing: the multitude of the heavenly host praising God in the highest and the little group of shepherds on the dark and wintry fields listening to the good news of a God who gives peace— peace to those whom his good will raises from the dunghill to make his children (2:14).

The third of the songs that St. Luke has preserved is the *Nunc Dimittis*, which Simeon sings when Mary presents her child in the temple and Simeon takes him into his arms (2:29-32). Two ages meet at this moment, the old and the new. The time of waiting has passed. The promise is fulfilled, the prophet dismissed. On the candlestick of the old covenant a new light has been enkindled, which shines not only for the chosen people but for the entire human race.

However, Simeon's last prophecy goes further than anything the Holy Spirit has announced thus far. It points to the dark hour when the sword will pierce the mother's heart (2:35), the hour of passion. At that time the thoughts of many hearts will be revealed (2:35). Those whom selfishness has hardened will fall. Those to whom selfless love has given the heart of a mother will rise (see 1 Kgs 3:16-27).

The image of the Passion is also indicated in the sacrifice of a pair of turtledoves, which the parents offer on this occasion (2:24). The ritual for offering fowl, which is so different from the offering of four-footed animals (see Lv 1:14-17), makes it clear that it is meant to be the sacrifice of those who suffer.[2]

The fate of the Messiah will be decided in Jerusalem. There he will die to save his people. Therefore, at their first visit to the city of David, the shadow of the cross falls over the child and his mother. When twelve years later the little family comes again to the temple, the cloud of the Passion rises for the second time to darken the hearts of the parents (2:41-52).

For three bitter days, foreboding through their number the days of the Lord's sufferings, Mary and Joseph seek the boy among their kins-folk and acquaintances (2:46). At last they find him in the temple, sit-ting among the teachers. At the age of thirteen a Jewish boy becomes a "son of the law," a responsible member of the covenant. Jesus chooses this time to manifest himself as the Son of his heavenly Father, eager to be "about his Father's business": the redemption of mankind through the sacrifice of the Son.

Brother of All

The "gospel of the infancy" announces that in the newborn Messiah the loving-kindness of God has appeared to all men. The rest of the Gospel is divided into three main parts: Christ's glorious activity as Saviour in Galilee (4:1–9:50); his journey from Galilee to Jerusalem (9:51–19:27); and his last days in Jerusalem, ending with the Passion, the Resurrection, and the Ascension (19:28–24:53). The latter part shows the struggle and the triumph of Christ's sacrificial love over the powers of darkness.

Selfishness divides the nations, incites the rich to exploit the poor, and leads to the degradation of women. In Christ, however, there is neither Jew nor Greek, neither bond nor free, neither male nor female, for they are all one in him (Gal 3:28). To make it clear that in Christ there is neither Jew nor Greek, St. Luke traces Jesus' genealogy beyond Abraham back to Adam (3:23-38; compare Mt 1:1-17). He shows that Christ is the brother of all men who therefore does not stop at the lost sheep of the house of Israel but goes to the Samaritans, whom the Jews despise most (9:52). For the same reason Luke relates how the Lord sets the one Samaritan who returns and gives thanks as an example for the nine Jews who do not (17:18). Again, in the beautiful parable it is the "Good Samaritan" who shows what real charity is.

In Christ there is neither bond nor free. The charity of Christ opens a new horizon beyond the division of social classes, of rich and poor. John the Baptist has already pointed out the basic demands of social justice in his sermons to the people, the publicans, and the soldiers (3:10-14). Our Lord goes much further. He sees in "mammon"— which has the meaning of our word *capital*—the great enemy of the human soul. The parable of the rich farmer (12:16-21) shows the foolishness of one who "lays up treasures for himself and is not rich toward God." The same is shown in the parable of the rich man and the poor Lazarus (16:19-31). The spirit has to triumph over mammon, so that through its good use we gain an incorruptible treasure (see 18:22; 19:26).

In Christ there is neither male nor female. If we remember that in the days of Christ it was not considered proper to greet a woman, we understand much better that the salutation of the angel, "Hail Mary, full of grace" (1:28), marks the beginning of a new era for woman, who receives a new dignity in a world transformed by the charity of Christ.

Nobody has made this clearer than St. Luke. He relates that women take their place in the constant company of Christ, "ministering to him out of their substance" (8:2-3). "Bewailing and lamenting him" (23:27), they follow Christ on his way to Golgotha. They stand "afar off" at his crucifixion (23:49) and assist at his burial (23:55). They are the first to receive the glad tidings of the Resurrection (24:1-7) and the first to announce them to the apostles (24:10).

Christ not only accepts the services of devout women, he also turns to them in a special way as their Saviour. He is moved by the sorrow of the widow who has lost her only son, and he gives him back to his mother (7:11-18). The story shows the power of a mother's tears over the heart of Christ, who is himself a mother's son. It also alludes to the power of the intercession that the Church offers for her children.

St. Luke is the only one to relate the visit of Christ in the home of Mary and Martha (10:38-42). The Lord praises Mary, who sits at his feet, listening to his teaching, for having chosen the better part. His words have effected a revolution. In the world of pagan antiquity the whole field of higher learning was reserved to man. Now, since the divine wisdom has taken flesh from a woman, it speaks to the woman's heart and is understood. The highest form of wisdom, the contemplative life, is opened to the bride of Christ.

In Christ there is neither Jew nor Greek, neither bond nor free, neither male nor female. Could we go a step further and say, "In Christ there is neither sinner nor saint"? It looks that way to Simon, the Pharisee, when the woman who is a sinner washes the Lord's feet with her tears (7:36-50). It looks so to many people when the Son of Man goes to be a guest of Zacchaeus, "the chief of the publicans" (19:1-10), and when he allows "all the publicans and sinners to draw near to him to hear him" (15:1).

The very word *Pharisee* means "the separated one." The Law has no power to save but only to condemn. The Son of Man, however, comes to seek and to save that which was lost (19:10). In the creative power of the Holy Spirit he makes new men out of sinners, that "where sin abounded, grace did much more abound" (Rom 5:20).

The three parables of the lost sheep (15:3-7), of the lost coin (15:8-10), and of the lost son (15:11-32) picture the saving activity of the Son (the shepherd), the Church (the woman), and the Father in all its creative power: "There is joy in heaven over one sinner, more than over ninety-nine just persons who do not need repentance" (15:7). The most beautiful of all, however, is the parable of the Good Samaritan (10:25-37).

Here the question of self-centered justice—"Who is my neighbor?"— was changed into that of creative charity—"Whose neighbor am I?" This question points to Christ himself, who gives the perfect answer when he leaves all his "rights" to take upon himself our sins. He makes himself our neighbor when he prays on the cross, "Father, forgive them, for they know not what they do" (23:34).

St. Luke closes his Gospel with the description of the risen Saviour revealing the secret of his saving charity to his disciples "at the breaking of the bread" (24:35), explaining to them the Scriptures (24:45) that they might understand how "it was fitting for Christ to suffer, and so enter into his glory" (24:26). The same life-giving "power from on high" that in the beginning of the gospel descended upon the virgin mother of Christ at its end is ready to descend upon the young Church, that she might bring remission of sins to all nations (24:47-49). His saving mission completed, the Saviour returns to his Father, leaving his blessing as a last pledge of his eternal charity.

TWENTY-FOUR

The Gospel According to St. John

In the four Gospels, or rather in the four books of the one Gospel, St. John the apostle, not undeservedly in respect of his spiritual understanding compared to the eagle, has elevated his preaching higher and far more sublimely, than the other three.... For the other three evangelists walked with the Lord on earth as with a man; concerning his divinity they have said but little; but this evangelist, as if he disdained to walk on the earth, just as in the every opening of his discourse he thundered on us, soared not only above the earth and above the whole compass of air and sky, but even above the whole army of angels and the whole order of invisible powers, and reached to Him by whom all things were made; saying, "In the beginning was the Word, and the Word was with God, and the Word was God."

With these words St. Augustine defines the difference between St. John and the other three evangelists. The Gospels of St. Mark, St. Luke, and St. Matthew are commonly called the "synoptics" because they are so closely related to one another, their parallel reports can be put side by side and viewed together in a "synopsis." St. John's Gospel, however, seems to be separated from these three by a wide gap.

Half of his text is original with him. Of the seven miracles reported by St. John, only two—the feeding of the five thousand and the walking on the waters—are mentioned by the other evangelists. While the events portrayed in the first three Gospels occur mainly in Galilee, St. John's report is almost wholly occupied with Christ's ministry in

Judaea. He gives an extensive account of Christ's discourses before the Jews in Jerusalem, yet the central theme of these discourses is not the preaching of the kingdom of God, as it is in the synoptics, but the revelation of Christ himself as the Son of God.

To this difference in content must be added differences in style and vocabulary. The Christ of the first three evangelists seems to speak a different language from the Christ of St. John. The first is a popular preacher who abounds in simple, striking parables, who avoids abstract discussions, who always remains practical. In the Gospel of St. John the teaching of Christ is nearly bare of parables. It moves instead around certain basic abstract concepts—life, light, truth, glory. Its deep spiritual meaning is far removed from the fleshly mind of the crowds.

"The Spiritual Gospel"

Some scholars have tried to solve the problem of the fourth Gospel by declaring it to be a construction without historical value, composed during the latter half of the second century. They speculate that it was written by a Hellenistic Christian, steeped in the philosophical concepts of the Alexandrian school, who intended to settle certain controversies that had arisen in the Church at that time. But any such theory contradicts the manifest testimony of the text itself and the continuous tradition of the Church.

The language of the fourth Gospel may differ from that of the synoptics, but it is not the language of a Greek philosopher. It contains clear indications that the author was bilingual and that his mother tongue was the Aramaic dialect spoken in Palestine at the time of our Lord. True, the whole arrangement of the material story in regard to place and time is peculiar to St. John, but closer examination reveals that the earlier evangelists are the ones who have streamlined the story for the sake of easier instruction.

The Synoptic Gospels arrange the events of our Lord's life into two chapters: his ministry in Galilee and his activity in Jerusalem. Many details in these Gospels indicate that this systematic arrangement does not correspond to the chronological order of the events, which is followed much more exactly by St. John. In the instances where St. John relates facts that are also reported by the other evangelists (the multiplication of the loaves, 6:1-13; Jesus walking on the waves, 6:16-21; the anointing in Bethany, 12:1-8; the entrance into Jerusalem, 12:12-19), it is evident that he, although he knows the synoptics, does not depend on them. At times he is more precise in indicating chronological order and the historical connection of events, and he adds certain details that show his report to be that of an eyewitness.

From this we cannot, however, conclude that St. John writes his Gospel in order to supplement the reports of the other evangelists. He moves on an entirely different level. Rather than aim at a complete record of the historical facts concerning the life of Christ, he selects a limited number of facts and teachings that he finds essential for the special purpose of his book: "Many other signs also Jesus did in the sight of his disciples, which are not written in this book. But these are written that you may believe that Jesus is the Christ, the Son of God: and that believing you may have life in his name" (20:30-31).

St. John's Gospel has rightly been called the "spiritual gospel" (Clement of Alexandria). He writes of what he has heard, what he has seen with his eyes, what he has looked upon, and what his hands have touched (see 1 Jn 1:1), but at the same time whatever he writes down is the fruit of long contemplation. He is a careful historian, but he penetrates beyond the external, material side of events into their deeper spiritual meaning. His "memory" does not simply register facts; it is illumined by the Holy Spirit, who reveals the significance of what has happened. Facts become "signs," meaning that they do not stand in themselves but have a higher meaning, pointing to or showing the glory of the Christ and Son of God.

One of the most important thoughts that the reader of St. John's Gospel must keep in mind is the relation of the Gospel to the Old Testament and its fulfillment in Jesus. Three Old Testament saints are mentioned in the course of the Gospel: Abraham, Moses, and Isaiah. These three are not taken casually; they are selected because they represent the totality of the old dispensation in its three most important phases. Abraham represents the promise; Moses, the Law; Isaiah, the prophecy.

John and Moses

The most important among these is certainly Moses. He is the first among the inspired authors, as St. John is the last. From Moses, the prophet, to St. John, the evangelist, leads one of those pathways that the divine wisdom, reaching from one end of human history to the other, has prepared for us. In following them our minds can be flooded with light and so grow into the length and breadth, the depth and height, of Christ.

Moses is in some way the key to understanding St. John, if only we keep in mind that, with St. John, we stand this side of the Jordan. Moses wrote of him whom John saw. As Moses was God's friend, St. John is the "disciple whom Jesus loved" (13:23). Anyone who understands the language of the evangelist knows that this love of Jesus is infinitely more than a special affection. Jesus' love for his disciple is an extension of the love with which the Father loves his Son. It is most perfectly expressed when Jesus, at the hour of his life-giving sacrifice, makes John his brother by giving him his mother.

As God's love once changed Moses, the love of Christ changes the natural ardor of John—whom Jesus called "son of thunder" (Mk 3:17) for wanting to call down fire upon the inhospitable Samaritans—into the patient strength of a true spiritual father, who stands next to Peter as one of the "pillars of the Church" (Acts 1:13). The love of Christ pours the ageless life of the Resurrection into St. John's soul as well as into his body. "I want him to remain until I come," our Lord says of him (21:22).

This becomes true in a deep spiritual sense. St. John, the youngest of the apostles, sees a new generation of Christians grow up, those who have not seen but have believed. They understand that Christ has come again, not on the clouds of heaven but in the visible body of his Church, where he is present in his sacraments and in his representatives. This second generation has once and forever broken with Jerusalem as the center of worship and doctrine, because they have seen the Holy City and its temple razed to the ground by the Romans in the year 70. They are no longer Judeo-Christians; they are truly members of the Church.

St. John is the bridge between the past and the future. Like Moses, he stands between the two generations: "I have written to you, fathers, because you have known him who is from the beginning. I have written to you, young men, because you are strong, and the Word of God abides in you" (1 Jn 2:14). He is more than one hundred years old when he dies, surrounded by his disciples, who have heard over and over again the sum total of his teaching: "Children, love one another, and if you do this it is sufficient."

As it was Moses', the commandment of love is John's last word. To John, however, this "old commandment" is new: "Dearly beloved, I am not writing a new commandment to you, but an old commandment which you had heard from the beginning.... Again a new commandment I write to you, which is true both in him and in you: because the darkness is passing and the true light now shines" (1 Jn 2:7-8).

The love St. John preaches is more than a commandment; it is "grace and truth" (1:14). It is life and light. To this love Moses pointed when he stood at the threshold of the Promised Land and prophesied: "The Lord your God will circumcise your heart, and the heart of your seed, to love the Lord your God with all your heart and with all your soul, that you may live" (Dt 30:6). Looking forward to the new age, when the holy name would dwell in the Holy Place, he said:

> It [the word of love] is not in heaven, that you should say: Who shall go up for us to heaven and bring it down to us, that we may hear it and do it? Neither is it beyond the sea, that you should say: Who shall go over the sea for us, and bring it to us, that we may hear it and do it? But the word is very close to you, in your mouth and in your heart, that you may do it.
>
> DEUTERONOMY 30:12-14

St. John sees the fulfillment of this prophecy. "The Word was made flesh, and dwelt among us, and we saw his glory"; and all those who believe in him receive the power to be born again, not of the will of man, but of God, in the new circumcision of baptism. "That which was from the beginning, which we have seen with our eyes, which we have looked upon, and our hands have handled, of the word of life ... we declare to you, that you also may have fellowship with us, and our fellowship may be with the Father and with his son Jesus Christ. And these things we write to you that you may rejoice, and your joy may be full" (1 Jn 1:14).

As the love of God lifted Moses to the heights of contemplation, likewise the disciple whom Jesus loved is filled with divine light. It opens his eyes to see the hidden depth of the life of the Lamb of God, which he himself had witnessed. Thus, "saturated with revelation," as St. Jerome says, he can write about it in his Gospel in such a way that the new generations, who have not seen with their eyes the glory of the only begotten Son, can believe that Jesus is the Son of God and the Christ expected by the Old Testament. Believing, they can have life (20:31).

The two visions Moses received—that of the burning bush, where the holy name, "I am who am," was revealed to him (Ex 3:14); and the other in the cleft of the rock on Mount Sinai, when the Glory passed by and proclaimed the divine mercy (Ex 34:6)—become one for St. John when he sees the One of whom his teacher, the Baptist, says: "After me there comes a man who is preferred before me, because he was before me" (1:30). The Baptist sees him "passing by" and says, "Behold the Lamb of God," and "the two disciples [John and Andrew] follow him" (1:35-37).

As the eternal Word, Jesus is before John. He is himself the "I am" (see 8:58; 13:19) who yet "passes from this world to his Father" (13:1) when he delivers himself up to the hands of his enemies to die as the Lamb for the sins of the world.

Miracles and Manifestations

The Mosiac writers saw in the number seven the symbol of the union between God (three) and the world (four), and this number dominates the whole structure of the Pentateuch. Likewise, careful study reveals that St. John uses the same number in his Gospel. For example, right in the beginning, St. John uses seven days, extending from the first announcement by the Baptist to the wedding feast at Cana, to introduce the "new creation" into the world. This he does to show that the new creation of grace is the fulfillment of the "old creation" of nature. Out of the infinite number of Christ's miracles, St. John selects seven, which he presents not only as manifestations of the omnipotence of the Son of God but as signs that reveal the secret of the Lord's saving activity to those who are able to understand.

The changing of water into wine at the wedding feast of Cana, the "beginning" of Jesus' miracles, is a sign of his entire activity. Changing the lower into the higher signifies changing the Law into the fullness of divine love; it indicates the dawn of the messianic age, the beginnings of faith transformed into love, the purification into union.

The other miracles unfold this beginning. The healing of the moribund son shows Christ as the physician, changing sickness into life and health for the sake of faith. The healing of the lame man in the sheep pool of Bethzatha (meaning "house of mercy") reveals him as physician for the spiritual sickness of sin and moral weakness. The multiplication of the loaves and the subsequent walking over the waters to the apostles' boat show him as nourishment for the hungry and as haven for the fearful. The healing of the man born blind in the water of Siloam (meaning "the one who is sent") reveals him as the light of the world. Finally, the resurrection of Lazarus reveals him as the source of life.

Closely connected with these seven miracles or signs are the seven self-manifestations, all introduced with the words "I am." They are indeed an unfolding of the holy name in connection with the miracles.

The first such manifestation takes place in the context of the multiplication of the loaves: "I am the bread of life" (6:35), pointing to the holy Eucharist, the nourishing power of his sacrificial love. The second is the revelation of his illumining power: "I am the light of the world" (8:12), the source of faith. The third and fourth show him as the door through which the sheep enter into the fold and as the Good Shepherd, who knows his sheep and who lays down his life for them (10:7, 11). The fifth proclaims him as "the resurrection and the life" (11:25) in connection with the raising of Lazarus. The sixth is directed to the disciples and is the summary of all: "I am the way, the truth and the life" (14:6). The seventh, pointing back to the first sign at the wedding feast of Cana, speaks of the "true vine" (15:1), the promise of final unity.

The importance of the number seven for the gospel can be seen especially in the last discourses (chapters 14–16), in which the teaching of Christ reaches its summit. Seven times the Lord repeats "I told you so." Seven times he uses the key words "in my name," "one," and "love."

The Mystery Solved

More striking still than the correspondence in the use of a formal principle, such as the number seven, is St. John's spiritual relation to Moses. The Christ of the fourth Gospel appears as the fulfillment of the most outstanding signs of the Mosaic writings. Right in the first line of St. John's prologue this relationship is manifest. The sentence "In the beginning was the Word ..." certainly refers to the first sentence of Genesis, "In the beginning God created the heavens and the earth."

However, St. John goes beyond Moses by asserting that the Word was in the beginning with God. We see that his "beginning" is not the beginning of creation but the eternal beginning of the Word. The Word, instead of being turned toward this visible world, is turned toward God, is equal to God, and reflects his eternal being. The Word is life and the light and therefore is universal, the source of all things.

Evidently the terms *darkness* and *light* used here by St. John also refer to the beginning of Genesis, when darkness covered the face of the earth until God commanded light to shine. The light was not overcome by darkness but "took turns" with darkness in the changing of day and night. This already points to death and resurrection, the Easter mystery.

We see here one of the fundamental rules that must be observed in order to understand St. John: Any event he describes, any beginning, contains in itself already the whole story. The first lines of the prologue refer to the Word and to the beginnings of creation, but at the same time they contain already the entire story of Christ's struggle with the powers of darkness, his temporary defeat, and his final victory. The fact that this interlacing of things has not been sufficiently taken into account has led to innumerable discussions among scholars about the meaning of the prologue.

For example, the sudden appearance of the Baptist has been a puzzle. Here we must remember that just as events are signs in St. John's

Gospel, so also are persons. John the Baptist stands in the prologue not just as an individual but as a type. In him the whole of the Old Testament is summed up. He is called the "man sent by God" to distinguish him from the Word made flesh. The Baptist here is the Old Testament. He is not the light; he is the witness to the light, the finger that points it out, the moon that shines not with its own light but as the reflection of the sun. This has always been considered the divinely intended meaning of the Jewish people and their teachers and fathers and prophets.

With the Baptist's testimony, repeated three times for emphasis, that after him will come one who was before him, the whole relationship between the Old and the New Testament is solved. This is a problem foreshadowed in the teaching of the Old Testament from the very beginning of the sacred history: the problem of the younger son preferred before the older one. The theme runs all through Genesis and Exodus and even the later writings. Abel is preferred to Cain, Isaac to Ishmael, Jacob to Esau, Ephraim to Manasseh, Perez to Zerah: Always the younger is preferred to the older.

This mystery is solved when St. John the Baptist says of Jesus: "He who comes after me is preferred before me, because he was before me." He comes after the Baptist, because he is the Word made flesh, who entered into the succession of time in his saving humility. The Baptist himself accepts in the selflessness of the true witness his role as the friend of the Bridegroom (3:29) and tells his own disciples that he must decrease, while the One who comes after him must increase (3:30). Thus he fulfills the meaning and mission of the old dispensation.

St. John the evangelist realizes that he is wholly a child of the divine love, who died for him that he might live. Could the mysterious anonymity of the author of the fourth Gospel not have its reason right here? Perhaps he speaks of himself in the third person because it is not he that lives, but the love of Christ lives in him. In any case, the expression "the disciple whom Jesus loved" means more than merely the fact that our Lord had a special affection for St. John. It marks the type of disciple he represents.

John and Peter

Each one of the apostles mentioned in the fourth Gospel stands for a specific kind of faith and relationship to Christ. Among them St. John is "the disciple whom Jesus loved," while St. Peter, with whom Jesus was so closely associated, could rightly be called "the disciple who loved Jesus" (see 21:15-17).

St. Peter's love springs from the natural impulse of his heart. It comes from below, out of "the will of the flesh." It is not the love with which the Father loves the Son, which causes the Son to give his life for his friends (15:13). St. Peter does not see why his Master should lay down his life for him; he wants to lay down his life for his Master. Therefore he does not understand why the Lord would kneel to wash his feet (13:6). He wants to save his Lord from arrest by striking with the sword at the high priest's servant (18:10); and when he sees Jesus bound, he thinks that all is lost and denies him (18:25). He is not present beneath the cross when Jesus dies.

But when they meet for the last time, the risen Lord tells St. Peter that he himself will one day be bound and led where he does not want to go. And so, through St. Peter's own death on the cross, the love with which Jesus has loved him will triumph in him (21:18).

On this occasion the Lord confronts the two disciples with one another, saying to Peter: "Follow me." Of the disciple whom he loves he says: "If I want him to remain until I come, what is it to you?" (21:22). To St. Peter he points out the laborious way of the active life as pastor of the flock, a way which will lead him to martyrdom. To the disciple whom Jesus loves is shown the hidden quiet of contemplation. This remains until the Lord comes, because it rises above space and time to anticipate already here on earth the agelessness of the eternal life.

The disciple whom Jesus loved typifies, indeed, all through the fourth Gospel, the contemplative life. In him the Lord's prophecy is fulfilled: "I shall love him, and I shall manifest myself to him" (14:21). His place is at the breast of the Lord, who shares with him the secrets of his heart (13:23, 25).

When, after the Resurrection, both St. Peter and St. John run to the empty tomb, it is St. Peter who enters first, but it is St. John who "sees and believes" (20:8). Again, at the last manifestation of the risen Jesus on the shores of Lake Tiberias, St. John is the first to recognize him and say, "It is the Lord!" Then St. Peter, hearing that the Lord is there, wraps his coat about him and casts himself into the sea to swim to him (21:7). St. John sees, St. Peter acts, because Jesus loves St. John and manifests himself to him, and St. Peter loves Jesus and works hard to reach him.

Therefore St. Peter receives the "power of the keys to bind and to loose." St. John, who has seen water and blood, the signs of faith and charity, of light and of life, gushing forth from the pierced heart of the Saviour, receives from the Holy Spirit the fullness of truth (16:13) and gives it to the Church in his writings. But nobody should separate Peter and John. Each represents one aspect of the Christian life, and only the two together are the fullness of the Church.

We can now easily see why it is important to realize that the fourth Gospel was written by the disciple whom Jesus loved and not by the disciple who loved Jesus. The latter would probably have started his book with a description of the misery of man and his longing for salvation, while the disciple whom Jesus loved soars like an eagle high above this world into the very bosom of the Father.

TWENTY-FIVE

The Acts of the Apostles

At Easter Christ, our Paschal Lamb, has been sacrificed. The neo-phytes have passed through the Red Sea of baptism. The Lord has brought them, and all of us who have celebrated these sacred myster-ies, into the Promised Land of spiritual liberty and abundance. The first spiritual food we receive in this happy state is the Acts of the Apostles, because in them St. Luke describes how the new Israel, the Church of Christ, breaks down the barriers of geography, nationality, and ritual to take possession of the universal kingdom of Christ.

There was a time when the Book of Joshua was read during Paschaltide. It describes the Israelites' taking possession of the Promised Land under the leadership of Joshua. The events that took place then bear a prophetic resemblance to those that, a thousand years later, took place after the descent of the Holy Spirit upon the apostles. The two books taken together form another one of those "pathways" on which Holy Scripture leads the mind into the fullness of the faith.

Joshua and Acts

The position the Book of Joshua holds among the writings of the Old Testament corresponds exactly to that of Acts in the New Testament. The Acts follows the four Gospels as Joshua follows the five books of Moses. In the Old Testament it was the Law, contained in the Pentateuch, upon which Israel's life as a nation was founded. In the New Testament Christ becomes the cornerstone of the Church, and his life is described in the four Gospels. After the foundations have been laid, God's people go into action. In the Old Testament it is a political conquest, that of the Promised Land under Joshua. In the New Testament it is a spiritual conquest, that of the whole earth in the power of the Holy Spirit, under the leadership and in the name of Jesus (Acts 3:6).

The name *Jesus* is the Greek form of the Hebrew *Joshua,* and it means "Yahweh makes room." The Hebrew verb "to make room" is usually rendered by the Latin *salvare* or the English "to save." The original Hebrew shows more clearly what the mission of Jesus-Joshua is: to make room for God's people to dwell in. In the Old Testament this room is Palestine. In the New Testament it is the whole earth, filled by the Holy Spirit.

To the marching order God gives Joshua—"Cross the Jordan here, you and all this people, into the land which I am giving them" (Jos 1:2)—corresponds the command the apostles receive from the risen Lord—"You will be given power when the Holy Spirit comes upon you, and you will be witnesses for me in Jerusalem and Samaria and to the very ends of the earth" (Acts 1:8). Three times is Joshua admonished "to take courage and be strong" (Jos 1:6, 7, 9). It is only through the supernatural hardihood of the Israelites and the contrasting faint-heartedness of their enemies that they are able to conquer the Promised Land. Likewise in Acts, the apostles are filled with "boldness" to preach the good tidings of redemption publicly and without fear (Acts 4:29; 28:31).

The Book of Joshua reports how twelve men are chosen, as the representatives of the twelve tribes, to gather twelve stones from the bed of the river Jordan to be set up as a memorial of the safe passing of the Israelites into the Promised Land (Jos 4:4). Likewise in Acts, we are told how the number of the twelve apostles is restored by the choice of St. Matthias (1:15-26).

In the Book of Joshua, Achan, of the tribe of Judah, is killed because he hid some spoils by burying them in the ground (chapter 7), intending to keep them for himself. To the death of Achan corresponds that of Judas, reported in Acts 1:16-20. Judas sells the Lord for thirty pieces of silver and then hangs himself in the field that has been bought with this "blood money." So the field is called the "blood field."

The fall of Jericho foreshadows the events that in the last age of history will bring about the fall of the city of this world. The Israelites, shouting when the horns are blown, point to the new Israel conquering the world through the preaching of the gospel. Rahab, the harlot, represents those of the gentiles who believe the glad tidings. She solemnly professes her faith by saying to the messengers who are sent by Joshua—prefiguring the apostles—"I know the Lord has given you the land, for the Lord your God is God in the heavens above and on the earth below" (Jos 2:11). The scarlet rope she is told to let out of her window to be saved is also a symbol of her faith. The Hebrew word for "rope" also means "hope," and its color points to the blood of Christ. While Achan, of the tribe of Judah, is judged, Rahab, the gentile harlot of Jericho, is saved (Jos 6). Their different fates foreshadow the passing of the Church from the Jews to the gentiles, when "the harlots enter the kingdom of God, while the heirs will be cast out" (Mt 8:12; 21:31). This is the theme of Acts.

In Acts the Spirit of the risen Christ compels the apostles to witness to Jesus as the Christ, that is, the Anointed One or Messiah of the Jews, and as the *Kyrios,* that is, the Lord of all mankind and of the whole universe. "Therefore," says St. Peter when he addresses his countrymen on the Day of Pentecost, "the whole nation of Israel must understand that God has declared this Jesus whom you have crucified both Lord and Christ" (Acts 2:36).

The Book of Joshua calls the ark, which the Levites carry through the Jordan into the Promised Land, "the ark of the Lord of all the earth" (Jos 3:11). The ark represents prophetically the risen Christ; by calling it "the ark of the Lord of all the earth," the Book of Joshua indicates that the conquest of the Holy Land is the "sign" of another, greater, conquest, that of the whole world through the "Lord Jesus" described in Acts.

The Book of Joshua gives a careful report of the distribution of the land to the various tribes (chapters 13–21). In Acts, however, Barnabas the Levite and others sell the pieces of land they acquired in Palestine and lay the price at the feet of the apostles (Acts 4:36-37). Through this action they profess that the "land" as such has lost its importance since the Spirit is filling the whole earth. The charity of Christ has now become the "home of the heart."

The Gospel of the Holy Spirit

The general theme and plan of Acts is indicated in 1:8: "You shall receive the power of the Holy Spirit coming upon you, and you shall be witnesses to me in Jerusalem, and in all Judaea, and Samaria, and to the very ends of the earth." The introduction (1:3–2:47) describes the descent of the Holy Spirit and the formal establishment of the Church. The first main part (chapters 3–7) shows the apostles giving testimony to Christ in Jerusalem. In the power of the Holy Spirit they work miracles, preach publicly and without fear, and give testimony before the authorities. Through their work the Church is confirmed in charity (chapter 5) and brings forth the first flower of martyrdom, St. Stephen (chapters 6–7).

Chapters 8–12 form the second main part, the spreading of the Church from Jerusalem into Judaea and Samaria. At the same time the passing of the Church to the gentiles is being prepared, through the conversion of St. Paul, "apostle of the gentiles" (chapter 9), through the reception into the Church of the first gentile family, Cornelius and his house (9:32–11:18), and through the formation of the first gentile congregation at Antioch (11:19-30).

The persecution of the Church by Herod Agrippa I (chapter 12) marks the transition to the third part of Acts, in which St. Paul replaces St. Peter as the leading figure (chapters 13–28). His three missionary journeys (chapters 13–19), his last journey to Jerusalem which ends in his imprisonment in Palestine (chapters 20–26), and his transfer to Rome and his imprisonment there (chapters 27–28) cover the years A.D. 44–63.

In all probability, Acts is written in this latter year by St. Luke, who has accompanied St. Paul on his eventful voyage from Palestine to Rome and is still with him when he is looking forward to his soon acquittal by the Roman court. St. Luke may even have a secondary purpose for writing the Acts, that of vindicating St. Paul by showing that not the Roman authorities but only the Jews are interested in the condemnation of the apostle.

The main purpose of Acts is, however, to show the power of the Holy Spirit working in the Church. For this reason Acts is also called "the Gospel of the Holy Spirit." It is the Holy Spirit descending upon the apostles on Pentecost who creates the Church (2:1-13).

Early medieval art liked to contrast the birth of the Church on Pentecost with the building of the Tower of Babel (Gn 11). On a church wall to the left is seen the beginnings of the tower rising, surrounded with tremendous scaffolding, with ladders leading up and men climbing from rung to rung, carrying heavy hods filled with mortar on their shoulders. It all looks like a tremendous effort, futile in itself, to reach heaven and to compete with God by heaping dirt upon dirt.

On the opposite wall the apostles are represented, with Mary in their midst, not climbing but sitting, not eager to make a name for themselves but praying together and thus giving glory to God. The rays of the Holy Spirit are descending upon them and settling on each one individually as a tongue of fire. The Church is not a monument built by the hands of men for the glory of men. She is the bride of the

Spirit, the New Jerusalem, descending from heaven.

When we study the beginnings of the Church, we are surprised to see how little human planning there is. St. Peter is not by any means the man to organize a worldwide propaganda campaign. He is not thinking in terms of world conquest. He does not set up an office to work out a scheme for impregnating the Roman Empire with the Spirit of Christ. He must be driven by the Holy Spirit into decisions and actions, the whole importance of which he does not realize.

Even St. Paul, who certainly is by nature a very active and indefatigable man, does not make the most momentous stop of his apostolic career, crossing the Bosporus to go into Europe, after long strategic calculations of his own. It just "happens." He is thinking of converting Asia when the Spirit stops him and he returns to Troas. There he has a vision. A Macedonian is appealing to him: "Come over to Macedonia and help us" (16:9-10). From this St. Paul concludes that God has called him to tell the good news to the people in Europe. He does not realize that he is setting out to conquer a key position for the Church. He simply obeys the divine call.

The Early Church

The fact that the Church is rather a gift of the Spirit than the fruit of human endeavor gives to the apostolic Church a unique position in the history of the Church and makes the Acts of the Apostles of vital importance to the Christians of all ages. We people of the "century of progress" do not look into the past to find there the pattern for the future. Accustomed as we are to think in terms of progress, any beginnings bear to us the mark of imperfection. The life of the Church, however, is not ruled by the laws of human progress. Not being built up from the ground, but descending from above, the growth of the Church is like that of a seed, the gradual unfolding of a fundamental structure that is wholly present already in the initial stage.

The risen Christ is the "seed" out of which the Church grows as an overflow of his abundance. From Christ the Church receives the divine life in the vessel of the sacraments—to be administered, not to be produced. From Christ she receives the full light of revelation as an unalterable deposit—to be handed down, not to be invented. The risen Christ sends to his Church the fullness of the Holy Spirit, so that St. Peter can truly state, on the very day when the Church is born, that this outpouring of the Spirit is the fulfillment of an event which, as Joel announced, would come about "in the last days" (2:17).

The apostolic Church is the Church of "the first love" (Rv 2:4). The apostles who govern her are endowed with a fullness of grace never to be given to any of their successors. The Church is built, once and forever, upon "the foundation of the apostles" (Eph 2:20).

For this reason the history of the Church is to a large extent the history of "reformations." Again and again the Church has returned to the apostolic pattern. To restore the spirit of the apostolic Church in its original purity and zeal was the avowed purpose of all the great saints and reformers. The Rule of St. Benedict is nothing but an attempt to reestablish the ideal apostolic Church within the confines of a monastery. St. Francis, St. Dominic, St. Ignatius, and the great number of their followers received the inspiration for their orders from the Acts of the Apostles.

The apostolic Church remains a model for our times, too—not that we want to turn back the wheel of history and copy the external forms of a past age, which is impossible, but because we realize that the waters of the Holy Spirit are nowhere as pure as at their source.

The Acts of the Apostles delineates clearly the ever valid pattern of Christian spiritual life. Its source is the Spirit of the risen Christ. He makes the apostles "witnesses of the resurrection" (1:22) and fills the minds of the faithful with the knowledge of Jesus as the Christ and Lord (2:36). In the power of this Spirit the apostles show to the faithful the pattern of redemption unfolded in the pages of the Old Testament and fulfilled in the Messiah Jesus (2:16-17; 13:16-31).

The Old Testament, interpreted in the light of the risen Christ, is the soil out of which the faith of the first Christians grows. The New Testament does not exist yet. The gospel is handed down as a living tradition, preserved and proclaimed by the Church. "I passed on to you the account I had received" (1 Cor 15:3). Not a book but the teaching authority of the apostles is the rule of faith.

Fruits of the Spirit

The glad tidings of redemption pierce the hearts of those who listen (2:37). Compunction is the first fruit of the Spirit in the hearts of those who are being saved. This compunction makes the first Christians willing to obey the authority of the apostles. "Stung to the heart, they said to Peter and the rest of the apostles: 'Brethren, what shall we do?'" (2:37). They receive the answer: "You must repent, and every one of you be baptized in the name of Jesus Christ, in order to have your sins forgiven. Then you will receive the gift of the Holy Spirit" (2:38).

How the gift of the Spirit transforms the hearts of the first Christians is shown in the beautiful report of the life of the apostolic Church:

> They persevered in the teaching and the society of the apostles, the breaking of bread and prayer. Everyone felt a sense of awe, and many wonders and signs were done by the apostles. The faithful all shared everything they had with one another, and sold their property and belongings, and divided the money with all the rest, according to their special needs. Day after day they all went regularly to the temple, they broke the bread together in

their homes, and they ate their food with glad and simple hearts, constantly praising God and respected by all the people.

ACTS 2:42-47

The Spirit of the risen Christ filling the hearts of the faithful inspires them to offer praises to God. As the evil spirit of this world induces men to seek their own glory, so the Holy Spirit impels the faithful to glorify God. Though St. Peter is doubtful whether the Spirit of God will really descend upon converts from paganism, he and his companions are convinced when they hear them "declaring the greatness of God" (10:46). The praises that are offered in the Spirit are not only private prayers but necessarily prayers in common and in public, because the Holy Spirit is essentially the Spirit of unity filling the whole earth. Besides the regular hours of prayer in the temple, the early Christians celebrate in their homes the "breaking of the bread," the holy Eucharist. The Mass is the center of their spiritual life.

Because the Spirit which they have received on Pentecost is the "power of the resurrection," he fills their hearts with joy and singleness of mind. Christ is their Shepherd leading them to the waters of refreshment. They taste the powers of a new age, after they have escaped the melancholic pessimism of those "who have no hope" (Eph 2:12). They do not know anyone but Christ alone. This singleness of mind gives them courage, strength, boldness, and the ability to endure persecution and suffering (5:41), which often is crowned with martyrdom (7:55-59).

The prophetic description that Psalm 133 gives of the community of the *Christos*, the Anointed One, is fulfilled by the apostolic Church. "Lo, how good and lovely it is when brethren dwell together as one. Like the goodly oil upon the head, which flows down upon Aaron's beard, that flows down to the edge of his robe" (Ps 133:1-2). The Holy Spirit unites the Christian community in the love of Christ.

An Ordered Life

Nevertheless, it would be wrong to think that the apostolic Church is a community of "pure love" to the exclusion of authority or juridical power. As no real community life among men is possible without law and order, so the Spirit does not remain in the Church without constantly "descending" from above through the channels of divinely appointed authority into hearts that are tested in concrete obedience. The first Christians recognize the fact that the Spirit of the messianic age is not a wildfire but is communicated from above through a system of "missions." As the Father has sent Christ, so Christ has sent the apostles.

Evidently the latter consider themselves a group of their own endowed with singular authority. St. Peter says to them with regard to Judas: "He was one of our number and a share of this ministry of ours fell to his lot." The proceedings of the first "council" at Jerusalem show clearly that the apostles consider themselves a governing body with full right of making laws that are binding for the whole Church (chapter 15). The office of preaching and of administering the sacraments is not conferred upon anybody by popular consent but by the laying on of hands on the part of the apostles, as the most expressive symbol of imparting the Holy Spirit who descends from above (6:6; 13:3). Juridical power in the Church, it is true, is not considered a means of self-assertion but as God's way to keep the source of the descending Spirit clear from all human attempts to change it.

The Spirit who descends from the head of Aaron to the edge of his robe by establishing authority and obedience in the Church creates at the same time a closely united family of brethren. The Spirit who wants to fill the whole earth frees the new Israel from all restrictions of race and of country. The dietary laws (10:11-15) and circumcision (chapter 15), which acted as a fence to separate the Jews from the rest of the world, are abolished.

Jews and gentiles, men and women, young and old, free and slave, eunuchs and magicians, rich and poor, are called into one kingdom. They have everything in common, not because they do not believe in the right of personal property, nor because they want to serve social justice by making the rich poor and the poor rich. Rather, they want to imitate Christ who has saved mankind by giving his own life. It is not a philosophy nor a law that makes them sell their fields, but the love of Christ urging them on.

We notice throughout the whole of Acts that the office of preaching and of administering the sacraments is always connected with ministering to the material needs of the faithful. In the last words that St. Paul addresses to the bishops of Asia when he leaves for Jerusalem, he says: "You know well enough that these hands of mine provided for my needs and my companions. I showed you in every way that by hard work like that we must help those who are weak and remember the words of the Lord Jesus, for he said: 'To give makes one happier than to be given to'" (20:34-35). Paul's work of preaching the gospel cannot be separated from the big collection he organizes for the poor in Jerusalem. Indeed, it is the institution of the deacons (chapter 6) to serve the tables that, to a great extent, is responsible for the success of the apostolic preaching.

The message of Acts for our time, and for every time in Church history, can be summed up in the admonition of St. Paul: "Do not extinguish the Spirit!" Let him illumine our minds with the knowledge of Jesus as the Christ and the Lord. Let him transform our hearts, piercing them with compunction, leading them to repentance, filling them with obedience to divinely appointed authority, inspiring them with gladness, courage, and singleness of purpose. May he keep us in the "breaking of the bread" and in the peace of Christ's love as one family of brethren. May he make the whole of mankind a field for us to conquer and the glory of God the last purpose of our lives.

TWENTY-SIX

The Letters of St. Paul

In the Old Testament Isaiah revealed to us the two great signs of salvation: the virgin mother and her child Emmanuel, and the Suffering Servant who bears the sins of many. In the New Testament the voice of Isaiah is superseded by that of St. Paul, who in the majestic words with which he opens his Letter to the Romans, announces that Isaiah's prophecies have been fulfilled in the Lord Jesus:

> Paul, a servant of Jesus Christ, called to be an apostle, set apart for the gospel of God, which he had promised beforehand through his prophecy in the holy Scriptures, concerning his Son who was born to him according to the flesh of the offspring of David and foreordained Son of God in power and in the spirit of sanctification, by the resurrection from the dead.
>
> ROMANS 1:1-4

Not only in these words but in all his preaching and writing, St. Paul announces as a present reality the messianic salvation that the prophets pointed to.

A Man of Contradiction

Paul, who is first made known to us under the name of Saul, is born at the beginning of our era at Tarsus in Cilicia (Asia Minor), "of the race of Israel, of the tribe of Benjamin, a Hebrew of Hebrews, as regards the law, a Pharisee" (Phil 3:5). He is educated partly at Tarsus, a famous university town and center of Greek civilization, but chiefly at Jerusalem, where he sits at the feet of Gamaliel: "a pupil of Gamaliel, and instructed according to the strict acceptation of the law of Moses" (Acts 22:3). His family is evidently of some influence, because Paul is born a Roman citizen. This unique combination of Hebrew race and scholarship, Greek culture, and Roman citizenship prepares Paul for his providential task: to tear down the wall of partition between Hebrew and gentile worlds, between East and West, and to make all, Jew and Greek, slave and freeman, male and female, one in Christ Jesus (Gal 3:28).

He is on the way to Damascus, "still breathing threats of slaughter against the disciples of the Lord" (Acts 9:1), when the call of Jesus reaches him and makes him the Apostle to the Gentiles (Acts 26:18). The grace of God hits him, like a bolt of lightning out of a blue sky, and turns Saul from a Pharisee into an ardent protagonist of liberty in Christ. His missionary journeys, of which we count three, bring him into nearly every part of the wide Roman Empire.

Evidently of poor health, with the thorn (of malaria?) in his flesh (2 Cor 12:7; Gal 4:13), weak in his bodily presence (2 Cor 10:10), and rude in speech (2 Cor 11:6), this amazing man accomplishes what must seem impossible even to a strong person. He travels thousands of miles by land and by sea, "in danger from rivers, danger from robbers, danger from my own people, danger from the heathen, danger in the city, danger in the desert, danger at sea, danger from false brothers, through toil and hardship, through many a sleepless night, through hunger and thirst, often without food, and exposed to cold" (2 Cor 11:26-27). Supported only by his Lord Jesus, whom he loves more than anybody else before or after him, he preaches the glad tidings of redemption to kings and governors, to Jews and gentiles; in palaces, in synagogues, in the marketplaces; among the philosophers of Athens, the friends of Caesar in Rome, the poor, the slaves, men, women, and children all over the world.

On his fifth visit to Jerusalem his presence in the temple causes a riot. Only the intervention of the Roman soldiers and his appeal, as a Roman citizen, to Caesar save him from the fury of the mob and from the snares of his Jewish enemies. After two years of imprisonment in Caesarea he is sent on the voyage to Rome, with Luke and another companion allowed to accompany him. Their ship is caught in a storm and finally wrecked on the coast of Malta, but all the men are saved.

The next spring they sail for Italy, landing at Puteoli, whence they reach Rome by land. St. Paul is kept there in light custody in a hired lodging, guarded by a soldier. For two years he remains there, "and he welcomes all who come to him, preaching the kingdom of God and teaching about the Lord Jesus Christ with all boldness and unhindered" (Acts 28:30-31).

The report of the Acts of the Apostles closes here, without giving any notice of the end of Paul's trial at the court of Caesar. He intends to go to Spain (Rom 15:24, 28), and, according to early tradition, he in fact does so. In his Letter to the Philippians, which he writes as a prisoner in Rome, he expresses his desire to go there shortly (Phil 2:24), and in the so-called pastoral letters we read that he goes to Corinth (2 Tm 4:20). We also read of a journey to Crete, where he leaves Titus to rule the Church and to set right anything defective (Ti 1:5), while he goes to Nicopolis to spend the winter (Ti 3:12). At the end of his life we see him again in Rome, a prisoner once more (2 Tm 2:9).

"As for me, I am already being poured out in sacrifice, and the time of my deliverance is at hand. I have fought the good fight, I have run the race, I have kept the faith. For the rest there is laid up for me a crown of justice, which the Lord, the just Judge, will award me on that day, and not only me but also all who love his coming" (2 Tm 4:6-8). According to universal tradition he receives the crown of martyrdom outside Rome and is buried nearby, where now the magnificent basilica of St. Paul-Outside-the-Walls guards his earthly remains, under a plain tombstone which bears the majestic inscription: *Paulus Apostolus Martyr.*

We stand overwhelmed before the inexhaustible richness and depth of this unique personality. To the superficial observer it seems to be full of contradictions. Now he is a Jew, now again an enemy of the Jews; now he observes the Law, now he rejects it; at one time he asks for money, at another he does not want it; now he offers sacrifice and has his head shaven in fulfillment of a vow, now he condemns with anathema those who do the same. First he administers circumcision, later he rejects it. In all these changes, however, his will remains always the same: the will to save all he meets.

> Though I am free from anyone's control, I have made myself everyone's slave, so as to win over all the more. To the Jews I have become like a Jew, to win Jews over; to men under the law I have become like a man under the law, though I am not myself under the law, so as to win over those who are under the law. To those who have no law I have become like a man without any law— though I am not without the law of God, but under the law of Christ—so as to win over those who are without any law. To the weak I become weak, that I might win over the weak. I become all things to all men, so as to save all. I do all things for the sake of the gospel, that I may share in its blessings.
>
> 1 CORINTHIANS 9:19-23

A Benjaminite

The key to St. Paul's personality, to his life, and to his work is the charity of Christ, which transforms Saul into "a vessel of divine election" and ordains him as "Apostle to the Gentiles." The nature of St. Paul's conversion can be understood much better when we see it in the light of his descent from Benjamin, which he himself stresses time and again (see Rom 11:1; Phil 3:5). The character of his ministry is greatly influenced by St. Stephen, whose death Saul consents to (Acts 8:1) but whose spirit he inherits.

As modern men we are not inclined to pay too much attention to people's names or to their descent. We consider names merely external labels, and descent a troublesome inheritance. In the Old Testament, however, names reveal the inner essence of things and persons, and descent leads to the root, that is, to the principle that largely determines the destiny of the descendant.

The God of the Old Testament is the "God of the Fathers." The chosen people continues the name and the spirit of its father Israel. Each of Israel's twelve sons determines the character and the mission of the tribe descending from him. Through his last blessing Jacob imparts to his sons the specific spiritual inheritance they will leave to their descendants (Gn 49:1-28).

There is Judah, for instance, the tribe of kingship, like a lion in his strength and courage, from whom the scepter will not depart until the one comes who will rule the nations (49:8-10). There is Zebulun, the tribe of the merchants (49:13), and Issachar, the strong ass, made for hard work but also enjoying the rest that is the fruit of all labor (49:14-15).

The youngest among them is Benjamin, the father of Saul. His mother was in great travail in giving birth to him, and when her soul was departing she called him Benoni—that is, "son of my sorrow"—but his father changed the name, after she died, to Benjamin—that is, "son of my right hand" (Gn 35:16-18). This change of name is indicative of the whole character of Benjamin. The destiny of the Benjaminites is conversion through the grace of God. That is what Jacob prophesies in his blessing over his youngest son: "Benjamin is a ravenous wolf. In the morning he shall devour his prey, and in the evening he shall divide his spoil" (Gn 49:27).

God's grace always turns to those whom nature seems to have neglected. It is of Benjamin that Moses says: "He is the beloved of the Lord" (Dt 33:12). He is the only one among the sons of Jacob to be born in the Promised Land (Gn 35:16); more than that, God chooses the territory of this youngest son of Jacob as the place where the court and the sanctuary and the Holy of Holies of the temple are to be built. This is the meaning of the beautiful words of Moses, which reveal God's design for the whole family of Benjamin, including Saul of Tarsus: "Benjamin shall dwell with him in confidence. The Lord shall establish his bridal chamber and the cloud of his presence between his shoulders" (Dt 33:12). What better place could there be for the love of God to celebrate its nuptials with the virgin Israel than the weak shoulders of Jacob's "baby"!

Benjamin is not only the youngest, but he is also the prodigal among the sons of Jacob. In the morning of his life he acts like a "ravenous wolf," committing a most grievous sin, which brings upon him excommunication from the covenant of the twelve tribes (Jgs 19–21). In the battle of Gibeah (Jgs 20:29-48) he fights against the other tribes with the fury of the wolf. He would be annihilated were it not for the mere pity of the other tribes and their mournful intercession "for Benjamin their brother" (21:6). Yet it is Benjamin who is chosen by God to give the first king to Israel (1 Sm 9:16), so that Saul, in surprise over so great a mystery of grace, exclaims: "Am not I a Benjaminite, of the smallest of the tribes of Israel? And my family the least of all families of the tribe of Benjamin?" (9:21).

Later in history it is again a Benjaminite, Sheba, the son of Bichri, who sounds the trumpet of rebellion against David and gives the word to the other tribes to secede from his house: "We have no part in David, nor inheritance in the son of Jesse: every man to his tents, O Israel!" (2 Sm 20:1). Yet after Solomon's death, when the secession of the northern tribes from the house of David becomes definite, Benjamin is the only tribe that stays with Judah.

The significance of Benjamin's loyalty to the house of David is explained by the prophet Ahijah. He meets Jeroboam, the first king of the ten rebellious tribes, and dividing his garment into twelve pieces, says to him: "Take to yourself ten pieces; for thus says the Lord God of Israel: Behold, I will rend the kingdom of Solomon out of his son's hands, and will give you ten tribes, and to this son I will give one tribe, that there may remain a lamp for my servant David before me always in Jerusalem, the city which I have chosen, that my name might be there" (1 Kgs 11:29-36). From then on Benjamin is the lamp that keeps alive in David's city the hope that the ten tribes will return, bringing with them the fullness of the gentiles.

Divine Election

It is easy to see how the destiny of Benjamin is fulfilled in St. Paul. In the morning of his life he acts indeed like a "ravenous wolf, devouring prey," "breathing threats of slaughter" against the sheep of Christ (Acts 9:1). As Rachel labored when she gave birth to Benjamin, so does Saul's true mother, the Church, suffer much from the wounds inflicted upon her by him. Then the "son of sorrow" is suddenly changed into the "son of God's right hand."

The time for him to "divide the spoil" begins for Saul on his way to Damascus. "Opening his eyes he can see nothing," and he is surrounded with the darkness of night for three days (Acts 9:8-9). Then it falls like scales from his eyes. God, who commanded the light to shine out of darkness, has shone in Saul's heart and given him the light of the knowledge of God's glory on the face of Jesus Christ (see 2 Cor 4:6).

The ravenous wolf, who has devoured the prey, begins to divide his spoils of victory, which the sacrificial love of Christ has won on the cross. St. Paul becomes the greatest of all the "dispensers of the mysteries of God" (1 Cor 4:1) by preaching the glad tidings of redemption to the whole world. The least among the twelve (1 Cor 15:9), like Benjamin he dwells in confidence with his Lord through faith in his charity (see Dt 33:27; Eph 3:7-17).

The fact that Benjamin is the only one of the sons of Jacob born in the Promised Land causes, in the history of his tribe, a tragic conflict between the universality of God's grace and the pride of being a native of the place of God's presence. Saul, the first king of the tribe of Benjamin, wants to build the young Israelite state on a purely racial basis. For this reason he does not tolerate the Gibeonites, who although they are not Israelites by blood have become members of the covenant (2 Sm 21:2).

As we have noted, the reaction against the nationalistic narrowness of Saul is David, who keeps a position above the twelve tribes by choosing Jerusalem, a city with a predominantly non-Jewish population, for his capital. The "city of David" is secured in the hands of the king by a royal guard of seasoned mercenaries of non-Jewish blood, the Cherethi and Pelethi (2 Sm 15:18). David atones for Saul's slaughter of the Gibeonites by delivering seven sons of Saul into their hands. They crucify them "on the hill before the Lord in the first days of the barley harvest," which means on Easter (2 Sm 21:9).

In view of this it cannot be considered a matter of chance that the other Saul, whose feelings as a Benjaminite were deeply hurt by St. Stephen's "saying things against the holy place and against the law" (Acts 6:13-14), is halted in his pursuit of the disciples by the same words with which David brought Saul to his senses when the latter was hunting him in the desert: "Who are you persecuting?" (see Acts 9:4; 1 Sm 24:14-15). When David revealed to his persecutor that he had saved his life, Saul's heart was pierced by David's love, and he became a prophet of his future kingship (1 Sm 24:20). The realization that he has persecuted the Son of David, who has given his life for him, turns Saul of Tarsus into an apostle of the rule of the risen Christ over all nations.

As Apostle to the Gentiles, St. Paul follows the footsteps of another great Benjaminite, Jeremiah, who was appointed by God "prophet of the gentiles." The words with which God called Jeremiah—"Before I formed you in the womb I knew you, and before you came forth I sanctified you: I have appointed you a prophet to the nations" (Jer 1:5)—are repeated by St. Paul in defense of his missionary activity among the heathen: "When God, who had set me apart from my birth and had called me in his mercy, saw fit to reveal his Son to me, so that I might preach the good news about him to the heathen, immediately instead of going up to Jerusalem ... I went off to Arabia" (Gal 1:13-17).

The divine election, through which a man becomes the instrument of universal salvation, precedes the birth in flesh and blood that makes him a member of a particular race. The "prophet of the gentiles" and the "Apostle of the Gentiles" both share in some measure the unique privilege of the Messiah who says of himself: "And now says the Lord who formed me from the womb to be his servant: I will give you for a light of the nations, that my salvation may be to the ends of the earth" (Is 49:5-6). The universality of the kingdom of God rests in the last analysis on the fact that the Messiah is "foreordained Son of God" before he becomes Son of David according to the flesh (Rom 1:4).

Benjamin's birth in the Holy Land should have been a sign to him of divine election. As soon as it was turned into a birthright, it became an obstacle to grace. Jeremiah, who showed his devotion to the land by buying a field in the land of Benjamin (Jer 32:6-15), protested vigorously against all earthly bragging about the temple (Jer 7:4). When he was accused of "saying things against the house and the city" (Jer 26)—just as Jesus was, and Stephen, and Paul—he lifted up his eyes to heaven and prayed: "You throne of glory, on high from the beginning! You place of our sanctuary! You hope of Israel, the Lord!" (Jer 17:12)—just as Jesus did, and Stephen, and Paul.

Saul of Tarsus, who can more than anybody else rely on his physical advantages as a Hebrew and a son of Hebrews, comes to count his former gains as loss for the sake of Christ. Thus he might be found in him, not having his own justice through the observance of the Law but the justice that is of God through faith in Christ Jesus. Him he wants to know, and the power of his resurrection and the fellowship of his sufferings, being made conformable to his death (Phil 3:4-10).

The Spirit of the Martyr

When St. Stephen, the first disciple of the Lord Jesus called to render witness to the universality of God's grace with his own blood, is being stoned for blasphemy by the defenders of the "place and the law," Saul is there to watch their garments. Holy Scripture ends the account of St. Stephen's execution with the momentous words: "And Saul entirely approved of his being put to death" (Acts 8:1).

If we consider that these words are written by St. Luke, St. Paul's intimate companion, we may easily guess that the apostle himself has insisted on this statement being made, as a matter of great importance to him. St. Stephen's death is the great crisis in St. Paul's life. By consenting to his death, Saul breaks down the barriers of his self-righteousness, and his soul becomes open to God's grace. It may be that St. Stephen's last words, "Lord, lay not this sin to their charge" (Acts 7:60), are the snare in which the divine Hunter catches his precious game. Who else could hear them better than Paul?

Anyhow, the spirit of St. Stephen lives on in the apostle. An intimate bond links the first deacon to the least of the apostles. The same glorified Lord whom Stephen saw standing at the right hand of the Father appears to Paul. Stephen was the first deacon of the Church, preaching the glad tidings (Acts 7:2-53) and serving the tables (Acts 6:3). St. Paul again and again calls himself the "deacon of God" or "deacon of Jesus Christ" (2 Cor 11:23), sent to announce the word rather than to baptize or fulfill priestly functions (1 Cor 1:14-17; Rom 15:16).

At the same time, Paul stresses his diaconal function of serving the tables of the poor saints of the Church of Jerusalem through a collection, which he takes up among the gentiles (2 Cor 8:19). Because they are partaking of the spiritual riches of Jerusalem, the mother Church of Christianity, through St. Paul's teaching, it is their duty to minister to the saints in Jerusalem with material things (Rom 15:25-27).

The function of the deacon, however, is not limited to the service of word and of tables. The truth to which he gives testimony and the charity with which he serves prepare him to become a sacrifice to God. As Stephen pours out his spirit before the Lord Jesus (Acts 7:59), so does St. Paul feel that his life is being spent like a drink offering to God: "As for me, I am already being poured out in sacrifice, and the time of my deliverance is at hand" (2 Tm 4:6).

In this ministry of his own blood for the faith of Jesus Christ, we touch the innermost secret in the life of St. Paul. Here is the ultimate source of his joy: "Even if my blood is being poured out as a sacrifice in the service of your faith, I am glad and rejoice with you, just as you also should be glad and rejoice in me" (Phil 2:17-18).

The Letters

The gospel that the Apostle to the Gentiles announced to the world has come down to us mainly in his letters. Naturally these do not form a systematic compendium of his teaching. With the exception of the Letter to the Romans, their contents are limited to the needs and questions of the moment. St. Paul's thinking, however, is so much dominated by one central idea that all thirteen of his letters[1] that have been preserved in the canon of the New Testament have one common root: the apostle's faith in the grace of Christ.

Saul's experience of conversion on the road to Damascus remains the guiding light of his teaching. There the mystery of Christ (Eph 3:4) has been revealed to him (Gal 1:22-24). There God, who in the beginning of the world commanded light to shine out of darkness, has by an act of pure grace kindled the light of faith in the mind of Saul to see Jesus as the gloriously reigning Lord (2 Cor 4:5-6), living and suffering in his disciples, replacing the emptiness of the Law with his personal presence, and breaking down the barriers of blood and of country that his name might be carried before gentiles and kings and the children of Israel (Acts 9:15). This indeed is the mystery that has been hidden in past ages and is now being revealed by the Spirit: that the grace of God has appeared to all men in the coming of the great God and Saviour Jesus Christ, who has given himself for us that he might redeem us from all iniquity; that we, not by reason of good works that we did ourselves but by believing in him, through the bath of regeneration and renewal by the Holy Spirit, might be purified as a people set apart for him, eager to do good works (Ti 2–3).

Romans

The most comprehensive exposition of the apostle's central theme of the grace of Christ is contained in the Letter to the Romans, which the Church ranks highest among the letters of St. Paul. St. Paul writes this letter during his third missionary journey, when he is revisiting Corinth (A.D. 58). His life has reached a turning point. He has "completed the preaching of Christ's gospel all the way from Jerusalem around to Illyricum," and there is no more work for him in that part of the world (Rom 15:19, 23).

His eyes turn to the West, as far as Spain (15:24); Rome seems to him to be the natural headquarters for this new campaign. In addressing himself to the Roman church, which has been founded in the capital of the gentile world without his help, the Apostle to the Gentiles rises to the whole height of his mission in the service of the glorified Lord Jesus. That Lord has breached the wall of separation between Jews and gentiles to unite all men in a common faith in the charity of God. In none of his letters is St. Paul more "catholic" than in this Letter to the Romans.

To the one who reads this letter for the first time, it seems a formidable maze of disjointed thoughts on all kinds of matters. But after a more intimate acquaintance with it, a definite structure appears, which we shall delineate briefly for the sake of the impatient reader. At the end of the introduction (1:1-17)—which consists of a salutation (1:1-7), a commendation of the church at Rome (1:8-12), and a declaration of his intention to visit it (1:13-15)—St. Paul states the theme of the letter: "The gospel is the power of God unto salvation to everyone who believes, Jew first and then Greek. It reveals God's way of justifying us, from faith to faith" (1:16-17).

In order to develop his main topic that the just live through faith in the justice of God, St. Paul shows first that humanity without Christ has no justice (1:18–3:20). The history of the gentiles proves that man left to himself is cut off from the glory of God (1:18-25) and given over to the lusts of the flesh (1:24-32). Such will be judged by God (2:1-11) according to the natural law written in their conscience (2:12-16). The Jews have the Mosaic Law, but it only brings to them the recognition of sin without being able to prevent transgressions. Scripture is right when it says: "There is not one just man.... All have gone astray" (Ps 14:1-3). Jews and Greeks are all under sin (2:17–3:20).

God, therefore, has brought to light his own way of justification by offering Christ to us as a means of reconciliation, so that all, Jews and gentiles, might lose all reason for boasting and instead put their trust in Christ's work of redemption (3:21-30). The universal saving power of faith is attested in the life of Abraham, who was declared just and father of all the nations through faith in God before he received circumcison (4:1-25). Through faith in Christ, who died for us in pure charity when we were yet sinners, the charity of God is poured forth in our hearts by the Holy Spirit (5:1-11).

We have become members of a new generation, which receives divine life from Christ as the new Adam (5:12-21). Through baptism we are planted into the death of Christ, which means that we are dead to sin (6:1-23), set free from the law that binds us to sin rather than giving us the strength to accomplish what is good (7:1-25), and freed from the inclination of the flesh through the Spirit of God, who raised Jesus from the dead (8:1-13). This Spirit makes us sons of God and heirs of future glory (8:14-17), which is attested by the yearning of all creation (8:18-22), of all of us (8:23-25), and of the Spirit within us (8:26-27). We are destined for this glory by God's eternal design (8:28-34), to which we are inseparably united through the charity of Christ (8:35-39).

Here where his faith has reached the peak of absolute confidence, St. Paul faces the most decisive objection to be raised against his gospel on the justice of God in Christ Jesus: the blindness of the Jews (chapters 9–11). The tragedy of the Jews (9:1-5) is no objection to the faithfulness of God, for the promises made to Abraham were not limited to the descendants of Abraham according to the flesh and therefore did not preclude God's free election of the "younger one"—that is, the spiritual Israel of the gentiles (9:6-13).

This election of the younger one is not against the justice of God, because salvation is a work of God's mercy and is therefore purely gratuitous (9:14-29). Moreover, the Jews themselves are responsible for their rejection, because they constantly wish to conquer justice for themselves through their own efforts and refuse to throw themselves into the arms of Christ, who all day long spread out his hands to a disobedient and gainsaying people (9:30–10:21).

Nevertheless, God has not cast off his people. On the contrary, the mystery of Jewish history is the greatest manifestation of his wisdom. Their present rejection is only partial. A "remnant" believes (11:1-12), which serves the purpose of grafting the wild olive branches of the gentiles into the original tree (11:13-22). This will not be final, but after the full number of the gentiles have entered, all Israel shall be saved (11:23-32).

Thus the history of the Jews is the triumph of the charity of God, who uses their rejection to reconcile the gentiles and will turn their final reception into the resurrection of all flesh (11:15). To contemplate the destiny of the Jewish people in the light of his faith in the justice of God is to St. Paul the greatest inspiration to praise the infinite depth of the riches of the wisdom of God (11:33-36).

After this doctrinal part of his exposition St. Paul briefly explains the practical fruits of the justice of God in the lives of Christians (12:1–15:13). The mercy of God in Christ Jesus transforms the lives of Christians into a continuous spiritual service (12:1-2), in which we give up our personal pride and humbly accept the place the grace of God has assigned to us in the community (12:3-8). We are to love one another and overcome all evil with the goodness of charity (12:9-21), which demands our obedience and justice in dealing with worldly authorities (13:1-7) and really is the fulfillment of the Law (13:8-10), urged upon us by the nearness of the day of salvation (13:11-14). Its most important test for the Roman Church is mutual tolerance in relations among Jewish Christians and gentiles in the community, so that the church of the Jews and the church of the gentiles can with one mouth glorify the God and Father of our Lord Jesus Christ (14:1–15:13).

Guiding the Churches

The gospel of the grace of Christ, which the Letter to the Romans explains so comprehensively, is in the other letters of St. Paul applied to more limited circumstances and problems. Next in importance, after the Letter to the Romans, are the letters to the Corinthians.

Corinth is at this time the most prosperous center of Greek civilization, the lights and the shadows of which are also discernible in the life of the Christian community founded there by St. Paul. The cult of the human mind and body, characteristic of Hellenism, leads easily to sophisticated individualism and to moral corruption.

In the first part of the First Letter to the Corinthians, St. Paul bids Greek intellectualism to surrender to the wisdom of the cross (1:10–4:21). In the second part he shows how the spirit of the risen Christ shakes off impurity (chapter 5), makes our bodies members of Christ (chapter 6), and gives a new meaning to marriage (7:1-24) and a new dignity to holy virginity (7:25-38). The Spirit replaces the impurities of idol worship with the new spiritual bread and the spiritual cup of the Eucharist (chapters 8–11). From a great variety of spiritual gifts he forms the unity of the mystical body of Christ (chapters 12–14) and finally transforms our mortal bodies in the resurrection of the flesh (chapter 15).

The Second Letter to the Corinthians is St. Paul's answer to the critical attitude toward spiritual authority that is also characteristic of the Greek mind, and which has led to disobedience toward the apostle in the church of Corinth. In brilliant colors he depicts the glory of the spiritual ministry of the New Testament, which is essentially a service in charity, not a rule in power. Charity, however, does not impair authority, as spiritual authority does not exclude charity.

As Apostle to the Gentiles St. Paul has not only the mission to lead the mind of the Greek captive in the obedience of Christ but also to defend liberty in Christ against captivity under the Law. In his Letter to the Galatians he shows the superiority of the new grace over the old Law, which cannot give life.

How the grace of Christ builds the unity of the Church as a temple of the Holy Spirit is the topic of the Letters to the Ephesians, Philippians, Colossians, and Thessalonians. Ephesians shows the foundation of ecclesiastical unity in Christ as the head, in whom all things in heaven and on earth are reestablished. Philippians, the most personal and intimate of all Pauline letters, gives a picture of the growth of this unity, while Colossians defends it against false teachers. The two letters to the Thessalonians, chronologically the first St. Paul wrote, seek to strengthen this young community against present (1 Thes) and future (2 Thes) persecution, preceding the second coming of Christ.

The last group of letters, often called the pastoral letters, explain the grace of Christ in the responsible leaders of the Church, the bishops and deacons (1 and 2 Tm, Ti). To these may be added, last but not least, the short Letter to Philemon, in which St. Paul exhorts a Christian master to make of his runaway slave a brother in Christ. St. Paul can indeed not render a more convincing testimony to the grace of Christ, which abounds "beyond all measure" in him "in all wisdom and prudence" (Eph 1:8), than he does in these letters.

TWENTY-SEVEN

The Seven Catholic Letters

Christ "being put to death in the flesh, was made alive in the Spirit" (1 Pt 3:18). At his resurrection the human nature of Christ was filled with the glory of divinity. The Second Adam became "a quickening spirit" (1 Cor 15:45). He ascended into heaven that the whole earth might be filled with his Spirit. "It is better for you that I should go away. For if I do not go the Paraclete will not come to you, but if I go I will send him to you" (Jn 16:7).

Through his ascension Christ became truly the Head of his mystical body. As Head he rules over the Church, not in the manner of an earthly king who lays down the law in dead letters, but in the power of the Spirit, who writes the new law of love in the hearts of the faithful. Fifty days after the chosen people passed through the Red Sea, they received the Law on Mount Sinai. Fifty days after Christ had passed through death into the new life of the Resurrection, he sent the Spirit of love to replace the tablets of stone. The Spirit of the risen Christ is the inner life of the new Israel, which has been redeemed in his blood.

It is fitting, therefore, that the Church formerly appointed the seven catholic letters to be read during the weeks immediately preceding and following Pentecost. The whole purpose of these letters is to impress upon the minds of Christians the fundamental fact that the "salvation" they received in baptism is a new life that can be achieved only from one source, the risen Christ as the head of a new generation. This life in turn can be lived only within the one "body," which is formed by the life-giving Spirit of Christ, the Church.

We children of this modern age are inclined to consider salvation something that lies in the future and has to be worked out chiefly by us individually, although we may need the help of the teachings and the sacraments of the Church. The apostolic doctrine, expounded in the seven catholic letters, will correct any such shallow concept that we may have of our true nature as Christians. It will make us realize that salvation is not an assistance only to be better men, but a transformation into divine life, which St. Paul calls our "being sealed by the Holy Spirit of God unto the day of redemption" (Eph 4:30).

Corresponding to the traditional division of the Old Testament into the Law (five books of Moses), the Prophets (including the historical as well as the prophetic books from Joshua to Malachi), and the Sages (Job, Proverbs, Psalms, and so on), which are concerned with the spiritual life of the people of God, we can distinguish three groups of writings in the New Testament: the Gospels, the Acts, and the letters of the apostles, in which the practical wisdom of Christian living is explained. Among these latter the seven catholic letters form a group apart from the letters of St. Paul, not only because they have other apostles as their authors[1] but mainly because they are of a different character.

The letters of St. Paul are real letters, directed to definite congregations or persons, dealing with problems that have arisen in the concrete circumstances of life. Most of the seven catholic letters are treatises of a universal character, directed to groups of churches or to all Christians. St. James sends his "letter" to the "twelve tribes in the dispersion" (1:1), a symbolic expression for the Christians of the new Israel, who are living as strangers and pilgrims here on earth. The First Letter of St. Peter is addressed to the "elect who dwell as foreigners up and down Pontus, Galatia, Cappadocia, Asia and Bithynia" (1:1). The First Letter of St. John does not mention any specific addressee at all.

This general and elementary character has given to these writings the name of "catholic letters." That there are seven of them is more than a matter of chance, because seven is always the number of earthly universality or of "catholicity." It is indeed remarkable how these seven letters form a complete whole in themselves, representing the life of the Spirit in all its fundamental aspects.

A short survey of their general contents will show this reality immediately. The Letter of St. James is the most general of them. It is closely related to the Book of Jesus Sirach (Ecclesiasticus) in the Old Testament and to the Sermon on the Mount in the New. It is the New Testament "book of wisdom." "If anyone of you want wisdom, let him ask of God, who gives to all men abundantly" (1:5).

The First Letter of St. Peter points out to Christians facing persecution the sure hope that is theirs through Jesus Christ. "Blessed be the Lord and Father of our Lord Jesus Christ who has begotten us anew unto a living hope through the resurrection of Jesus Christ from the dead" (1:3). The Second Letter of St. Peter—together with that of St. Jude, which it incorporates nearly entirely—warns the Christians to preserve the purity of faith against heretical doctrines. "I was under the necessity to write to you: to beseech you to contend earnestly for the faith that was handed down, once for all, to the saints" (Jude 3). The letters of St. John expound the topic that is closest to the heart of the apostle whom the Lord loved: "Behold what manner of charity *(agape)* the Father has bestowed upon us" (1 Jn 3:1).

The seven letters, therefore, develop the complete pattern of spiritual life: the wisdom that descends from God and brings everything back to him; and the three theological virtues of faith, hope, and charity, which transform, direct, and animate the whole life of man to fill it with the *plenitudo divinitatis,* the fullness of the Godhead.

The Letter of James

The Letter of St. James explains, in the language of a man who has been trained in the school of the prophets and the sages of the Old

Testament, the elementary rules of life that a Christian should observe. The first and fundamental truth, which St. James, and with him all the other apostles, states in an emphatic manner, is that Christian wisdom descends from God; it does not rise out of the hearts of men. The human heart is the source of temptations, of passions, of pride, and of sin. Whatever gifts are worth having come to us from above, from the Father of all, who gives light (1:5, 17). Of his own accord he has brought us into being by the word of truth, so that we might be a kind of first fruits among his creatures (1:18).

Christians must be ready listeners who, in a humble spirit, let the word, which has the power to save their souls, be planted in their hearts (1:21). After they have received the word, they must act upon it. Who could be brought to life by the word of the Father and not become a father to the orphans and the widows? How could he cater to the rich and refuse to become a father to the poor? How could he set up himself as a merciless judge of others (1:27–2:13)? Faith without good works is indeed like a body without a soul, a dead thing (2:14-26).

In a simple but forceful "down-to-earth" manner, St. James warns his fellow Christians of the blatant inconsistencies that so often exist between their faith and their conduct in everyday life. The tongue is a little organ, but of greatest importance in human life. It is given to us to praise God. How could we use it to curse men made in God's likeness (3:1-12)?

Bitter feelings of jealousy and rivalry are incompatible with the wisdom that descends from above, which is chaste, peaceable, considerate, full of compassion and good deeds (3:13-18). Likewise the cravings of our lower instincts can never be on friendly terms with the Spirit God has put in our hearts (4:1-5).

Those who are born anew from above must become enemies of the world. They must humble their pride before the Lord, and the Lord will raise them up (4:6-10). Pride is also the root of detraction, which infringes upon the exclusive rights of the one Judge who has the power to save and to destroy (4:11-12). Pride lets us take our lives into our own hands as if no God existed, and it makes us forget that we are no more than a mist, which appears for a little while and then disappears (4:13-17).

The worst fate, however, awaits the wealthy who have withheld wages from laborers and have lived luxuriously and voluptuously here on earth. They have fattened their hearts for the day of slaughter (5:1-6).

Incompatible with the concupiscences and the pride of life, which fill this world, the wisdom from above has created another world, which the apostle describes in the last part of his letter (5:7-20). The world of salvation rests on the firm foundation of the patience with which we wait for the coming of the Lord, as the farmer waits for the rain from above. The fact that human history can come to an end at any moment, with the advent of Christ, fills the hearts of Christians with courage and endurance in all adversities. It prevents us from complaining of one another and causes us to be sincere, so that our *yes* is a plain *yes* and our *no* a plain *no*.

The heart of this new world, however, is prayer. "Is anyone of you sad? Let him say a prayer. Is he cheerful in mind? Let him sing a hymn!" (5:13). As patience is waiting for the wisdom from above to come, so is prayer its very presence among us. If anyone, therefore, is sick, he should call in the priests of the Church and have them pray over him and anoint him with oil in the name of the Lord (5:14). The "wisdom from above" will act as a good physician, taking care of the body as well as the soul of the sick man. Mutual confession of sins, mutual intercession, continual prayer, and zeal to save the souls of those who have gone astray make up the new world of salvation where the true wisdom loves to dwell.

The Letters of Peter and Jude

There is no other letter written by the apostles that depicts with equal enthusiasm the splendor of that heavenly gift of salvation that we have received in baptism than the First Letter of St. Peter. Written probably in Rome ("Babylon," see 5:13) at the beginning of the persecution of Nero (A.D. 64), this letter is truly the word of a spiritual father to his newborn children in Christ. These he wants to prepare for the time of trial that is close at hand.

At that solemn moment on Saturday in Easter week when the neophytes put off their baptismal robes to face the trials of daily life, the words of this letter were used to impress them with their dignity as a kingly priesthood, a holy nation, people set apart. In our days the message of this letter is more important than it ever has been in the past, because it is the Magna Charta of the Christian "laity," that is, of the members of the united, organized body of the people of God. The successors of St. Peter in our day want so much to see these laity become conscious again of their dignity and their responsibility.

We cannot read the first chapter of St. Peter's letter without realizing that it is the "rock" upon whom Christ has built his Church who speaks here. His aim is to inspire his fellow Christians with the rocklike firmness that emanates from the risen Christ. In baptism the Christians have been born anew from an imperishable seed (1:23), the Spirit of the risen Christ. They have received, therefore, a sure hope, which is not like that of the heathen, a timid and uncertain looking forward to something they do not have and might never receive. Christian hope is, on the contrary, a firm possession, through faith, of an imperishable inheritance kept safe for us in heaven.

The Spirit of Christ received in baptism is the advance installment of that inheritance. With perfect calmness should Christians fix their hopes on the grace that will be offered to them when Jesus Christ is revealed (1:13). He is like a living stone, upon which we can be built like living stones, into a spiritual house for a holy priesthood, to offer spiritual sacrifices that through Jesus Christ are acceptable to God (2:5).

Like a lighthouse in the raging sea of the gentile world should this holy nation stand, a shining witness to the glory of God. The liberty acquired in Christ does not make them revolutionaries but staunch supporters of the social order, as citizens submissive to legitimate authority (2:13-17), as slaves serving their masters (2:18-25), as wives subject to their husbands (3:1-6), as husbands showing deference to their wives (3:7), as brothers and sisters being all of one mind (3:8-11). Even the pressure of persecution will not turn Christians into rebels but will let them share in the spirit of martyrdom that Christ himself showed when he died for our sins, the just for the unjust, to bring us to God. He was put to death in the flesh but was made alive in the Spirit, and so shall we be who through baptism have part of his triumph (3:14-22).

As Christ suffered in the flesh, so should we mortify our sensual nature, dying to the desires of men and living according to the will of God (4:1-6). Mortification is always accompanied by edification, through which the new spirit of brotherly love builds up the Church by ministering to the brethren as good stewards of the manifold grace of God (4:7-11).

In a moving final appeal St. Peter exhorts his dear friends in Christ to stand up under the test of fire that is being applied to them, as men who know that when they share the sufferings of Christ the glorious spirit of God is resting upon them (4:14). Addressing himself especially to the "elders," being himself a "brother elder" and witness to what Christ suffered (5:1), he implores them to carry their charge—not like drudges, not tyrannizing, not as hirelings, but cordially and generously as God would have it done—that they might receive from the prince of shepherds a never-fading crown of glory (5:1-5). If the younger ones also show deference to the elders and humility toward one another, if they all throw their care upon God, then the God of all mercies will, after a little while of suffering, perfect, confirm, and establish the whole Church like a rock, standing fast in the true grace of God (5:6-14).

The Second Letter of St. Peter was evidently written with that of St. Jude at hand, for it incorporates the latter with some slight changes (2 Pt 2:1–3:14). Both letters have as their objective the preservation of the true faith against the false teachings of heretics. A deep sense of their apostolic responsibility moves the authors to warn Christians lest they lose the firm hold that a divinely inspired faith has given them (3:17).

Nothing could be more contrary to the doctrine of these letters than the idea so often proclaimed in our days that matters of faith and doctrine are irrelevant to salvation. The reason for the apostles' uncompromising attitude is not arrogance or narrow-minded sectarianism but their fundamental conviction that the whole meaning of Christianity is to let us share in the divine nature (1:4). Therefore, only that faith can be truly Christian which is authentically divine, approved by the Father and handed down by faithful witnesses (1:17-18). "No prophecy has ever originated in the human will, but under the influence of the Holy Spirit men spoke for God" (1:21).

Heretical teachings are dangerous because they are "of man's invention" (1:16) and therefore powerless to change men's lives (2:12-22). Men who "deride anything they do not understand" are like "rainless clouds driven before the wind" (2:17; Jude 12), because by being cut off from the divine light they have also lost contact with the divine life. From the mouth of the apostle Jude rings out, therefore, the solemn warning to Christians of all ages: "Make your most holy faith the foundation of your lives, and go on praying in the power of the Holy Spirit. Keep in the love of God, and wait for the mercy of our Lord Jesus Christ, with eternal life as your goal" (Jude 20-21).

The Letters of John

In the three letters of St. John the general warning against false teachers becomes more specific. The great theologian among the apostles turns against those "who will not acknowledge that Jesus Christ has come in human flesh" (2 Jn 7). These "aristocrats of the spirit" look down upon the average Christians as "animal men" who are unable to ascend to the heights of a "purely spiritual" idea of God. They believe in the innate goodness of human nature and abhor the Christian belief of redemption through the blood of Christ. Their spiritual pride induces them to segregate themselves from the *hoi polloi* and to form exclusive religious circles. The wrong spiritualism of the gnostics, as they call themselves, causes them to deny the Incarnation and to destroy, at the same time, the bond of brotherly love among those who are redeemed. They follow a wrong light that does not impart life and is unable to unite men in love.

Against them St. John shows in the first of his letters that God is charity. Further, the incarnation and the passion of the Son of God are the channels through which this charity of God descends to men, redeeming them from sin and uniting them in brotherly love. Whoever, therefore, denies the Incarnation separates men from God and destroys the bonds of brotherly love. The charity of God, the incarnation of Christ, and the unity of the Church are inseparable.

This fundamental doctrine is developed by the apostle in his letter under the three different aspects of light, life, and love. In the first section (1:5–2:28) he shows, in opposition to the gnostics' claim to be really "enlightened" while other Christians are still living in darkness, that God alone is light, and that those who live in fellowship with God do not live in darkness (1:5-6).

The true light, however, is not some kind of higher theoretical knowledge; it is practical sanctity, and the darkness opposed to it is sin. True knowledge, therefore, cannot be separated from observing the commandments (2:4), nor can it be separated from brotherly love. He who hates his brother is still in darkness (2:9). No compromise is possible with the "love of the world," which is concupiscence of the flesh, concupiscence of the eyes, and pride of life (2:16). True light is that of the faith that has been handed down to us through tradition (2:24): that Jesus is Christ, the Son of the Father. Whoever disowns the Son through false teachings regarding the nature of Christ is not in the light, which is God.

In the second section of the letter (2:29–4:7) the same fundamental truths are explained under the aspect of life. God is Father, the source of life; we are not only counted as God's sons, but we really are his children, here and now, although it has not yet appeared what we shall be (3:2).

The life that makes us children of God is opposed to sin, which makes us children of the devil (3:8). The surest sign that we have the life of the Father in us is the fact that we love our brothers and sisters, because the Father has made us his children by his Son's laying down his life for us. For that same reason it is of vital importance that we keep the faith, which teaches us that Christ has come to us in human flesh (4:2).

That we are light and that we have life depend, therefore, on the fundamental truth St. John explains again in the third part of his letter (4:8–5:12): God is charity, and we remain united to him as long as we love one another. God revealed the inner secret of his love when he sent his only begotten Son into the world, that we may have life through him (4:9-10). This love, for which the New Testament writers coined the word *agape* to distinguish it from the love the fallen world knows under the name of *eros*, consists not in our having loved God but in God's loving us first and sending his Son as an atoning sacrifice for our sins (4:10).

Human love, in this state of fallen nature, is self-centered. It has been overcome by the selfless love in which the Father offered Christ when man was his enemy. On the cross, in water and in blood, Christ has won the victory, in which we take part through faith.

Our faith, which has triumphed over the world, is faith in the charity of God as manifested in the Son. In him life has been revealed. The apostle has seen it with his own eyes and touched it with his hands. He announces it to us that we may also have life by believing in the Son of God (5:13-21).

In this marvelous letter the teaching of the seven letters reaches its climax. What the apostles want to impress on their audience—and we are of their flock, sitting at their feet—is the divine reality of our life in Christ, which is not only observance of commandments but life "in the power of God." God's sovereign love has drawn us to himself through his Son, in the power of the Holy Spirit. Made partakers in the divine nature, it is now up to us to "ratify God's calling and choice of us by a life well lived" (2 Pt 1:10).

TWENTY-EIGHT

The Apocalypse

The fifty days between Easter Sunday and Pentecost constitute, according to the mind of the Church, one continuous feast. As the number forty is symbolic of this present age, so the number fifty represents eternity. Therefore the forty days of Lent, devoted to fasting and fighting and to the commemoration of Christ's *Pascha* or "passage" through this world, are followed by fifty days of feasting to celebrate the "exaltation" of Christ. The Church of old used the term exaltation to comprehend, in one word, the various phases of Christ's glorification: his resurrection, his ascension, the descent of the Holy Spirit, and the second coming. The angels had told the "men of Galilee," when they saw the Lord ascending into heaven: "This Jesus who is taken up from you into heaven, shall so come as you have seen him going into heaven" (Acts 1:11). The Christians of the first centuries, therefore, considered these fifty days as the time the Lord would choose for his second coming. To prepare themselves for this greatest of all events in the history of our salvation, they used to read the Apocalypse.

The word *apocalypse* means "a revelation." We often use this word in the plural to speak of revelations received by a saint, meaning supernatural communications of a more-or-less private nature, usually containing some spiritual advice. Here, however, the word is used in the singular. The Apocalypse is not a private communication but an official revelation that God gave to Jesus Christ and that the latter makes known to John through the mediation of an angel (1:1). It does not contain private spiritual advice, but it is the disclosure of God's

349

mysteries regarding "the things which are and which will come to pass hereafter" (1:19). The "things which are" refer to the spiritual condition of the Church and the dangers that threaten her from within (chapters 2–3). The "things which will come to pass" are revealed in the rest of the book and concern the attacks launched against the Church from without and her final victory.

Popular conception usually considers this latter part of the Apocalypse a prophetic picture of the whole history of the Church in her struggle against the opposition of the world. Thus the Protestant Reformers of the sixteenth century saw the papacy prefigured in the scarlet-clad harlot seated upon the beast. Some of their opponents decided that the name that underlies the mysterious number of the Antichrist, 666, was that of Luther! Adventists, Anabaptists, and many other sects made the prophecy of chapter 20, on the "reign of the thousand years," the cornerstone of their doctrine, claiming that with their own appearance in this world Satan had been chained. Their hopes ended sooner or later in disappointment.

The Apocalypse indeed is not a matter of counting the times and the seasons. Any genuine interpretation of this most difficult of all books of Holy Scripture has to start with describing the historical situation in which it was written.

The Book of the Martyr

When St. Luke finished writing the Acts of the Apostles, around the year 63, it had not yet been determined what attitude the Roman Imperium would take toward Christianity. Acts described how the Spirit, who fills the apostles, compels them to preach publicly and with all boldness that Christ Jesus is the Lord *(Kyrios)* in whose name every knee should bend. The book ends, however, before Caesar has passed judgment on Paul.

During the thirty years that elapsed between the writing of Acts and that of the Apocalypse, the Roman Empire developed more and more into a totalitarian state. The Caesars, especially Nero and Domitian, assumed the title "lord and god." This made the conflict between the two "lords," Caesar and Christ, inevitable. When the empire imposed upon Christians as a test of loyalty the performance of religious ritual in the worship of the emperors, the apostle—witness of the risen Lord (Acts 1:22)—necessarily became a martyr. The Apocalypse is the book of the martyr.

Living in exile on the Island of Patmos, John[1] shares the tribulations the persecution under Domitian (about A.D. 95) has brought upon his brethren in Christ. There, on a "Lord's Day," the day when the whole Church renders public homage to the risen Christ as the Lord of the whole universe through the solemn celebration of Mass, John is rapt, in ecstasy (1:10). Hearing a "great voice" from behind him, he turns and sees the "Son of Man" in his heavenly glory, surrounded by the symbols of his universal rule, the seven stars and the seven candlesticks (1:12).

We are reminded of a similar event in the life of St. Stephen, the first martyr. He, confessing before the public authorities the lordship of Jesus, saw heaven open and the Son of Man standing at the right hand of God (Acts 7:55). The trial of the martyr, which was staged to reveal his guilt to the eyes of the world, turned into a revelation of the glory of Christ, who triumphed in the martyr's steadfast confession.

On the other hand, the true satanic nature of the powers of this world showed itself in all its brutality. Thus the trial of the martyr was in itself an "apocalypse," an image of the last universal revelation of the forces of good and evil, which will take place at the end of history before the tribunal of God. In the martyr, therefore, present and future merge into one. Spiritually he lives in the "last days."

The same is true of any period in the history of the Church in which the powers of the world strive for total domination; it is true of our own age. We have seen hundreds and thousands of Christian martyrs in Mexico, in Russia, in Spain, in Yugoslavia, in Communist China, turning their trials into manifestations of Christ's glory. We are living indeed in an "apocalyptic age." Spiritually we are contemporaries of John. That is what makes the study of the Apocalypse so vital to us.

Letters to the Churches

We should, therefore, listen carefully to the message the Spirit has for the churches in the first part of the Apocalypse (chapters 2–3). In each of the seven letters that contain this message the divine Author presents himself under a different aspect, all of which, taken together, make up his complete personal description (see 1:12-16). In a similar way each of the seven churches shows a characteristic trait, while taken together they represent the universal Church.

The first letter is directed to the church of Ephesus, the "first city of Asia." She has "done much." Her orthodoxy is beyond reproach. But she has lost the "first love" and therefore needs to be invigorated by eating the fruit from the tree of life, the holy Eucharist. Otherwise Christ, who appears here with the symbols of his universal power, will remove her lampstand from its place—that is, deprive her of her rank as the leading church in Asia. To be strict against heresies is not all; it is not even enough as long as the "first love," spontaneous enthusiasm, is lacking. That "first love" can be restored only through the fountain of genuine Christian love, the holy Eucharist.

In the letter to the church of Smyrna, Christ appears as the martyr, "who died and came to life again" (2:8). This corresponds to the spirit of Smyrna, the church of the martyrs, rich in apparent poverty, deeply alive in apparent death. Hers is the "crown of life."

Pergamum is the seat of the Roman authority in Asia and the center of the imperial worship. To her Christ appears as wielding the sharp, double-edged sword of the gospel, because she needs to be cleansed from heretical doctrines. Therefore, the hidden manna of contemplation is promised to her.

Thyatira, by nature an unimportant and unattractive little place, has become a military outpost of the Roman army, with the immorality and superstition common to such places. To the church there Christ writes as the Judge, whose eyes blaze like fire and search men's hearts and minds. He turns her attention from military drill to the spiritual power and authority which is derived from the Father.

Severe rebuke is directed against the church in Sardis, a former capital of Asia. The city lost its power when its otherwise unconquerable fort was taken by surprise by night. Again, the church of Sardis seems to be asleep. The "one who holds the seven spirits" warns her therefore: "If you do not wake up, I will come like a thief, and you will not know at what hour I am coming upon you" (3:3).

The city of Philadelphia is the gateway to Phrygia and inner Asia. The church there is addressed by him "who is holy and true, who carries the key of David" (3:7). He has opened the door of missionary activity to this church, because she has kept faithfully the message of the cross (3:10).

Laodicea has always been a city devoted to commercial interests and to the material side of life. The Christians of that city are evidently affected by the same spirit. They think that they are wealthy, that they need nothing (3:17), when in the eyes of the Lord they are beggars, blind and naked. The most bitter of reproaches, however, is followed by the most tender of pleas: "Here I stand knocking at the door. If anyone listens to my voice and opens the door, I will be his guest and dine with him, and he with me" (3:20).

The View From Heaven

These seven letters are, as we have seen, an examination of the spiritual condition of the Church. The following chapters (4–22) show us the meaning of history in the messianic age. This new part is introduced by a vision of the heavenly world (chapter 4), because everything that is happening on earth has its ideal preexistence in the mind of God, which is symbolized by the book with the seven seals. Only the Lamb is able to open it, because Christ, our Paschal Lamb who died for us and rose for us, is the beginning and the end of God's designs. He is the only key to the mysteries of history, because he alone did in all things the will of the Father.

The seven seals (chapters 5–8) present a moving picture of the endless miseries that afflict mankind in the course of history. Conquest, wars, dearth, death, famine, earthquake—they all pass before our eyes in a fearful procession, interrupted only by the cry of the innocent victims: "How long, O Lord, how long!" (6:10). However, the only reaction to this tragedy on the part of those of this world is fear, not repentance (6:17).

At the same time another development takes place: the sealing of the elect (7:1-8). It is a beautiful vision of the sacramental activity of the Church, which forms the other side of human history. The angel rising from the east signifies the priesthood as representing the risen Christ on earth. He seals the 144,000 with the seal of the living God in baptism and confirmation.

The number 144,000 is not to be taken literally but symbolically, indicating the completeness of salvation. The seer does not want to give the number of Jews to be saved, but as the following vision of the blessed in heaven shows (7:9-17), he wants to give a picture of the universality of salvation, of which the number twelve has always been a symbol.

A new call to repentance is directed to the world with the sounding of the seven trumpets. They herald tremendous cosmic catastrophes. Heaven seems to attack the earth with nuclear bombs (chapters 8–11). The effect is the same as before: The rest of mankind, those who did not perish by these plagues, does not repent (9:20).

Over the clouds of dust and debris—the aftermath of the seven trumpets' blast—another awe-inspiring vision arises: an angel of sovereign strength, with a cloud for his vesture and a rainbow about his head, with a face bright as the sun and feet like pillars of fire. Setting his right foot on the sea and his left on the dry land, and lifting his right hand toward heaven, he swears by him who lives through endless ages that time (delay) should be no more (chapter 10). God's patience has come to an end. The last series of plagues, described in the seven cups (chapters 15–16), are not a warning anymore nor a means to lead to repentance. They have the character of punishment, the "bowls of God's wrath" (16:1). Obdurate beyond repentance, men blaspheme God in their unbearable pains (16:9, 11).

Before this last series of plagues—which remind us of the plagues of Egypt (Ex 7:14–11:10)—has been loosed upon mankind, seven signs appear in heaven and reveal the true nature of the opposing forces of good and evil (chapters 12–15). The dragon (chapter 12) is— throughout the Old Testament, beginning with the first pages of Genesis (3:1)—the symbol of Satan (see Is 27:1). The beast rising out of the sea (13:1-10; see Dn 7:3) represents political power in the service of Satan. At St. John's time it was the Roman Empire with its Caesars, who blasphemed God with their titles of divinity.

The beast coming up from the land (13:11-18) is later constantly identified as the "false prophet" (19:20). It signifies the forces of evil in the intellectual field: the theologians, priests, and propagandists of the Antichrist, who strive to induce men by means of force, deceptive publicity, and economic pressure (13:17) to worship the image of the beast. The false prophet is the satanic reverse of the priesthood. As the angel marks the redeemed with the sign of the living God, likewise the false prophet marks men with the mark of the beast (13:16), the number 666, which "indicates a certain man" (13:18).

According to most commentators this man is Nero, because the Hebrew letters of this name render the numerical value of 666. Even if this application to a historical person should not be true, the number six is half of twelve and therefore essentially incomplete. As 144,000 is salvation fulfilled; 666 is the symbol of definite, absolute frustration.

To the signs indicating the forces of evil belongs also the great harlot (chapters 17–18), the "church" of the Antichrist. Whether it happens in Babylon, Rome, Paris, Berlin, London, New York, or any other big city, the accumulation of men, of wealth, and of power in the service of Satan shows the same characteristics everywhere. They form always the "harlot" who sells everything; without love, without faith, without lasting principles of truth and of morals, she caters to those men in power, providing a marvelous opportunity for politicians and international merchants (18:9-19). The glittering facade of wealth and passion covers only hatred and destruction. Her very princes hate her and eat her flesh (17:16).

In John's time the memory of Nero is still alive. Legend has it that he will return after his death (17:8). He does return, and he still returns, not in person but in those who do what he did: who in the guise of saviours usurp power, claim divine honors for themselves, and eat the flesh of those whom they have "liberated."

The Glorious Victors

The signs of the forces of evil—the serpent-dragon, the beast, the harlot—express the subtlety, violence, and faithlessness of godforsaken selfishness. They are opposed by the three signs of good: the woman clothed with the sun, the Lamb, and the rider with the two-edged sword of the gospel. They represent in turn the faith, the sacrificial love, and the wisdom upon which the kingdom of God is founded.

The woman clothed in the sun, with the moon under her feet and a crown of twelve stars on her head (12:1), is the Church, the true Israel of the Old and New Testaments. The twelve stars upon her head are the twelve tribes of Israel (Gn 37:9), to whom correspond in the New Testament the twelve apostles. Both represent the complete number of all the elect.

The moon at her feet is the symbol of this world in need of salvation. Because the moon shines through the light of the sun, it is also a symbol of faith in Christ as the risen Lord, the Sun of Justice. Faith makes the soul shine in the light of the risen Christ.

The child whom the woman brings forth, as well as the dragon who persecutes them, point to the "protoevangel" of Genesis 3:15: "I will put enmity between you (the serpent) and the woman, between your seed and her seed." The child of the woman is the Messiah, together with those who are being saved through him. In ancient symbolism the community is always identified with the individual in whom it is most perfectly represented.

The interpretation of the woman as a symbol of the Church does not, therefore, exclude its application to Mary, the Mother of God. The fullness of grace that is hers has wrapped her in divine light as in a garment. She is the mother of the "seed" who will crush the serpent's head. She is the mother of all the redeemed, symbolized in the twelve stars. She is the bridge between the "sun" and the "moon," between the Word of God and mankind. Her own life reflects the history of the chosen people: As Israel had to flee into the desert before Pharaoh, so Mary had to flee with the newborn Saviour before Herod (12:6).

The sign of the woman is completed by the vision of the Lamb standing on Mount Zion (chapter 14). The Lamb is the symbol of God's sacrificial love, in which he saves mankind by offering his Son as victim for our sins. Therefore the Lamb stands in the center of the throne "as if slain" (5:6). The accuser has been conquered "because of the Lamb's blood" (12:11). Now the Lamb is the center of God's kingdom. It is surrounded by the 144,000, who in the splendor of holy virginity follow the Lamb wherever he goes and sing the new canticle of the Lamb.

After the fall of Babylon (chapter 18), the wedding feast of the Lamb is announced (19:7). It consists of seven visions describing the consummation of history (chapters 19–22). The Word of God—clad in the blood-sprinkled garment of his love with the two-edged sword of the gospel as his weapon—leads the celestial armies to victory (19:13-15). The beast and the false prophet are cast into the lake of fire. The dragon is chained for a thousand years, while those who belong to Christ reign with him (20:2-5).

St. Augustine, who explained this entire paragraph in book 20 of his *City of God*, referred the thousand years to all the years of this age between the first and the second comings of Christ. During this time the devil is chained because he cannot seduce the Church, and those who rise in the "first resurrection" (20:5) of baptism really reign with Christ.

Immediately before the final judgment a last persecution takes place, when "Gog and Magog" are stirred up against the "tents of God's people" (20:9). *Gog* means "house," as opposed to the tabernacle or booth. The house is the dwelling place of those who "take care of themselves." The tabernacle serves those who throw all their cares upon God, trust in his help, and do not plan any harm against anybody else. The people of God, therefore, live in tents. The final struggle between the "house" and the "tent" is the eternal struggle between those who only trust in themselves, and therefore fight against everybody else, and those who trust in God and therefore live in peace with others.

After the final judgment (20:11-15) a new heaven and a new earth arise, "and there is no longer any sea," because the sea is the residue of chaos in this world (see Gn 1:9). The New Jerusalem descends from heaven, because she is built by God's love and not, like the Tower of Babel, by human efforts. She is the chosen vessel of God's sacrificial love, the "bride of the Lamb," built on the measure of twelve, the symbolic number of God's will to save.

There is no temple in her, because the temple is only a symbol of God's presence in a world that has lost him. No sun, no moon, shine in her, because they separate the times (Gn 1:14) and have therefore no meaning in eternity. The river of the Holy Spirit waters the city. The Tree of Life gives her all the beauty of the Garden of Eden. But New Jerusalem is more: a city.

The end of history excels over the beginning. From the garden the way has led to the city of God, whose lamp is the Lamb, because she receives all her light from the ever-burning love of God. "There we shall rest and see, we shall see and love, we shall love and we shall praise. Behold what shall be in the end without end!"[2]

Nevertheless, before this Sabbath comes, whose end shall not be the evening but the Lord's Day, we shall cry, "Amen. Come, Lord Jesus!" that he soon may come as we have seen him going into heaven.

Notes

Words of Eternal Life: How to Read the Scriptures

1. St. Leo, *Sermon* 52, 1.
2. Rule of St. Benedict, 11, 9.
3. *Homily,* 46, 1.
4. See Origen, *Commentary on the Psalms,* frgm. 39, 8.
5. Pascal, *Pensées,* ch. 6, 15.
6. *Sermon* 141, among the sermons of St. Augustine.
7. St. Jerome, *Letter* 107, 12.
8. See Isaiah 34:14: "I meditate like a dove."
9. *Summa Theologica* Ia, 1, 10.
10. *Introduction au "Livre de Ruth"* (Paris, 1938), 81.
11. St. Augustine, *On John* 9, 3.

One
Genesis 1–11: Primeval History

1. These five books have traditionally been attributed directly to Moses. Most scholars today agree that Moses did not actually write the books. They were probably compiled over a period of many centuries and edited into their final form around the time of the Babylonian exile. However, portions of the books may actually date back to Moses, and as a whole, they are so filled with his influence and person that they can still be called the Mosaic writings.

Two
Genesis 12–50: The Patriarchal Period

1. W.F. Albright, *From the Stone Age to Christianity* (Baltimore, 1940), 183.
2. See Genesis 31:42, where Jacob refers to God as "the God of my father Abraham and the Awe of Isaac."

3. St. Augustine, *City of God,* 16, 32.
4. St. Augustine, *City of God,* 16, 26.
5. St. Augustine, *Against Lying,* 10.

Three
The Book of Exodus

1. Martin Baber, ed., *Ten Rings: Collected Hasidic Sayings* (New York, 1947), 22.

Four
The Book of Leviticus

1. Origen, *Homily 7 on Numbers,* 2.
2. Origen, *Homily 5 on Leviticus.*
3. Origen, *Homélies sur la Genèse,* Sources chrétiennes 7 (Paris, 1944).
4. Origen, *Homily 9 on Leviticus,* 5.
5. Origen, *Homily 9 on Leviticus,* 9.

Seven
The Book of Joshua

1. See W.F. Albright, *Archaeology and the Religion of Israel* (Baltimore, 1946), 94.

Eight
Judges and Ruth

1. *Quaestiones in Heptateuchum VII,* q. 49.
2. See bin Gorion, *Die Sagen der Juden, Juda und Israel* (Frankfurt a.M., 1927), 43.

3. See A. Jeremias, *The Old Testament in the Light of the Ancient East* (New York, 1911), 11, 166.
4. *Questions on Ruth (Migne, P.G., 80, 518-19).*

Nine
The First Book of Samuel

1. John Henry Newman, *Parochial and Plain Sermons,* 111.
2. *Parochial and Plain Sermons,* 111.

Twelve
Tobit, Judith, and Esther

1. During the Reformation, most Protestant churches returned to the Hebrew canon, and so removed Tobit, Judith, and portions of Esther from their Bibles to place them among the "apocryphal" books. The Catholic Church still considers these books to be inspired Scripture and counts them among the "deuterocanonical" books. The citations to the deuterocanonical portions of Esther that are given in this chapter refer to the Vulgate numbering and will not always correspond to modern Bibles.

Thirteen
The First and Second Books of Maccabees

1. bin Gorion, 349-50.
2. Leo Baeck, *The Pharisees and Other Essays* (New York, 1947), 7.
3. Quoted by Baeck, *The Pharisees,* 21.

Fourteen
The Book of Job

1. Edward J. Kissane, *The Book of Job* (Dublin, 1938), xxx.

Fifteen
The Book of Psalms

1. Rashi's *Commentary on Genesis,* translated by Abraham ben Isaiah and Benjamin Sharfman (Brooklyn, 1949), 23; Benno Jacob, *Das erste Buch der Tora* (Berlin, 1934), 90-91.
2. S.R. Hirsch, *Die Genesis* (Frankfurt, 1867), 60; E.T. *The Pentateuch* (London, 1959), 59-60.
3. Berakoth 31a.
4. Hermann Gunkel, *Einleitung in die Psalmen* (Göttingen, 1933).
5. Sigmund Mowinckel, *Psalmenstudien* (Kristiania, 1921-24).
6. Hans Schmidt, *Die Psalmen* (Tübingen, 1934).
7. E.A. Leslie, *The Psalms* (New York, 1949).
8. J.G. Herder, *The Spirit of Hebrew Poetry, II* (Burlington, 1833), II, 94-95.
9. St. Augustine, *Enarrationes in Pslamos,* 144, 1.
10. Pessachion 117a.
11. J. Abrahams, *The Glory of God* (Oxford, 1925), 19.
12. See J.H. Newman, *Sermons on Subjects of the Day,* Sermon 18.

Seventeen
The Prophecy of Isaiah

1. G.A. Smith. *The Book of Isaiah* (New York, n.d.), 1, 22-23.
2. Most modern scholars agree that Chapters 40–66 of Isaiah were not written by the prophet himself. They refer to that portion of the book as "deutero-Isaiah." At the time Fr. Damasus was writing,

some disagreement on this question still existed; accord-ingly, he here attributes the entire book to Isaiah.

Twenty-Two
The Gospel According to St. Mark

1. St. Ignatius of Antioch, *To the Philadelphians* 5, 1.
2. *Didache* 8, 2; *II Clement* 8, 5.
3. *The Great Commentary of Cornelius à Lapide* (London, 1893), General Preface, xxxi-xxxvi.
4. *Adversus Haereses* 3, 11, 8.

Twenty-Three
The Gospel According to St. Luke

1. Dante, *De Monarchia* I, 16.
2. See pp. 68-70 of this book, on the sacrifices of Leviticus.

Twenty-Six
The Letters of St. Paul

1. Thirteen New Testament letters bear Paul's name, but scholars question whether he actually wrote them all. The Letter to the Ephesians, the two Letters to Timothy, and the Letter to Titus may have been written in Paul's name by a secretary or disciple, possibly even some years after his death. Whether or not the letters come directly from Paul's hand, they clearly reflect his influence and ideas, and therefore are included in the body of his writings. The Letter to the Hebrews, once thought to be Paul's, is now considered the work of a separate author and so is not discussed here.

Twenty-Seven
The Seven Catholic Letters

1. The authorship of some of these letters, particularly the two Letters of Peter and the Second and Third Letters of John, is disputed. Such disputes do not, however, lessen their authority as inspired Scripture.

Twenty-Eight
The Apocalypse

1. We do not know whether the John who wrote the Apocalypse was the apostle John, author of the fourth Gospel.
2. St. Augustine, *City of God,* XXII, 30, end.

Index